ERASERHEAD

THE DAVID LYNCH FILES: VOLUME 1
The full story of one of the
strangest films ever made.

By Kenneth George Godwin

ERASERHEAD, THE DAVID LYNCH FILES: VOLUME 1
By Kenneth George Godwin
Copyright © 2020 Kenneth George Godwin
No part of this book may be reproduced in any form or by any means, electronic, mechanical, digital, photocopying, or recording, except for inclusion of a review, without permission in writing from the publisher or Author.

Published in the USA by:

BearManor Media
4700 Millenia Blvd.
Suite 175 PMB 90497
Orlando, FL 32839
www.bearmanormedia.com

Paperback ISBN 978-1-62933-539-1
Case ISBN 978-1-62933-540-7
BearManor Media, Orlando, Florida
Printed in the United States of America
Book design by Robbie Adkins, www.adkinsconsult.com

Eraserhead: An Appreciation and *The Making of Eraserhead* originally appeared, in edited form, in *Cinefantastique*, Sept. 1984
Eraserhead: An Appreciation was reprinted in this version in *Film Quarterly*, Fall 1985

To David Lynch,
whose first feature changed the course of my life.

Table of Contents

Introduction vii
Eraserhead: An Appreciation. 1
The Making of Eraserhead 11

Interviews 70
David Lynch 71
December 8, 1981. 73
December 9, 1981. 113
December 15, 1981 134
February 11, 1982 142

Cast and Crew. 155
Jack Nance 156
Fred Elmes 171
Catherine Coulson. 192
Alan Splet 209
Doreen Small 215
Jack Fisk 225
Laurel Near. 228
Jeanne Bates 231
Peter Ivers. 235

Additional Interviews. 244
Ben Barenholz 245
Mel Brooks 247
Stuart Cornfeld 249
Jonathan Sanger 252

Introduction

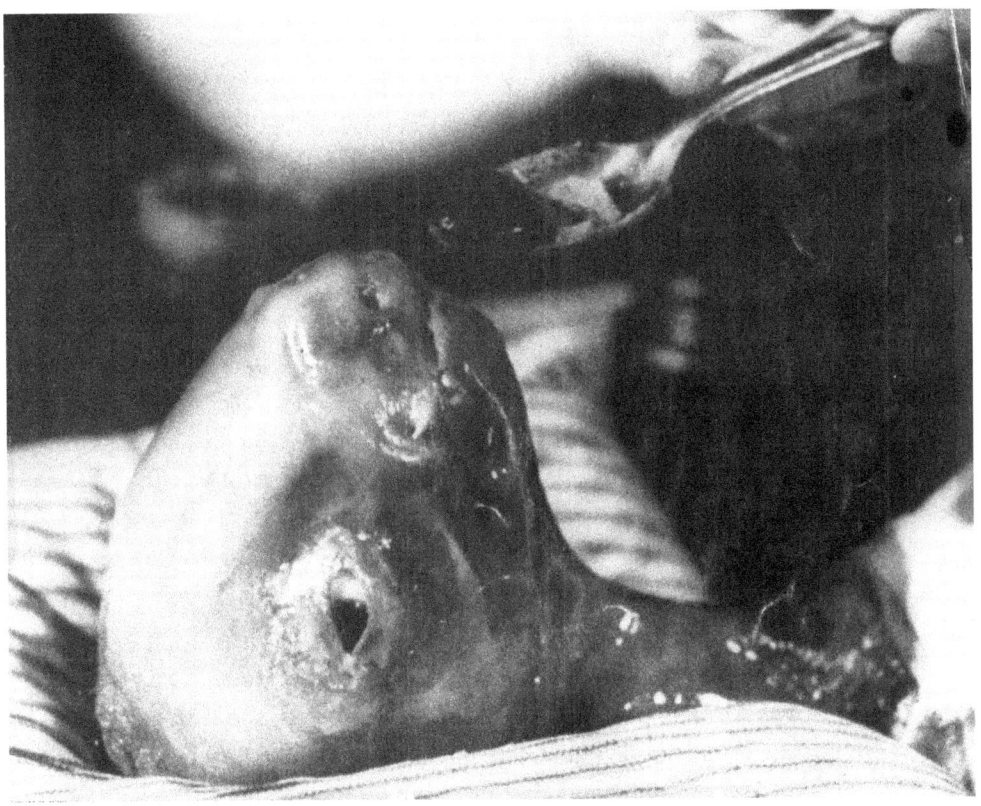

The Eraserhead *baby, nicknamed Spike by Jack Nance.*

In the summer of 1980, David Lynch's first feature, *Eraserhead*, showed up at what was at the time Winnipeg's main repertory cinema, The Festival on Sargent Avenue. The theatre was run by Greg Klimkiw (later Guy Maddin's original producer) whom I knew from our in-print rivalry as film reviewers for the two University student newspapers – Greg for the University of Manitoba's *Manitoban*, and me for the University of Winnipeg's *Uniter*. Although we had occasionally tossed barbs at each other, there was no actual animosity and when Greg took over the Festival, he handed me a "free lifetime pass".

The initial booking for *Eraserhead* was just for a weekend. Having read something about it in the previous year or two, I was eager to see it and went with a friend to the first showing. I was hooked from the opening image, found myself sucked into a remarkably dense, sustained imaginary world every detail of which fascinated me. My friend, however, was bored and restless and I had to spend much of the screening very deliberately ignoring his hints that we should leave. I went back the next night by myself and once again found myself immersed in Lynch's world.

During that summer, Greg brought the film back repeatedly for weekend midnight screenings and I ended up seeing it a total of eight times in about three months. Most of those subsequent screenings were in the company of another friend, Tim Kulchyski, who was equally impressed. We'd often walk about until dawn talking about the film, trying to parse its meanings, ending our discussion over breakfast at Salisbury House.

Months later, while staying with my brother and his family in Hong Kong, I found myself unable to shake off my obsession and I set out to explain to myself what I thought and felt about *Eraserhead*. The result was an essay which, when I returned to Winnipeg in the Spring of 1981, I submitted to *Cinefantastique*, a magazine I'd subscribed to since its first issue in 1971 and which I admired for the general seriousness of its approach to genre films. The editor/publisher Fred Clarke replied quite quickly, explaining that my essay wasn't really the kind of thing they usually printed. However, he'd been trying to do a piece on *Eraserhead* for several years and had not had any luck with the notoriously secretive Lynch; the director was well-known for not wanting to talk about his work, particularly about how he did things technically, which was one of the focuses of *Cinefantastique*'s approach.

But what Clarke had done was to send a copy of my essay to Lynch as an indicator of how seriously they took his work, and to prove that they wanted to approach him with respect. I wasn't entirely sure how I felt about being rejected and used at the same time, but the outcome was certainly to my advantage. Lynch finally responded to the magazine by saying that he would be willing to cooperate on an article – but only if they used me as the writer. Quite a coup for someone with no journalistic experience beyond rather amateurish weekly reviews for a student paper.

Initially, Clarke asked me to send along a list of questions I'd need answered and he would get his man in Hollywood to go over and put them to Lynch. This was satisfactory to neither myself nor Lynch. Terms were eventually agreed on: I had to buy my own ticket to Los Angeles, while the magazine would pay for my hotel and a rental car for a week. And so, with no prior experience as an interviewer, I flew south and booked into the Beverly Garland Howard Johnson's next door to Universal Studios, where Lynch was already preparing for his upcoming *Dune* production.

The next day, I went to the studio, briefly met Lynch and his assistant Steve Martin, and was sent to a private screening room where I was shown Lynch's first two short films – *The Alphabet* and *The Grandmother*. There was a genuine sense of unreality about the experience which, I think, added to the power of the two films. Then after lunch, I settled into Lynch's office, turned on my cheap Radio Shack cassette recorder, and began a conversation which went on for more than three hours. We had a second, equally long session the next afternoon, plus a couple of brief phone follow-ups during the course of the week as I met and interviewed other *Eraserhead* alumni who had been given permission by Lynch to speak to me.

That week in Los Angeles was a remarkable experience for me which further deepened my appreciation of Lynch's work. When I returned to Winnipeg, I spent weeks transcribing all my tapes (initially writing by hand, then typing them out), during which time I mapped out the article which I finally sent to *Cinefantastique* (after passing it by Lynch to check the accuracy of what I had written) in early Spring 1982. My biggest frustration in the whole process was the subsequent delay in publication; the article finally came out in the Fall 1984 issue of the magazine, by which time – partly because he had already opened up to me – Lynch had gone on to speak to other writers. Although I was the first to hear the full story of the making of *Eraserhead*, much of what I had heard and written about had already appeared elsewhere by the time my article appeared.

Included here are my original essay and the full text of the article as written (both were heavily edited by Fred Clarke at *Cinefantastique*), plus the full transcripts of all the interviews I did in researching the article.

Eraserhead: An Appreciation

Henry Spencer (Jack Nance) finds his Heaven in Eraserhead.

A man lives in a seedy one-room apartment located in a nondescript urban wasteland. One day he gets a call from a girlfriend he hasn't seen in some time. She has given birth to a baby. Her mother insists on marriage. He agrees – or rather doesn't disagree. Unable to cope with the demanding baby, the woman leaves. The man looks after it through an illness. He has a brief sexual encounter with a neighbour. Increasingly insistent visions of a strange woman who exists behind the radiator in the apartment impinge on his claustrophobic world. Finally, he kills the baby – an act which shatters the world and frees him to join his vision-woman in Heaven.

Eraserhead, writer-director David Lynch's first feature, has been baffling and disturbing audiences since its release in 1976. It has become one of the most persistent and successful cult films on the midnight and art house circuits. Yet, while it shares many characteristics which might be attributed to cult films as a class, it differs in some significant ways.

A common characteristic of many cult films is their air of exhibitionism – the relentless grotesquerie and pseudo-mysticism of *El Topo*; the innocent decadence of *Rocky Horror*; the not so innocent decadence of John Waters' outrageous entertainments. These films invite the audience to throw off their inhibitions and join in an assault on generally accepted standards of good taste. The ultimate example of this is the participatory cult which grew up around Jim Sharman's *Rocky Horror*, the complete identification of the audience with the film, the shared knowledge and rituals which brought the audience together in a communal experience, a new and alternative culture.

Yet *Eraserhead*, while it dwells on shocking, even perverse images, seems in-turned, obsessively introspective. It provides an auditory and visual assault which isolates each viewer. The experience becomes intensely personal, unshared. Lynch achieves this by relentlessly applying alienating devices. Foremost among these is the setting of the film in a bleak world not recognizable as our own. The action which takes place there offers no narrative with an externally meaningful coherence. The simple "story" of Henry Spencer's forced marriage to Mary X is utterly banal – yet it is couched in a collection of bizarre, seemingly meaningless images and inconclusive scenes which shatter the story's familiarity and make it frighteningly strange.

Exhibiting an artistry and technical skill almost unique in low budget filmmaking – *Eraserhead* is shot in beautifully atmospheric black-and-white, enhanced with a remarkably intricate, expressionistic soundtrack – Lynch has structured the film in a series of almost circular movements, taking the viewer on detours which seem to lead back to our starting point – but not quite. Early in the film, Henry stares at the radiator in his room. A menacingly slow tracking shot moves along the base of the radiator, accompanied by a low, threatening hum and a harsh hissing of steam; sound and image attain an intensity which warns of some imminent event. But nothing happens. Yet later the radiator becomes increasingly prominent as the location of Henry's vision of Heaven. Expectation is fulfilled, but in an unexpected way and displaced in time.

Later, after Mary has walked out, exhausted by the baby's demands, Henry wakes in the night to find her shivering feverishly beside him. He stares at the wall and the camera passes into it; the wall becomes an alien landscape where a worm-like creature rises up to swallow the camera. We emerge from darkness to look back out of the wall at Henry. But Mary is no longer there.

Henry's neighbour, having locked herself out, invites herself into Henry's apartment. They embrace in a bed which is transformed into a pool of milky fluid into which the couple submerge. Henry now enters his Heaven for the first time and approaches the deformed woman who inhabits it. His head abruptly explodes from his shoulders and sinks into a pool of blood, emerging into daylight where a small boy grabs it and runs. The boy sells the head to a pencil factory where it is found to be made entirely of rubber. From here we find ourselves suddenly returned to Henry's apartment where he lies alone, no sign of the neighbour.

In effect this is a kind of cinematic sleight-of-hand. Lynch diverts our attention and then alters a detail of the scene. But the distraction is far out of proportion with the slight change that he makes. What then are these detours? Simply strange, meaningless intrusions into the film's world? But here either everything is real, or nothing is. We can discern no degrees of reality because there is no baseline to which we can point as rational. There can be no distinction between what really happens and what someone thinks is happening because here thought is instantaneously manifest as event. We find ourselves in *Eraserhead* in a kind of psychological quicksand, unable to find the correct footing, emotional or intellectual, from which to view the events we see. In fact, it seems that very little actually does happen in the film, although something momentous is always about to happen. Yet the cues we are given by the characters themselves indicate that this world is "normal".

This gives the film a kind of humour like that of Beckett and other Twentieth Century absurdists, a humour arising from people behaving as if meaning exists in a meaningless world. Henry responds to his child as any doting father might – yet it is a strange reptilian thing, armless, legless, a head attached by a thin neck to a shapeless, bandage-wrapped body – not a human mutant but a perfectly formed something else.

The actions and responses of the characters during Henry's visit to the X's exhibit an almost complete incongruity in each character's behaviour – a breakdown or even a complete absence of communication between one mind and another which is nonetheless accepted by the characters as communication. Mrs X asks Henry, "What do you do?" to which he replies ingenuously, "Oh, I'm on vacation." Mary has a seizure which her unconcerned mother treats by brushing Mary's hair. Henry is asked to carve a chicken which is only the size of a fist; when he tries to comply the bird twitches to life and spews out an oily liquid. And so it goes on – nothing seems to fit.

At its most accessible level, the film seems to be a strange domestic comedy in which the little annoyances of daily life are blown up to monstrous proportions, with poor bemused Henry stumbling through it all, trying his damnedest to appear inconspicuously normal in situations where he is not certain just what "normal" is.

But this humour is not funny, because it is wedded to dark, bleak imagery, an almost obsessive interest in biological matters – the textures of internal organs, physical deformity. This biological concern and the bleak, post-industrial landscape in which the film is set, are reminiscent of the paintings of the Swiss surrealist H.R. Giger (who, not surprisingly, has called *Eraserhead* "one of the greatest films I have ever seen"). Giger's paintings depict people trapped in mechanical complexes, often being absorbed into the machinery; creatures half-organic, half-mechanical; landscapes of glistening flesh; decaying biological matter.

This parallel offers a means of deciphering Lynch's seemingly impenetrable film. Its coherence is not the external one of narrative form, but the internal one of dream images which may represent any number of things simultaneously with no single meaning negating any of the others. It seems that Lynch has managed to capture the processes of dream consciousness with remarkable precision. *Eraserhead* is not simply a fantasy related to us and labelled dream: it is the dream experience itself.

But whose dream? The film itself presents us with no one who stands outside the events of the dream. Henry, at the centre, is not the dreamer but rather the dreamer's dream identity (it is very much a male dream). Perhaps it is this absence of the dreamer which makes the film so immediate and so disturbing: the viewer becomes the dreamer.

Looked at in this way, the film's meanings begin to emerge clearly. *Eraserhead* is about corruption – the corruption of the natural world and of man as a part of that world. At the root of this corruption is man: the human mind, or intellect, or consciousness – that part of man which causes him to perceive himself as apart from the rest of nature, a separateness which causes him to believe that he is free to interfere with and alter nature in any way he desires, with impunity. In the film, the consequences of this meddling well up in vivid nightmare terms. The world of *Eraserhead* is a dead one, bleak and sterile. Man's interference has made it actively hostile to life, and this process has rebounded on him in the form of a perversion of the most basic of life's forces: sex. The symbolic progress of the film reveals an ever-deepening fear of sex (as the agency by which life perpetuates itself), leading ultimately to a disgust which can only be remedied by a complete escape from it – into death.

The physical world depicted in *Eraserhead* offers virtually no images of life. From the very start, we see only a bleak, grimy urban wasteland; concrete expanses, tenements in a narrow street, relieved only occasionally by open space – treeless waste ground. These open spaces are either mere expanses of mud or wire-enclosed compounds containing a litter of technological debris. There are no bird sounds, just the occasional metallic rattle of some idle device off in the shadows. Just once dogs are heard to bark, an angry off-screen outburst from which Henry ducks away nervously. The only animals actually shown are a bitch and her pups in the X's house; the sound accompanying the pups' suckling seems wrong, like the squealing of rats.

The "ornaments" in Henry's dingy room are themselves dead: a mound of dried grass on top of the dresser, a mat of the same beneath the radiator, and on the bedside table a heap of dirt from which protrudes a dry, leafless twig. Above this hangs a picture of a mushroom cloud – the ultimate symbol of death.

Even when we are shown a garden (in front of the X's house), it is as bleak as the rest of this world: dark and shadowy, with a high wire fence pressing in at the side through which murky, unwholesome steam drifts from railway yards, it contains only dead, withered flowers and shrubs.

The scene which takes place inside this house presents the film's themes in miniature. Far from being a cozy family home, it offers little comfort, no haven from the grim world outside. Situated right beside the tracks, it is bombarded with the filth, noise and vibration of passing trains. The interior is cluttered with clumsily placed pipes which further shrink the small rooms and get in the way of movement. This is just another aspect of the inefficient, decaying technology of the film's world – seen again and again, in the empty rotting industrial sites, in the barely functioning elevator in Henry's building, in the violently burning-out light bulbs (in the X's house, and later in Henry's room as the world is coming to an explosive end).

When Mary's father, Bill, first enters from the kitchen, he bursts into a sudden diatribe which is quickly drowned out by the roar of a passing train. He says that he has seen the area pass from meadows to the hell-hole it is today. And then adds significantly that, as a plumber, he put most of the pipes in himself, ruining his knees in the process.

Bill offers a further symbol of this corruption: as they sit down to dinner, he asks Henry to do the carving. He explains at length why: "The girls have heard this before, but" ... some years ago he had an operation on his arm. The doctors told him he would never recover the use of it ... "but what do they know?" He rubbed it every day and bit by bit he regained movement until now "it's as good as new." Except that there is absolutely no feeling in it; he will not carve because he is afraid he might cut himself. The arm has a semblance of life, but is in reality little more than animated dead matter. (One thinks of the grandmother sitting in the kitchen, a vegetable appendage to the family, moving only when Mrs X manipulates her lifeless hands to toss the salad.)

The dinner itself is a kind of perversion. It consists of chickens – of a sort. They are only the size of a fist and, Bill says, man-made. "Damnedest things, but they're new." Man, trying to extend his manipulation into every corner of nature, has produced a parody.

The film's central symbol for that active part of the human mind, responsible for the disruption and perversion of the natural world – and for the unbalanced, faulty technology which has been the agency of that perversion – is the Man in the Planet. This figure, a grotesque mutant, is a barely moving, twitching creature who sits in a ruined, decaying room with control levers in front of him. He is the repulsive inhabitant of man's own mind. By manipulating his levers he initiates the action of the film; he is "in charge" of this world whose motion has become mechanical rather than living. In the film's final moments, it becomes clear that the Planet itself is not even spherical, but distorted, elongated – shaped something like a head, a dark inorganic head. This creature, embodying the force responsible for corrupting the natural world, stands as the film's devil. But he is also a vital part of man. The horror of this nightmare is the horror of man facing the monster in himself, a confrontation which finally leads to an act of self-destruction to end the horror.

Opposing this devil is a second symbolic figure, Henry's "angel", the sexless woman who inhabits his vision of Heaven. The devil's second appearance in the film blocks Henry's attainment of this Heaven. His third and final appearance shows his control lost, the world destroyed and Henry "freed" at last. But before this sequence can be understood, and the nature of the climactic act of self-destruction comprehended, the second aspect of the film's vision of corruption must be examined.

The perverse sexuality which pervades the film is the key to understanding the meaning of *Eraserhead*. To begin at the beginning: the film opens with images of conception and birth. In the beginning there is space, the Planet – and Henry floating in nothingness. The conception is already corrupt; the sperm comes not from the penis, but is rather drawn mechanically from Henry's mouth (the head) by the Man in the Planet's manipulation of his levers. The head which attempts to reshape the natural world here tries to control the very processes of reproduction. The sperm itself is an over-sized, clumsy parody of the real thing. It drops into a water-filled cavity in the Planet's surface, submerging in a stream of bubbles which fade to darkness.

The birth consists of a vertical rising from this darkness through a circular hole in the ground, moving up into light and open space. We, like Henry, like the as yet unseen child, have passed from a state of non-existence into the physical world – a world which becomes increasingly claustrophobic and from which Henry longs to escape back into non-existence.

The grotesque sperm appears twice more in the course of the film. The first time, it helps to define the nature of the place Henry so longs to enter – the stage which exists in the wall behind the radiator. Although the stage's presence is hinted at just after Henry receives the message from Mary that he is expected for dinner, we do not actually see it until Mary and the baby have moved in and Henry's world has been reduced to the size of the dingy little apartment – until he has become totally trapped within this bleak world.

The stage is as seedy as the apartment, but it is lit by a stark white light which banishes shadows. At the centre is the deformed blonde woman of Henry's vision; sexless, with a shapeless body and a bland, childish expression, she performs a stiff little Shirley Temple-like dance. As she dances, the sperm-things drop about her. She steps around them daintily with a coy smile until the music stops; she steps on one of the things and it squishes a milky fluid out on to the stage. She does it again ... and Henry's Heaven is defined. A warm, moist, safe, enclosed place: the womb. But a sterile womb. Its sexless inhabitant and guardian eliminates the intruding sperm, thus guaranteeing that no conception will occur – and so no birth, no entry into the hated outer world.

At its third appearance, the sperm has become actively malignant. Mary has walked out, yet Henry wakes in the night to find her beside him, tightly wrapped in the sheets, shivering with a fever. Henry, a look of worry, even fear, on his face, reaches beneath the covers and begins to pull something out – a sperm, pulled free apparently from Mary's vagina. It is now a parasite, a source of sickness. Henry pulls it, and then several more, out of Mary – reversing the normal course of sex – and hurls them at the wall, killing them.

Not surprisingly, birth itself is presented in a series of progressively more negative images. Initially, in the opening sequence, it is a journey from darkness into light – a vertical ascent. The second birth image follows one of the film's circular diversions, occurring immediately after the scene described above. As Henry stares at the wall where the crushed sperm have left their smears, the small cabinet beside these marks opens and we see a little worm he earlier found in his mailbox. This worm is itself significant, so I will here make a brief diversion of my own to deal with it.

As the cabinet doors open, the worm (which, a woman once commented to me, resembles a very young foetus) comes to life and crawls off into darkness, emerging onto a cratered landscape. It slips into one hole, rises from another, repeating the action several times. And each time it reappears, it has grown larger and fatter – like a penis swelling to erection. This awakening of the penis, as it were, leads directly into the scene which follows (involving the neighbour) and to the climactic self-destructive action. The original finding of the worm – in a dark place (the mailbox) – and Henry's furtive concealment of it, represents the first moment of sexual self-discovery. The circular craters which so stimulate it to growth are an obvious female symbol. Finally, the end of the worm opens into a rapidly widening mouth, an image of extreme appetite, also perhaps becoming a symbol of the vagina, which swallows the camera in complete darkness.

We emerge from this in a way which echoes that first birth image; the camera pans slowly until an opening comes into view, through which it travels. Here, however, instead of rising vertically it tracks horizontally, and we emerge not into light and open space but into Henry's cramped, dimly lit room.

The third birth image is more shocking. Henry, having finally reached the stage-Heaven, is decapitated. His head lies in a pool of blood. Abruptly, it plunges down into the liquid, emerging into that apparently different outer world where it is found that Henry's head consists entirely of rubber. Here we have not only violence, blood, and a descending movement – we have a stillbirth; its product is not alive, indeed may not even be organic.

Given all this, it is equally unsurprising that the vagina occurs as another central image. Its first appearance comes during the dinner scene – the opening into the body cavity of the little chicken which comes to life and oozes a thick oily liquid which might be blood. Henry finds the sight distasteful. Yet Mrs X is aroused by it to the point of sexual climax, after which she frightens Henry by making a sexual advance. There is a complex fear here: of menstruation, of female sexuality, and of its links to reproduction.

Subsequent appearances of the vagina image are less threatening, as should be the case, given Henry's desire to re-enter the womb. It becomes an image of absorption (the craters on the Planet's surface, the mouth of the worm) which culminates in what is perhaps the film's only moment of beauty, as the bed becomes a pool of milky fluid into which Henry and his neighbour sink in an embrace.

It is at this point that Henry first reaches his Heaven. He journeys through the vagina to emerge into the womb. Standing among the crushed sperm, the deformed blonde sings her brief song about Heaven and then reaches out towards Henry. But he is blinded by a fierce light and the Man in the Planet takes her place. Henry backs away and his head explodes from his shoulders, replaced by the baby, its insistent cry more plaintively demanding than ever. Henry has reached his Heaven, but he cannot possess it – because he penetrated to the womb through an act of sex. But here sex (as the means of procreation) is forbidden. Henry is violently expelled in that image of stillbirth.

This brings us to the image which dominates the film, which becomes its centre as it becomes the centre of Henry's life: the "baby". This inhuman (yet still oddly human) creature, which lies unmoving on the table from its first appearance, somehow seems to be in control. It wears Mary down with its incessant demanding cry, finally driving her away. Yet Henry accepts its presence passively. What is this bizarre reptilian thing? From its shape and its position in the film's structure of symbols, it can be only one thing: the penis (complete with scrotum – the bandage-wrapped sac to which the head is attached by a thin neck). But it is the penis grown out of all proportion; it has become a separate entity, all appetite. Its cry for attention hardly ever stops. It even disturbs the neighbour as she is willingly giving herself to Henry. Mary is driven away by its need, she rejects its demands (and Henry's slightest sexual move) and is, as a punishment, "infected" by its product, the malignant sperm.

After Mary has left, the baby continues its wailing. Henry wants to leave the apartment, the claustrophobic trap of his tiny airless room, but every time he reaches for the door the baby cries out again. Henry turns back to discover it a mass of repulsive blisters. "Oh," says Henry with a mild concern, "you are sick." He attempts to treat it, his actions as mild and ineffectual as ever. But perhaps in that moment he has his first glimmer of where his true problem lies. For it is this thing which blocks his access to Heaven. He is ruled by the penis, the source of the dreaded sperm, agent of reproduction; and is thus unworthy. This is the meaning of the decapitation sequence. Control by the penis is complete.

This is reinforced later. After his "return" from Heaven, he cannot stop thinking about the neighbour (sex). He jumps at every sound from the hall. But when he finally does see her again, she is about to enter her apartment with another man, one with a disfigured face who is touching her salaciously (sex has lost its glow). Henry stares; she stares back. And what she sees is the penis-baby rising in place of Henry's head.

Now the film moves into its climax. Why does Henry take up the pair of scissors and cut open the bandages in which the baby is wrapped? His movements are hesitant. Is his interest clinical? an attempt to diagnose his sickness? Is he trying to punish the baby for trapping him and making his life hell? Or is it a deliberate act of self-release? Certainly, the outcome is release of a kind – the kind, in fact, which Henry longs for. The act itself is self-castration: destroy the appetite by destroying the organ. All the poisons flood up out of the dying thing, and its death throes cause chaos. Because, in destroying the penis, Henry also destroys the tool of continuity, the means by which the world (the particular inner world of the dream) is sustained. Without the support of this organ, the world flies apart. The result is death. But of course this is what Henry desired. The nothingness of the sterile womb, Henry's Heaven, is death itself.

How does this all relate to that other theme, of the world corrupted by man's mind? Quite simply, the kind of control involved in man's heavy-handed manipulation of the physical world is unable to harness the forces of life. The attempt (seen in the mechanical act of conception which initiates the action of the film, in the man-made chickens) results in gross parody – and, worse, in a great conflict with those forces which continue to express themselves in their own terms. The horror of sex which is so pervasive in the dream – from Henry's discomfort around women to the grotesquely distorted sexual imagery – arises from the perception that this particular force is beyond the control of man's rational consciousness (the twisted Man in the Planet). Instead of trying to come to terms with it in a way which would acknowledge its rightful place, consciousness fears sex, tries to suppress it; and down in the subconscious, the place of dreams (the realm of the film) it becomes distorted, even more fearsome. Because it is beyond this kind of control, sex is perceived as a monster. And the only way to escape it is to eliminate it entirely. But self-castration not only obliterates sex – in cutting off the links to life's vital forces, it also kills the castrating consciousness. And so, at the very moment of victory, as sex is finally defeated and Henry sinks blissfully unconscious into the arms of his sterile angel, the Man in the Planet pulls desperately at the controls of his disintegrating machine and flies, with his world, into a million fragments.

Eraserhead is, then, a depiction of the self-defeating tensions which result from man's inability to reconcile his intellect with other, equally potent, aspects of his nature. What makes Lynch's achievement so impressive is that he states this entirely through suggestion – and with a good deal of dark, skewed humour – manipulating his symbols with remarkable dexterity in a surreal vehicle which is organic and unified – and frighteningly alive – without ever reducing the message to the level of a tract. As H.R. Giger put it: *Eraserhead* is one of the greatest films I have ever seen. An obsessive, haunting work made by a remarkable, original talent, it is completely *sui generis*.

The Making of *Eraserhead*

Henry Spencer (Jack Nance) adrift in an urban wasteland.

At the 1976 Filmex in Los Angeles, a startlingly original film appeared, apparently out of nowhere. Dark and brooding, its moody black and white images slipping seamlessly from mundane reality into nightmarish fantasy and back again, it wielded a powerful effect on its audience, leaving many stunned and disturbed. Few could fail to be impressed by the assurance and skill with which the filmmaker manipulated both picture and sound to create an imaginary world of such depth and conviction.

But who was the filmmaker? And where did this film *Eraserhead* come from?

David Lynch was thirty at the time of the Filmex premiere of *Eraserhead* and he had only two previous short films to his credit (*The Alphabet*, four minutes; *The Grandmother*, thirty-four minutes – both combining live action with animation). His interest in film had been slight. Unlike the generation of directors epitomized by Lucas and Spielberg, he had not been enthralled by the Saturday matinees of his childhood and filled with an ambition to recreate those thrills. His first love was painting and his work with film began as an extension of his exploration of painting techniques.

During his high school years in Virginia, Lynch shared a studio with his best friend, Jack Fisk, and on weekends he would go over to Washington, D.C., to study painting at the Corcoran School of Art. After high school, he went on to the Boston Museum School, which he attended for a year. Dissatisfied with that, he set out on a three year visit to Europe which lasted just fifteen days.

"I didn't take to Europe," Lynch recalled. It might have been different if he had "just gone to see it, but I was all the time thinking, 'This is where I'm going to be painting.' And there was no inspiration there at all for the kind of work I wanted to do." So he returned to the States, finding himself cut off financially. He did not want to go to school and his family were unwilling to give him money.

During this period, he went through a number of jobs – at an art store; printing blueprints; in a frame shop. "And I kept getting fired from these jobs because I couldn't get up in the morning." Finally, while working for a man named Michelangelo, Lynch was fired again for scratching a frame – and then rehired as a janitor. This Michelangelo had a bell installed in Lynch's apartment with which he could wake Lynch in the morning. This arrangement seemed to work well, although instead of being paid, Lynch was simply given food money. "Then he would make me show him my food, because he didn't want me spending it on just paint and not eating. Well, I wasn't going to do that. I mean, I was hungry!"

It was while Lynch was working as a janitor, living on peanut butter, bread, and milk, that Jack Fisk turned up one day at four-thirty in the morning. At that time, Fisk's name was Luton; the two of them were called at the same time for their draft physical. "I never would have woken up for it," said Lynch, if Fisk had not got him out of bed. Fisk had gone to Philadelphia after high school to attend the Pennsylvania Academy of Fine Arts. "And out of school or in art school," said Lynch, "you're not in school. Art school didn't hold any weight. So we were both called in."

It was on the bus ride to the physical that Lynch's friend told him about the Academy in Philadelphia. His interest was fired. He gathered together his portfolio and with a little money from his father, he took a bus to Philadelphia and enrolled in the school in late 1965.

"It was a great, great time to be at the Academy," Lynch recalled. "Schools have waves and it just happened that I hit on a really rising, giant wave. There were so many good people at the school; it was real exciting. And that really started everything rolling. I kind of got a feeling for things in terms of painting, and my own style kind of clicked in."

Lynch works in a number of different styles, from what he terms "industrial symphony" drawings, complex mosaics of sharply drawn geometric shapes, to action painting, in which he hurls black paint at the canvas and then adds hard edged elements amongst the spray patterns. "I do a lot of figures in quiet rooms," he added. "I really like figure painting.

"But somewhere along the line in the painting I wanted to do an animated film." Every year, the Academy had an experimental painting and sculpture contest. In his second year there, Lynch entered this contest with his first attempt at animation, not so much a film as a moving painting, a loop which could repeat itself endlessly. Accompanied by the sound of a siren, it consisted of six "figures"; three sculptured surfaces based on casts of Lynch's head done for him by Fisk, with film overlapping them, and three purely film figures. "It was more like a painting," said Lynch, with eighteen or twenty animated elements working in it. The figures caught fire, got headaches, their bodies and stomachs grew, and they all got sick.

Lynch's experience in making this film-painting did not ignite any filmmaking passion. "That was going to be the end of my filmmaking experience," he said, "because that cost me $200 to do, and that was just too expensive. The sculptured screen itself cost $100." In preparing for the film, he had shopped around for a 16mm camera, surprised at the varying prices he was quoted "because I thought all 16mm cameras were the same." He finally found a "weird" little camera with a fifty-foot cassette, "a little turret, and a real nice little Cook lens." It also, of course, had a single-frame capability. The dealer had to show Lynch how to operate it, although even "he didn't know how to run it really."

"How am I going to light this business?" Lynch asked.

The man gave him two photofloods and told him to set them at forty-five degree angles to his working surface and to "look out for glares."

The next problem arose from the camera's lack of reflex viewing. Lynch was working on the seventh floor of an old downtown hotel which was a part of the school. That floor for a long time had been used only to store old furniture, so "it was a great place to work. It was real quiet." He set up his makeshift animation stand, a big board which he fixed to a radiator, and taped the camera down to a dresser that he dragged in, figuring that its weight would hold the camera steady. Then, having marked the positions of the board and dresser to ensure that neither shifted out of place, he set to work animating. But because the camera had only a rangefinder, he had to set it far enough back to be confident that the whole board would be in frame. When the film was developed, it turned out that the whole board had been caught – along with a lot of the wall and the radiator.

When the film was shown, the sculptured screen had to be hung in the middle of the stage so that all the excess would simply fall away behind it.

Lynch was pleased with the final results, but because of the relatively high cost and the technical difficulties, he was not inclined to pursue film any further. "It was much nicer to paint than to make these movies," he thought. "But this was one of those things, a crossroads, where you say, 'Well, that's the end of it.' But then something happens and you say, 'No, that's not the end of it.' Because this guy came along and he said, 'I want one of these for my house.'" A commission from a rich patron who had seen that first effort at the Academy. (Interestingly, another person who saw that single screening was Jonathan Sanger, who would later be Lynch's producer on *The Elephant Man*.)

Armed with almost a thousand dollars, Lynch bought a new camera and set to work creating a new piece along similar lines – a sculptured screen with a repeating loop of animation. His patron would hang the screen, a piece of sculpture in itself, set up a projector, screw it down, and at the flick of a switch he would have a moving painting whenever he wanted it.

Lynch spent two months animating. The day came to get the developed film back from the lab and he was excited. "I opened it up," he recalled, "and I quickly held it up to the light to see some frames – and there weren't even any frame lines. It was just a blur." The camera, "although a really good Bolex," was broken. Instead of the usual intermittent action, it slid the film through in a continuous motion. The film was ruined, two months' work wasted.

Yet this setback turned out to be a very positive thing in terms of Lynch's work with film. When he called his backer to explain the situation, he was told to "take the rest of the money and do whatever you want." With a little extra money from his father, who wanted only a print of the finished film in return, not necessarily with a sculptured screen, Lynch made a four-minute animated short, *The Alphabet*.

If the initial commission had worked out, "I daresay there again that would have been the end of it," said Lynch, "but now I had this little film and this guy told me about the American Film Institute. 'You ought to apply for a grant. All you have to do is write a script for a film you want to do and send them previous work.'" So Lynch wrote a script which was "very weird because I'd never written anything before. It was just little images and stuff, sort of like shorthand and poetry." He sent it, along with a print of *The Alphabet*, to the AFI in Washington.

At that time, early in 1968, Lynch was still living in Philadelphia, with a job printing engravings. He was now married to his first wife, Peggy, and they were "really poor." He was twenty-two and unknown when in the mail he received notice of the first group to be given grants by the AFI. The recipients were all older than himself, had already made names for themselves, had done things – people like Stan Vanderbeek. Lynch said to himself, "Man, I am so embarrassed that I even applied to this place. This is ridiculous," and he just wanted them to send his film back and forget about it.

Until one day he got a phone call at work. The second group of grants had been awarded – the AFI gave them out every quarter of a year. The call was from George Stevens, Jr, and Tony Vellani at the AFI in Washington. Lynch had submitted a proposed budget of $7118 and they wanted to know, "Can you do it for $5000?" "You got it," Lynch replied.

Later, George Stevens, Jr, told him how the offer had come about. When weighing applications, the AFI sorted the various films into categories. And this time, after they had arranged them all into their various piles, there was one little film left over in a pile of its own: *The Alphabet*. So they said, "We gotta give this guy a grant."

Lynch now set to work on *The Grandmother*, a mixture of live action and animation, black-and-white and colour. The $5000 grant was not enough, but the AFI subsequently gave him another $2200 to complete the film.

Though smaller in scale than *Eraserhead*, *The Grandmother* is more audacious in its use of flamboyant surrealistic images. It declares itself forcefully as the work of an artist secure in his imagination, unselfconscious in his willingness to put highly personal, even painful images up on the screen. There is an openness, even an innocence about the film, which gives it not only a genuine charm, but also a poignancy which enables the viewer to feel a direct emotional connection with the often abstract, dreamlike images.

The film, using only images and sound effects – it contains no dialogue – tells of a lonely young boy whose parents are distant, too caught in their own concerns to pay any attention to his emotional needs. Seeking attention, the boy repeatedly wets his bed, but receives only anger from his father. Then he discovers a seed which emits a plaintive cry; he plants it in earth on an attic bed, waters it, and watches it grow into a huge root-like stump. Eventually this thing gives birth to the Grandmother (in a scene strongly reminiscent of the pods giving birth in Kaufman's remake of *Invasion of the Body Snatchers*, a film which *The Grandmother* pre-dates). The Grandmother is a kind, affectionate figure who gives the boy the emotional warmth he needs. But she sickens and dies – at least physically. What she represents still exists, but the boy is unable to see it; he is alone again, his isolation coming from within.

As *Eraserhead* would later do, the film combines mundane reality with strange fantasy; its central character feels trapped and longs to escape – a longing which takes on concrete form as dream becomes indistinguishable from reality. But where *Eraserhead* strives always to maintain a firm sense of realism within its own dreamlike world, *The Grandmother* flies headlong into stylized surrealism. The emotions and mental states it deals with are fully recognizable, but the people are cast in animal, even at times in vegetable, terms. The shifts between animation and live action, the various camera techniques, including pixilation, force a constant awareness of film as a medium. It is, more than anything, like a moving painting. Where conventionally film technique attempts to be as unobtrusive as possible so that the viewer might be drawn as deeply as possible into the content of the film, here Lynch's techniques become as prominent a part of the film as the images they convey. In this, *The Grandmother* recalls the great German expressionist films, such as *Caligari*. What is surprising is that Lynch had no experience of those films prior to making *The Grandmother*. He rediscovered the approach by coming to film through painting. This is an important point if one is to appreciate his work fully: the medium is not simply a vehicle for conveying the image; both medium and image are integral parts of the whole, bound to each other and subsumed to the intention of the work – the creation of what might be called "mood".

Lynch's intention is to use images and sounds in various combinations and juxtapositions to call up in the viewer a pattern of emotions and psychological states which together create an overriding mood, as the notes in a piece of music combine to create a symphony. His style places composition above narrative.

For David Lynch, *The Grandmother* was important for a number of reasons. Although he now sees it as "innocent and sort of primitive," like a painting by Rousseau, the experience of making it gave him the confidence in his filmmaking skills which he would need for the protracted and arduous task of making his first feature. It was also this film which put him in a position which would enable him to make that feature. When the initial grant had been running out, Lynch had invited Tony Vellani up to Philadelphia to see what had been done so far; Vellani was very impressed and okayed the extra funds. He also told Lynch about the newly formed Centre for Advanced Film Studies which the AFI had set up in Los Angeles. Lynch applied and although he did not get in immediately, he was accepted by the Centre in its second year.

Finally, it was *The Grandmother* which introduced Lynch to soundman Alan Splet who was to become a major collaborator in turning the director's vision into cinematic reality. When Lynch was making *The Alphabet*, he rented a little Uher tape recorder, which incidentally was broken and so produced certain peculiar sounds which he kept and used in the film. But he did not know how to cut and mix a soundtrack himself. He went to Calvin Productions in Philadelphia, an industrial film company. A man there named Bob McDonald cut the sound effects for him, while another named Bob Collom did the mix.

When Lynch was ready to start working on the sound for *The Grandmother*, he went back to Calvin. He was already creating effects, but he wanted to work with Collom again to create more, and to use the company's library. Collom told him, "Fine. When you get your stuff together, come on by." But when Lynch arrived at the door of the sound department, Collom met him and told him that he was not available, that Lynch would have to work with his assistant, Alan Splet.

"I thought," Lynch recalled, "'Oh brother, I'm being shunted off to this assistant.' And so there's Alan; a strange looking guy. He's very, very thin, and I remember he had a synthetic black suit and real short hair and a strange look to him. I shook his hand and I felt all the bones shaking in his arm. I thought, 'Oh brother, this guy is an oddball, the squarest guy I've ever seen in my life, and we're going to try to make some nifty sound effects. This isn't going to work.'"

But Lynch talked to Splet, explaining what he wanted to do, to use the library as raw material to be played with and altered. That sounded good to Splet, who said he would gather some things together, and they made an appointment to start a couple of weeks later. When that time came, according to Lynch, they began work at nine in the morning and finished at seven or eight that evening. And continued to work straight through the next seven weeks, weekends included.

They created most of the sounds themselves, using the library to supplement their work. Although there were only five tracks, by the time they were through the reels of white leader they began with had been completely transformed into reels of solid brown magnetic tape. "And in a lot of cases," Lynch commented, "that was very intricate cutting. Alan loves cutting little bits and taking just a half frame of this sound and cutting it in, just getting it to sync in and feel just right, all this painstaking stuff. Way more than most people would even hear." And all that work came at a bargain price; despite week after week of long hours, Calvin only charged Lynch the in-house rate of $250 per effects reel – even though a typical ten-minute reel might contain only a half-dozen effects, while Lynch's contained wall-to-wall sound. "So that was an awful good deal," said Lynch. "Otherwise it would have been thousands of dollars."

In creating the sounds, they would scour the company in search of useful materials; a plastic box to crush, a pencil sharpener, a staple gun. But Calvin being an industrial film company, there was not a lot of equipment around for the sophisticated manipulation of sound; Splet and Lynch were left to their own ingenuity much of the time. As in the case of *The Grandmother*'s whistle: "We wanted a little reverb to it," said Splet, "and we didn't have a reverb device. That was just beyond our means. So we got the sound basically by re-recording the whistle through a piece of aluminum heat ducting which we just happened to find in the shop. We re-recorded it maybe fifteen times through this piece of ducting to get the little bit of echo on it that we wanted."

Much of their work together on *The Grandmother* and the two features which followed was essentially a matter of trial and error. But it was not entirely a haphazard process; their roles were complementary. Lynch would have an abstract idea of what was necessary to aid the picture in evoking the required mood. "You have so many possibilities," he commented, "but really you only have one sound that's right for that scene. And when you hear it, you really know it. But before you hear it, you at least know that it's not this. It's a sound that kind of does this, and it's low or it's like a whistle, or it's like something that starts off rough and then smooths out ..." Lynch would even do little drawings to indicate the "shape" of a sound.

Then Splet, the engineer, would have the task of locating something concrete to coincide with Lynch's concept. "I have to start probing a little bit just to get it a little more concretized," he said. "Then when I think I've got it, I'll try something on David. He'll say, 'Ah no, no, no. It should be such and such.' Then I think back and I'll approach it again and try something different." They would repeat this process until they finally narrowed it down to the sound that Lynch wanted – at which point they would start on the next effect.

For Lynch, sound is a vitally important part of the whole, not simply an enhancement of the picture. As in his use of visual images, his approach to sound is essentially expressionistic. Lynch's manipulation of sound transforms effects into a kind of music which serves the purpose usually fulfilled by the score, as a guide to the viewer's emotions, but without being abstractly detached from the visual image as music is. Lynch himself sees it in terms of a spectrum, with music as "brittle" and sound effects as "liquid". His use of sound lies somewhere in the centre, the area of plasticity where the liquid is beginning to solidify.

The collaboration between Lynch and Splet on *The Grandmother* was so successful that the film went on to win prizes at the San Francisco, Bellevue, and Atlanta film festivals, and the Critics' Choice Award of a panel voting on the twelve best filmmakers to be given grants by the AFI. Also, George Stevens, Jr, and Tony Vellani were so impressed that they offered Splet the position of head of the sound department at the new AFI Centre in L.A. Although he resisted for a while, Splet finally accepted.

So, in 1970, Lynch, his wife and baby daughter, Splet, and Jack Fisk all headed for California together.

The AFI's Centre for Advanced Film Studies was at that time located at a mansion in Beverly Hills. Its program was a mixture of classes, seminars, and practical filmmaking experience. It exposed the students to a large variety of films and filmmaking techniques, bringing in people from the industry to pass

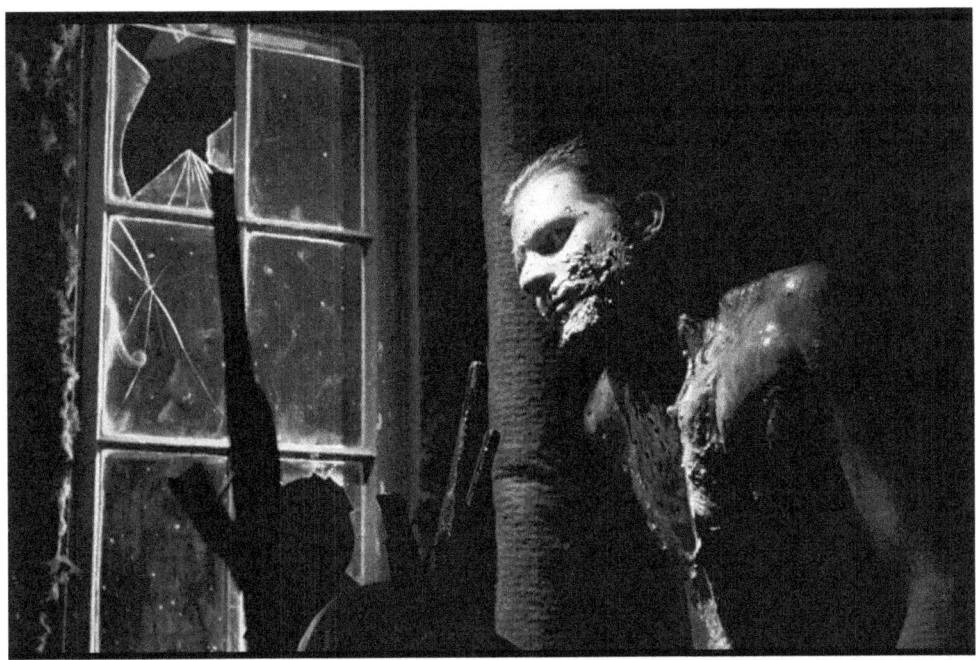
David Lynch's friend Jack Fisk in uncomfortable makeup as the Man in the Planet.

along their experience and knowledge. In those early years, it was a fairly loose situation; now it has moved to a new location in Greystone, California, has larger numbers of students in attendance, and the program is more regimented. There is now a large emphasis on the use of video systems for experimenting with film techniques, but a smaller percentage of students are permitted to actually make films in their second year than was the case in Lynch's time. Although Lynch is himself now on the board of directors, he is grateful that the school was less formal when he attended as a fellow in the early Seventies.

"I'm thankful that I went when it was more loose," he said. "If you wanted to learn something, somebody would be around to tell you about somebody that knew that or you could drop in on a class if you wanted to, but you could do a lot of your own work." Lynch is not a great believer in schools, "even though they're fun places to be because of the inspiration of other painters and other filmmakers." There are people who can teach a lot about the forms and techniques of art and film, much can be learned in a classroom situation; but there is a tremendous amount that can only be learned through direct experience – and what is learned from teachers in a classroom can only be truly validated by that experience. The great value of the AFI's independent grant program, under which *The Grandmother* was made, was that it allowed the filmmaker to learn by doing. "You go off and you just do it," said Lynch, "you make your own mistakes. You do your budget, get it together, and because they give you that responsibility, not treating you like an idiot, you try to do a good job."

For Lynch, the most influential part of the Centre's curriculum was the film analysis class given under the tutelage of Frank Daniel, former dean of the Czechoslovakian film school. A film would be screened and each student would be assigned the analysis of one aspect of it: sound, editing, camera, acting, etc. "And you would really watch the film from the editing point of view," said Lynch, "or the sound point of view, or the music point of view. And then give your idea of how the guy thought about music and how he used music and how it fit in or it didn't fit in with the story." Then Daniel would sum up and add his analysis. And they would also talk about structure. All of which Lynch found invaluable, coming as he did from a painting background. "All these things registered. Even though I never really thought about it so much, I think that a lot of this stuff sunk in." Indeed, the influence is apparent in some of the differences between *The Grandmother* and *Eraserhead*; where the first is essentially a flow of images spurred by the painter's mind, the second has a definite structure of incidents. However, despite this emergence of a narrative sense, *Eraserhead* relies on its system of images for the bulk of its power; its meaning is contained more in those images than in its spare narrative.

In applying for admittance to the Centre, Lynch had to submit previous work plus a script – as he had done in applying for the original AFI grant. *The Grandmother* of course constituted the previous work, while the script was a piece called *Gardenback*. As it turned out, Lynch spent most of his first year at the Centre working on that script. Caleb Deschanel, subsequently the cinematographer on such films as *The Black Stallion* and *Being There*, was at the AFI at that time and he introduced Lynch to a producer at Twentieth Century Fox who became interested in expanding *Gardenback* into a feature. "But," Lynch recalled, "it wasn't a film that was really meant to blow up. I couldn't think in a regular enough way, with regular dialogue, to make it work for them. A lot of people tried to help me, but the bits that I liked started floating further apart and in between was the stuff I didn't like."

Finally the frustration became too much. Lynch went down to the sound department and told Alan Splet, "That's it," and the two of them walked out. They went to a restaurant and ate a big meal. And when they walked back to Lynch's house, his wife Peggy told them that the AFI had been calling: would Lynch go back and at least talk to them? So Lynch went back to talk.

"Okay," they said, "everybody's gotten upset, but you've been calm and reasonable. Now if you're upset, something must be wrong. What do you want to do?"

"Well," Lynch replied, "I don't want to do *Gardenback*. This is ruined. I don't want to do it. I want to do this thing called *Eraserhead*."

And they replied, "Go ahead and do it."

One further difficulty stood in Lynch's way. That year, a student at the Centre named Stanton Kaye had been picked out of a group which included Jeremy Kagan, Matthew Robbins, and others, to do the first feature film at the AFI, a thing called *In Pursuit of Treasure*. Everybody at the Centre worked on it in some way. Lynch, because of his experience in casting, was sent to Kanab, Utah, for two days which stretched into two weeks, to cast ten thousand gold bricks. He worked up to twenty hours a day in a basement with a man called Happy. This relatively expensive film project "turned out to be quite a fiasco," said Lynch, "which almost shut AFI down." A lot of money was spent, the film was never made, and "feature" became something of a dirty word at the AFI. There was a reluctance about giving money to directing fellows as a result.

Lynch knew that his film would be a feature, but because of his compressed scriptwriting style, his emphasis on image rather than narrative and dialogue, the *Eraserhead* script was only twenty-one pages long. So the AFI said the film would be twenty-one minutes long. Lynch said, "I think it's going to be a bit longer than that." "Well, okay," they replied. "Forty-two minutes." According to Doreen Small, who became the film's production manager, the bargaining went a little further, with Lynch offering to shoot in black-and-white if they would let him shoot in 35mm. But given Lynch's strong advocacy of black-and-white, such a deal would not have entailed any sacrifice.

Eraserhead bears a number of similarities to *The Grandmother*. It too is about loneliness, fear, a longing for security, a desperate need to escape from a grim life which entraps the central character. But in *Eraserhead* these things expand to fill a whole world, a bleak, dying post-industrial wasteland. The family, however, still figures large in its scheme. But where in *The Grandmother* it is distant and unfeeling, isolating the boy, in *Eraserhead* Henry Spencer finds it threatening; not simply closed to him, its interactions a mystery, but ready to actively assault the dull cocoon of his life. His marriage to Mary X does not provide him with a little warmth and companionship, protection from the bleak outside world – it brings hostility and resentment from Mary and leaves him with a demanding, insatiable child which traps him more deeply in the world from which he longs to escape.

Each apparent way out (Mary's leaving him; the visit of a sexually available neighbour; the seeming escape into some other, outer world in the Eraserhead dream sequence) only leads him back into the trap, the failed promise of escape making it even tighter, more claustrophobic than before. At the centre is the baby, not threatening but helpless; its dependence on Henry is what holds him; he is bound by responsibility. In the end, Henry inflicts a horrible death on the baby, repudiating that responsibility, an act which shatters his world and allows him to escape to his sterile Heaven.

Judging by these films, one might expect David Lynch to be a dark and brooding figure, perhaps resembling in intensity pictures of the young Orson Welles. Or, as Mel Brooks put it, "I expected to meet a grotesque, a fat little German with fat stains running down his chin and just eating pork." The actuality is quite different from the expectation: a "clean American WASP kid; it's like Jimmy Stewart thirty-five years ago."

Lynch is a friendly, rather boyish man in his mid-thirties, who appears to have stepped out of the *Happy Days* Fifties of drive-ins, sock-hops, and cruising the strip on a Saturday night. His speech is littered with words like "neat" and "nifty". There is nothing in his appearance to suggest the bleak intensity of his films.

In late 1981, when Lynch finally agreed to tell the full story of the making of *Eraserhead*, he was based at Universal Studios in a large, airy office in which he was preparing the *Dune* project. His desk was a litter of papers and on the wall behind him hung some modular drawings he calls "rickies". On the office door was tacked a note which read, "Gone for a short hike for woodpeckers. D.K.L." and on the black office couch sat five stuffed toy woodpeckers – Chucko, Buster, Pete, Bob and Dan; "the boys" (who later would be relocated to Mexico for the shooting of *Dune*) – one of whom held a pencil with which, Lynch pointed out, he had scrawled in a moment of treachery the names of Lucas and Spielberg on one of the walls. It was apparent that the man had a sense of humour, but he hardly seemed disturbed. And the childhood he spoke of was almost idyllic.

"When my parents saw *The Grandmother*," he said, "they were very upset because they didn't know where this came from. I had a sort of golden childhood." Born in Missoula, Montana, January 20, 1946, into an "extremely happy" family, his memories are of blue skies, red flowers, white picket fences, and green grass, with birds chirping in the trees and a plane droning overhead. He would take afternoon naps and watch red ants crawling on the cherry tree. His parents never argued, he got along with his brother and sister. His toys were all new, paint gleaming, and he wore "clean little corduroys". All his grandparents got along and when they visited in their nice Buicks they brought treats. A general aura of happiness suffuses Lynch's memories of those days. "And I think what happened was that I went to a big city and it scared me." He began to sense that what he knew was only a small part of the "real world" and that the rest of it was not quite so rosy. "And," he said, "it was real frightening."

The idea of the city as a frightening, alien place runs through *Eraserhead*. But if Lynch is to be believed, this is not the calculated expression of an idea. He speaks a great deal of feeling and intuition, indeed he seems to distrust words to some degree and although highly articulate, he claims that "I can't talk about things so well." Again, much of this stems from his painting background. He thinks in terms of visual images and there is a fear that translating those images into words will at least partially sterilize them by pinning down only a fraction of the meaning they convey. By refusing to verbalize he can leave the images largely uninterpreted so that they maintain their original power, their multiple associations which might vary widely from viewer to viewer. Lynch will not even say how he interprets *Eraserhead*, what he intended to say with the film, because to him it is like a Rorschach test and every viewer's interpretation is as valid as his own; he does not want the film to be pinned down, its meanings fixed by an "orthodox" interpretation.

Even during production, he did not tell any of the cast or crew what he was trying to say with the film. "He would give me little clues as to what it meant," said Fred Elmes, the film's second cinematographer, "or how this related to that. He gave me enough to keep me involved, to keep me hooked with it." But Lynch would deal chiefly only with the surface level, the physical expression of the image. "You can do a whole lot of stuff scene by scene," said Lynch; "if it has resonance in different levels, you can talk mainly on this level and if it's true" the validity will carry into the other levels. "But you don't ever have to really talk about this." Everybody who worked on the film accepted this and trusted that what they were doing was far more than just a film school exercise. "Everybody seemed to tune into what it was that we were doing," Lynch commented, "and we never really sat down and did any heavy kind of intellectualizing. Like Jack (Nance) says, 'We'll leave that to the smart guys back east.'"

Nonetheless, it is possible to see where the main impetus of the film came from. As Lynch himself said, "*Eraserhead* is the real Philadelphia Story. Philadelphia itself was a place I never wanted to go to – ever. It was really a frightening city. There's an atmosphere in every place that you go. And it's hard to imagine the atmosphere, but once you're set in it, you say, 'I see what you're talking about.'" In Philadelphia "it's mainly an atmosphere of fear, just all-pervading fear."

Lynch was an art student living a hippie existence before hippie times. "We lived in strange ways and strange parts of town," he recalled. But the hostility between police and hippies had not yet surfaced. "One time I was walking around at night with a stick with nails driven through it and a squad car pulls up alongside of me, and he says, 'What've you got there?' And I showed him this stick with nails driven through it. He said, 'Good for you, bud,' and took off.

Lynch lived in an industrial area, virtually deserted after dark but for occasional echoing footsteps and the odd passing car. It was little narrow streets and tall buildings without lights. Brick and soot-covered windows. Underpasses and railroads. He lived kitty-corner from the city morgue, a few blocks from where Edgar Allan Poe once lived. And next door was Pop's Diner, where Pop lived with his son, Andy, and another man who had little dogs. "You know how ticks fill up with blood?" Lynch asked. "The dogs were like that, totally ready to burst, like water balloons with legs. Everybody in Philadelphia, the people that lived there, especially in these areas, were extremely strange. All this started taking its toll."

He lived in Philadelphia for five years. He met and married his first wife there and their daughter, Jennifer, was born there. And all that time, he was poor and struggling to survive. Whatever fears and tensions he might have felt through those years emerge in the densely compressed images of *Eraserhead*. But the film should not be seen as simply a bizarre autobiographical piece. Lynch is an artist, not a reporter. He himself is not present in the film. He has essentially gathered together a number of psychological states related to the city, to fear and isolation, and embodied them in concrete images which will stir up in the viewer echoes of any of those states which he may himself have experienced.

For all the reality which Lynch gives to the world of the film, it is obviously not a realistic film. What Lynch does is to distort what is familiar; at first one perceives it as strange, but as one gradually comes to see its familiarity, one is forced to reevaluate what is usually accepted without question. By showing us the familiar in the strange, he makes us aware of what is strange about the familiar. Normalcy is a habit; but what is normal to the people of *Eraserhead*'s world seems strange to us. Yet they view it all with the same habit of acceptance that we ourselves have in relation to the "real world". Thus we become aware of the habit itself as a distinct part of our own experience. In the film's world our own rules no longer apply; we have to seek out the rules by which this new world operates, and so become aware again of the rules we have come to take for granted. If people do not really act as they do in the film's world, by what rules do people really act?

In seeking the rules of the film's world, we begin to take notice of any and every little detail; is this, we wonder, significant? Lynch himself finds the extent of this searching both surprising and amusing. Early in the film, Henry puts his right foot in a mud puddle, but when he gets home it is his left foot which is wet. The viewer takes note of the fact and wonders if it means something. In this case, Lynch laughed, "that's accidental. Both socks were wet, but we couldn't remember which shoe went in the puddle. You know, it's hard to believe that someone looks at your films so closely." But in the world of *Eraserhead*, the viewer has no choice but to search amongst all the details for what is significant.

By shifting the familiar, what we call "reality", a few degrees over, Lynch knocks us off balance and the resulting uneasiness forces us to reconsider what we normally accept without thinking about it. We discover that the frightening, claustrophobic world of *Eraserhead* is not so different from our own experience as it first seemed. Lynch essentially just gives an external concrete form to familiar mental states: the baby which entraps Henry becomes an insatiable monster; fear of sex becomes a parasitic disease in the form of "foetuses"; the longing for escape into a comfortable security becomes a strange sterile Heaven.

Hanry Spencer (Jack Nance) in a contemplative moment.

Given approximately $10,000 by the AFI, Lynch had to be very careful if he was going to see his film to completion. Yet at the start he had no idea just what a long haul it was going to be. Early in 1972, he began to make preparations. Below the main mansion at the Centre, there was a cluster of stables, garages, quarters for maids and mechanics, and a huge hay loft, plus a greenhouse and the grounds around it. It was there that Lynch established what amounted to a small studio. "We had," he recalled, "about five or six rooms and this giant loft where all the other sets were built; a miniature soundstage and studio."

The set-building began immediately, with Lynch being assisted by his brother, John, and Alan Splet. For $100, he had bought a lot of flats from a studio which was going out of business and these were used again and again. When one set was done with, it was taken apart and the pieces used to build another. The same area of the loft served for the pencil factory, the pencil company front office, the lobby of Henry's building. "All these rooms were the same space with different sets built in it," commented Catherine Coulson, the film's camera assistant. "And now I work on union films and I see these art departments with ten people doing the same thing, not quite as well sometimes. David really pretty much did everything himself. He has tremendous energy; he can just go and go and go for something that interests him."

Lynch derived a lot of pleasure from this work, building a wall out of *papier-mache* and finishing it so that it looked as if it might be "forty feet thick, but it's only a sixteenth of an inch thick. That's what I loved about the whole *Eraserhead* thing; faking it, but still taking the time to get it right and get the mood." Yet, if a set cost thirty or thirty-five dollars, it was counted expensive.

The baby was also created during this pre-production period. An alien, reptilian creature, little more than a head attached by a thin neck to a soft, shapeless body, it is not so much a deformed human as a perfectly formed "something else". The illusion of life which Lynch managed to instill in the creature provides the film with much of its power. But Lynch, always reluctant to discuss technical matters, particularly in the area of effects, flatly refuses to discuss the baby, even to the point of declining credit for having designed it. "In a way," he commented, "nobody designs anything. All these shapes are found in nature, something like archetypes that everyone can relate to even if they can't intellectualize why." Lynch talks a great deal about being something like a channel through which ideas and images flow. If asked where he came up with some detail – like the bowl of water in Henry's drawer, or the X's vegetable grandmother – he replies, "I can't even take credit for these things. When you get an idea and you go with it and later on you find out that the proportions were correct, you can't really take credit for it because it's happening so much out of your control. If you let ideas flow, they flow, and you get them when you need them."

But Lynch's reluctance about talking of the technical aspects of the film is as simple as Ray Harryhausen's reticence: a feeling that explaining the magic act destroys the illusion. The baby in *Eraserhead* seems appallingly alive; but to reveal how it was done – "it's all logic and common sense anyway," said Lynch – would reduce it to a simple technical accomplishment, knowledge of which would strip away much of its effective power. As with Harryhausen's animation, the principles could be found with a little effort by anyone who wanted to devote the time to the problem; but Lynch himself refuses to undercut the effect he so painstakingly worked to create. He prefers to leave people wondering because their interest may bring them back to the film again and again.

As preparations continued, Lynch began to gather together the people with whom, and equipment with which, he would give his ideas cinematic life. Because of the size of the project, it would no longer be possible for him to photograph it himself, as he had done with *The Alphabet* and *The Grandmother*.

Lynch had met cinematographer Herb Cardwell at Calvin Productions in Philadelphia. One day Alan Splet happened to mention that Cardwell would like to get out of industrial films. "Are you kidding?" Lynch said. "Herb would be great." So Cardwell, who died a few years after his work on the film, became the project's first cameraman.

Doreen Small, the film's production manager during the first year, came to the project through Jack Fisk, for whom she had worked while he was art director on a black exploitation film called *Cool Breeze*. Small had moved to L.A. from New York where she had worked in an art gallery. She got into movies through a neighbour who was an assistant art director on *Cool Breeze*. Fisk told her about Lynch, saying that he needed help getting props, organizing things – the sort of work she had been doing under Fisk. When she came to *Eraserhead*, no shooting had yet been done. Henry's room was still being constructed, and it was necessary to find the "decorations" for it: the picture of a nuclear explosion which hangs on the wall; the matted substance which lies under the radiator, "a kind of sticky, oily hair stuff" found at a "kind of oil well over on Robertson Avenue." She also helped to build a lot of incidental props. And then Lynch suggested that she ask around at the AFI to find out how to be a production manager and script assistant.

The actors whom Lynch gathered for the film all turned out to be the first people he saw for the roles. Charlotte Stewart (Mary X) came to the film through her roommate at that time, Doreen Small. Judith Roberts (the Beautiful Woman Across the Hall), Alan Joseph (Bill X), and Jeanne Bates (Mrs X) had all been members of a theatre workshop, Theatre West. Roberts knew Lynch and recommended Bates to him. Bates at one time had been under contract to Columbia, where she had made twenty-two pictures; she had usually been cast as "the dear young thing and nice young – well, at that time young – mothers," she said. At first, she recalled, Lynch told her that she was too pretty. "She's great," said Lynch. "She would come in all dressed up and very stylish, come into the X's house, and she just didn't fit in." But she thoroughly enjoyed the experience of putting on moles and hair, making herself, with Lynch's help, look as dreadful as possible. "I thought it was wonderful," she said. "I wanted to get out of doing nice ladies." And by the first night of filming she fitted in perfectly.

Lynch's most important acquisition for the cast was unquestionably Jack Nance who, as Henry, is the centre of the film. Yet, as Lynch put it, "We didn't have that great an interview." Jack Nance is a very low-key character. He speaks with a slow drawl in a soft voice with a slight smile of ironic humour almost perpetually on his lips. Catherine Coulson, at that time married to Nance, commented, "Jack is not the kind of person who gets very enthusiastic unless something really catches his imagination." Having had experience of student filmmakers before, Nance was a little wary of Lynch. "I had done a couple of AFI projects before," he said. "We kind of kept our distance from one another at first. He wasn't sure and I wasn't sure." Lynch was "this crazy guy with a beat up straw hat and three neckties, and he started telling me strange tales."

Nance describes himself as a Boston Irish Catholic Yankee who, as a boy, was transplanted to Texas and, as a result, spent all his childhood re-fighting the Civil War. Beginning as a stage actor in Dallas, he recalls as the happiest time of his life his days on the road in the Southwest: small theatres, old vaudeville houses, one-nighters in small towns – the classic suitcase existence of the travelling player. Nance confessed that "I don't take movies seriously really." He has done a number of what he calls "Roger Corman hot rod movies and Chuck Norris karate pictures," but only three projects which he views with some pride: a Sixties *cinema verite* piece called *Bushman*, about the plight of a Nigerian tribesman who visits the States as a student during the period of student and racial unrest; *Eraserhead*; and Wim Wenders' *Hammett*, like *Eraserhead* a film plagued by delays and financial problems.

In the end, it was something unconnected with the film which decided Lynch to hire Nance. As they were about to part company in the parking lot, Nance, who owned a Volkswagen, saw an old VW which had been fitted with a big home-made wooden rack. "It was kind of an ingenious design," he said. "You could probably load as much on the VW as you could on a truck. I thought what a neat thing. So I said, 'Boy, whoever built that thing must be on the ball.' So David said, 'Thank you, Jack. I did that and you're hired.'" It was Nance's enthusiasm about the rack which enabled Lynch to see a whole other side of him, a side which had been dormant during the interview.

Nance himself had a personal reason for being at least curious about the project: the script. "I was reading all of these strange images," he recalled, "and then I got to the final scene where there's the giant baby head. And I was struck by that because it was describing in some detail a sort of hallucination that I'd had at one time when I was very sick and running a fever. I was taking codeine, and I was in a hotel room in Great Bend, Kansas, in a blizzard, dying, and I had a terrible nightmarish kind of delirium hallucination, that when I was reading that scene I thought, 'My god, this is exactly like that time in Great Bend.' And then later, when he introduced me to the baby, I went, 'That's it!'"

It was, incidentally, Nance who named the baby. First he just called it "a little light bulb", but then he came up with the name "Spike" and it stuck. Asked where it came from, he smiled and replied, "I think it's on the birth certificate."

Catherine Coulson, an actress who was to become an important member of the crew, staying with the film to the end, was originally brought in by her husband with a view to playing the part of a nurse in the film. "She was this crusty woman," said Coulson, "and Jack said to David, 'You should meet my wife; she'd be perfect for this part.'" Nance told her enthusiastically about Lynch, "an oddball who wears three ties and this hat. He's built all these sets already down at AFI and he's really quite, quite brilliant. He's real sweet and very innocent."

Coulson met Lynch to audition for the part of the nurse, wearing "a prim little dress and my hair back very severely." Lynch agreed that she would be fine for the part. Then he began to rehearse Nance and Charlotte Stewart in the scene in which Henry arrives home as Mary is having trouble feeding the baby – the first baby scene in the final version of the film. And Lynch gave Coulson a stopwatch and asked if she would time the scene. She stood on a rolled up carpet, made by Lynch himself, which would eventually adorn the lobby of Henry's building, and timed the scene "because he wanted to be sure that the film would be the right length," she said. "Which now is so amusing to me." If Lynch knew from the start that he was making a feature, some of the other people involved started out with the same view as the AFI: short script, short film. But even Lynch did not at that time have a realistic idea of the scale of the task on which they were embarking. "It was supposed to take a few weeks to shoot," said Coulson. "I think the original shooting schedule was six weeks."

As it turned out, the film would finally reach completion more than four years after Lynch started to build his sets.

Lynch began by rehearsing all the major scenes. "He worked very meticulously," Jack Nance recalled. "Every reaction and every look and everything that was happening inside Henry's head – we had to get into that in great detail. I don't think it was analyzed. We had these long strange conversations, skull sessions, and things would reveal themselves to us a lot as we were going along. Lynch is really wonderful at drawing images. He doesn't have a theatrical background; he has an art background. He can communicate with actors. Actors react to imagery. They see themselves in the big picture and so the best directors always give very visual kinds of images that you can work with. Lynch is just great at that."

Of working with actors, Lynch said, "I like an actor that I can talk to and get what I want from. I don't want to say, 'My way,' and not listen to anybody else's point of view. If somebody does something that is super and it works, I hope I'll be able to see it. But if they're doing something that doesn't work – I know the rest of the film and the way it's going and this is wrong – they've got to be able to do it so it's right. Otherwise you just turn them loose."

As the production progressed, everybody seemed to develop a sense of the rules of the world Lynch was creating. "Because the rules were so strong and the world was so real to us," said Lynch, "it was real easy to tell when you were doing something wrong."

"Sometimes we didn't know what was happening," Nance commented. "I remember one particular shot, a very simple, quick shot. I was supposed to say, 'No kidding,' or something and turn and walk away. And we worked on it take after take after take, a whole reel of film. Herb Cardwell, the cameraman, had to change magazines, so he just opened up the magazine and started throwing the film out on the floor, and he said, 'Well, at least we won't have to look at that shit in the screening room.' For some reason, it didn't work. It played all right, but there was something that wasn't there. We had a lot of that; unless we knew exactly what was going on in Henry's mind, it was no use cranking up the camera."

"Henry is a total blank," said Lynch. "When Jack had any kind of expression, it was wrong. The more he could empty out, the closer it got. I just consider myself super fortunate to have had Jack. There's no other person, in my mind, that could ever do it."

"Henry was very easy," according to Nance. "It was like putting on a comfortable suit to put on that character." In fact, "I would put on the suit and the tie and there was Henry. In spite of the fact the world in *Eraserhead* is strange and very bizarre and Henry is a very bizarre character, the fact is he was just a regular guy. A real ordinary joker."

Like any ordinary workaday guy, "he was fairly responsible, held down a job, and got along in the world. He had his own ideas of what was cool. He had a haircut that he probably thought was cool and he probably thought that the white socks with the suit was kind of flashy. And he had hip taste in music." An ordinary everyday guy in an ordinary everyday story: "Happens all the time. It's basically your boy meets girl story."

By the time shooting began, on May 29, 1972, Catherine Coulson, who as Nance's wife had often been present during the rehearsals, had been absorbed into the crew. Lynch would make suggestions: "Well, since you're going to be here, would you like to maybe hold the boom or push the dolly?" There were so few people involved that quite quickly any distinctions between jobs broke down. Everybody simply did what they could whenever necessary. Soon Lynch suggested that Coulson take some production stills, so Cardwell taught her how to do it. She held the boom and pushed the dolly a few times, and began to learn about lighting. "I started learning what inkies and babies and 2Ks were," she recalled, "and how to hang them." When it became apparent that bringing in take-out food was not the best way of feeding the crew, she began making dinner for them all. "We had a little hotplate and a frying pan and we just made every meal. By the time we were really in the thick of it, we were making breakfast, lunch, and dinner. That sort of took care of my nurturing self, and then my art self was also getting satisfied by doing these other jobs."

After the first few weeks of shooting, the original camera assistant left the film. Coulson was drafted. "It was a scene with Henry in the hallway," she recalled, "walking down the hall toward his room. Herb said, 'This is the follow-focus knob and as he walks toward us, you have to hit the number on the lens how many feet away from the camera he is.' So he taught me how to tape off the hallway and then he said, 'As he comes forward of course, you turn the knob faster.' That was really my first instance of doing what I later found out was a highly technical job!"

"The day shooting began, a number of AFI people – Frank Daniel, Tony Vellani, and some others – looked in at the stables," Lynch recalled, "and kind of peeped in and sort of smiled. And then they left." They also watched the first dailies, but "they never said anything about either one. They thought everything was under control." This was in part because both Herb Cardwell and Alan Splet were very experienced men, in part because everything looked so good; sets had been built at the AFI before, but none so complete as these. Lynch and Splet had devised very effective sound blankets, using fibreglass insulation in burlap bags to cover all the walls not in a shot, which resulted in their obtaining extremely clean sound. "It just looked like we were really rolling," said lynch. "And we were." But another factor to which he attributes the lack of interference from the AFI was the fact that they felt placatory towards him after the failure of *Gardenback*. And, of course, they were busy with the running of the school.

Because the grounds, garages, and greenhouse were also used by the Beverly Hills parks department, the area was very noisy during the day, with trucks and equipment coming and going. It was decided that they would shoot on a night schedule – a decision also influenced by Lynch's own preference for working at night. This enabled members of the crew to do other jobs at the same time: Splet had his position as head of the sound department at the AFI; Coulson would work as a waitress during the day. It made for a strenuous life, Coulson recalled. "I always say I met David as a young woman and by the time I finished *Eraserhead*, I had aged. We worked long hard hours."

Yet Coulson said that her only real regret about the film was that she did not get the credit: "Mr Nance's hair by ..." In truth, though, the concept for Henry's hair-style was Lynch's – as indeed almost every detail in the film belonged to Lynch, the crew serving to execute his highly specific designs. Of course, some of the credit in this instance must go to Jack Nance's hair. Lynch wanted Henry to have it "short on the sides, tall on the top." What he had in mind was just a couple of inches. Nance had his hair cut in preparation two weeks before the start of shooting, allowing it to grow back out a little. When the first night of shooting arrived, Coulson teased it, getting, she said, "a kind of maniacal pleasure from back-combing his hair." Lynch was in another room at the time, and when he entered he found the crew all laughing. "They thought it was totally ridiculous," he recalled. "Obviously it was going to have to be cut down." But Lynch's instincts told him that this was the genuine Henry look – straight up five or six inches. "'By god, that's it.' And they said, 'No, no, no, you can't do that.' And I said, 'No, we've got to do this. This is unbelievable.' And in a couple of hours it literally became ordinary." Lynch considers himself very lucky in having found Nance. "How many people's hair would do that?" he asked. "And he was a dream to work with."

"One of the hardest things," Coulson recalled, "was keeping Jack's haircut all those years. When he wasn't shooting for a long time, he would let it go, but then poor Jack would have to have another haircut before starting to shoot again. My family didn't know him any other way really, except with that goofy hair, which he would try to comb down. But it really never looked very good. We have a lot of family pictures at Christmastime with Jack with this goofy haircut." Coulson herself learned how to do the cut when the trips to the barber became too expensive.

The first scene to be shot that night was Henry's visit to the X's, where Henry sits awkwardly on the couch beside Mary and has a "conversation" with Mrs X. "So, Henry," she asks, "what do you do?" "Oh," he replies, "I'm on vacation." Despite the peculiarly unnatural pacing Lynch wanted in the dialogue, the sense of disconnection between question and response, the actors had no

Charlotte Stewart as Mary X, awaiting the arrival of Henry.

difficulty in establishing the relationships between characters. "It didn't cause any kind of problems with 'what you're saying has nothing to do with what I'm saying'," Nance recalled, "because that's what we were doing." What was required from the cast was essentially straightforward because Lynch could convey so clearly to them just what was going on in this world.

The first shot of the production was done in a single take.

From May 29, 1972, shooting continued quite steadily for almost a year. During that time the concept of the film went through only one major change from Lynch's original conception. Most of the ideas had already been developed before shooting started, and the film was to remain faithful to them through to the end. In part this derives from Lynch's refusal to analyze; he believes in allowing the subconscious to shape his work with as little interference as possible from the conscious. "I think that's part of these rules," he said. "You try to stick close to that original thing, unless it really starts feeling wrong, because that idea came with some power to it. You'd be closer to the truth of something if you try to be true to those original ideas." Because he had essentially unlimited time, no outside interference, and the complete confidence of the cast and crew, Lynch was able to maintain that integrity; he was never required to explain what he was doing and so was able to keep as much of the subconscious purity of the images as was possible. But if other concepts emerged during the filming which seemed valid, he was ready to incorporate them. "You could say, 'Well, gee, that makes it totally different.' But the thing is, the film isn't done 'til it's done." What happened during that first year was a certain lightening of the film's mood.

"It was much less of a dream," said Doreen Small, "and much more of a nightmare when we began." At that time, said Small, Lynch smoked a lot of cigarettes, drank a lot of coffee, and woke up in a foul mood – "we used to rotate who would wake David up." Jack Nance recalled that Lynch could be extremely temperamental if things were not going just the way he wanted. But then he took up meditation.

"I had everything going for me," Lynch explained. "I was supposedly doing what I wanted to do more than anything else: making films. I practically had a little studio and we were working – and I just wasn't happy. I was real innocent in metaphysical things and suddenly someone mentioned meditation. And I knew it was for me."

In the original conception, Henry's longing for escape had no object. The film would end with the killing of the baby and the disintegration of the world. But as Lynch pulled himself out of his personal gloom, a little light penetrated the world of *Eraserhead*. "One day," he recalled, "I was sitting in the food room and

I just drew this little lady, and little foetuses were falling out of her. And I wrote the lyrics for the song 'In Heaven'. And I thought she would live in the radiator, where it's nice and warm, and this would be a real comfort for Henry. So I went running into this set which was just across the hall and I looked at the radiator and, lo and behold! there was this little square in it. It was perfect. And not only that; we had shot scenes with Henry looking at the radiator two different times. There was no loss and there was nothing extra we had to shoot. It fit in perfectly." So Henry's longing was answered by Lynch's subconscious and an entirely acceptable "happy ending" appeared virtually out of nowhere.

For all his confidence in his vision, his assurance in handling cast and crew – even with long-time professionals like Jeanne Bates, he "did not doubt for a moment that he could tell them what to do," according to Doreen Small – Lynch did have what he termed "an insecurity thing." Its detrimental effects were cleared up by the meditation, but it also showed up in a number of other ways, like the old straw hat and three ties which he wore at that time. "I still like to have my collar buttoned," he commented. Lynch, said Jack Nance, "is the most ritualistic person I know. Even coffee used to be a ritual. 'Jack,' he'd say, kind of excited, 'let's have our coffee now.'" Lynch has a daily routine of giving himself a little treat every afternoon. "For a while," Nance continued, "it was grilled cheese sandwiches, the same time every day. He tried a number of things before he settled on Bob's shakes." Lynch's dedication to the chocolate shakes at Bob's Big Boy is now widely known.

The most positive aspect of this side of Lynch's character appears in the meticulous way he works, the careful planning, the painstaking attention to the smallest of details. "He had very precise ways of doing things," said Catherine Coulson. "I started helping him in the afternoons to build things. The first thing I had to learn was how to wash paint brushes. And I remember he taught me how to hammer."

Fred Elmes, who joined the film after nine months of shooting when Herb Cardwell had to leave for financial reasons, told of coming on to the set without knowing the already well-established ground rules. "Everybody," he said, "knew where everything was and what everything was and how David worked – what to do and what not to do. So I went into it the way I normally would, which is to, in a very quiet way, take charge of what needs to be done and to do it myself. In the case of *Eraserhead* I really had to do it myself because there was nobody else to tell to do it. We were doing a closeup of the baby and David had looked through the camera and lined it up and it was all ready to go. And I went over to the table and I moved this little prop over so that it was not hidden so much by something else. And Catherine turned to me and said, 'Fred, we don't move things on that table.' And I said, 'Well, it's just that it was blocked and I wanted to see it more clearly.' And she said, 'Well, David has never moved anything on the table.' So I put it back," he laughed. "Heaven forbid David should see!"

Lynch's fastidiousness extended to care of the budget as well. But as tight as the money was, he was determined that no one should work for free, so he insisted on paying everyone a small stipend – although Herb Cardwell, during his tenure, received a true salary. "David was kind of wonderful," Jeanne Bates recalled. "He was very conscientious about wanting to pay the actors a stipend. That was one of the things that was kind of dear about him." The people involved accepted the small sum because they knew that it mattered to Lynch and they cared about what they were doing. "It was a real artist's film," said Coulson, "a film being made by a wonderful human being who I think is quite a genius." He had a clear, strong vision tempered with enough consideration to let people help him to realize it, but always with enough ego to make it very clear that it was his film. It was rewarding to work with him, Coulson asserted, "because you knew he wasn't ripping you off. He has the ability to jump into the other person's place and be compassionate and loving. I had worked on other AFI films where it was just assumed that the actors and technicians worked for free, but David took his initial money from AFI and paid everybody. And I was making $25 a week, but when we ran real low on money, we cut everybody's salary in half, and I was making $12.50 a week. Which of course I always put back into the food. We would all kind of pool our money to some extent. I never felt that it was right any other way. It really did seem like our film, even though it was David's film. There was a sense of collaboration."

There were of course ways to get around such a tight budget, at least in some areas. Lynch would send Doreen Small out to swap meets and such, to see what she could find in the way of knick-knacks. The more bits and pieces, the better; it gave him more to choose from when dressing the sets. "She got a whole box-load of these things for $5," he recalled, "and she got an electric fan that I really liked." Then there was the little duck which floats in a bowl of water as the X's dining table centrepiece, and the tailless mounted fish on the X's wall.

The Salvation Army and Goodwill Industries proved a useful source. "Henry's whole wardrobe was gotten at Goodwill," Lynch recalled. "It was like we were going shopping, and we got his shoes and his socks and his pants, his penholder and all his pens, and got him all geared up with his little tie tack and his tie. And we got Bill X's hat and some neat things for his belt."

Another valuable source was Catherine Coulson's aunt, Margit Fellegi, a flamboyant designer of bathing suits who lived in a big seventeen room Beverly Hills house "and had years and years' worth of stuff. She loved David," said Coulson, "and really supplied a lot of props." She gave them the vaporizer for the sequence of the baby's illness and some old worn sheets for Henry's bed. "One of the first jobs I had," Coulson recalled, "was dying these sheets so that they weren't 'white' white. We were shooting black and white and you don't want to have 'white' white. So I was dipping them in tea and coffee to make them the right colour." Aunt Margit also supplied the old, ragged blanket which covers Henry's bed. This was a source of continuity problems because, like Jack Nance, the blanket aged during the years of filming, gathering more and more holes.

Nance and Coulson even gave up their living room furniture for the film. It appears in the lobby of Henry's building. "When we would give something up, it would be gone for months," said Coulson, "because we would have to take it so slowly. It wasn't because of any kind of inefficiency, just because the job was being done basically by a couple of people."

One of the biggest strokes of luck Lynch encountered came when a friend mentioned that the studios threw out a lot of sound stock. "To them it's really nothing," Lynch said, "but to us it was pure gold. So we were going around in the trash at Warner Brothers and we filled my Volkswagen with raw stock. And Alan got it all into nice big reels with very few splices in them and he degaussed them all and we had all the raw stock we needed."

They began working on the sound early in the production. When it became apparent later in that first year that the initial money would be insufficient, one of Lynch's efforts at fund-raising involved bringing in a producer to show him what had already been done, in the hope that the man would put some money into the project. Among the mass of loosely edited footage was one scene which had been finalized, complete with sound; the first part of Henry's visit to the X's. "We wanted to get a real finish," recalled Alan Splet, "full sound and picture. We built that scene completely. We got all the sounds and we even did a mix on that section." The plan, unfortunately, did not work out as Lynch had hoped. The producer "got real upset," according to Lynch, "and he started giving me and Tony Vellani a lecture on filmmaking."

Jack Nance described the scene: "The guy blew his stack. He was enraged, he was offended. He went storming out of the screening room, and he was yelling, 'People don't talk like that!' He said, 'Look, I know people and people don't act like that! You people are crazy! People don't talk that way, people don't act like that. What do you think you're doing?'"

"He didn't put any money into it at all," Lynch concluded, adding wryly, "So there were indications that it was not going to be a blockbuster, that a lot of people weren't going to be able to relate to it." He recalled another incident: to all the people involved with the film, Henry's bizarre world seemed quite ordinary. But "one day we took Henry down to these oil tanks to get a shot, and he was all dressed up, with his hair up and all that. And as he was getting in the car, some secretaries came by and saw him." The looks on those secretaries' faces suddenly brought back the strangeness Lynch had experienced the first time he had seen Henry.

At one time or another, everyone on the film was struck by this contrast between the standards which the *Eraserhead* crew accepted as normal and the more general standards of the uninitiated. It was common practice when some technical problem arose for someone to call around the studios asking for advice. Catherine Coulson found herself with the task of finding the right substance to flow out of the dying baby at the film's climax. "I remember calling the Universal special effects department and saying, 'Do you have any suggestions as to how to fill a room full of mush?' And in my perspective that was a rather normal question to ask." The recipient of such a question would often find it rather peculiar.

Dinner at the X's: "Man-made" chicken.

Coulson recalled another such incident: "One time when David was editing the film a friend of mine was working next door in another editing room (at the AFI), and she got a call one night from David and Alan, asking, 'Do you have a radiator in your room?' And she said, 'Yes.' And they said they needed the sound of a radiator. And she said, 'I don't know if it's that kind of radiator.' And they said, 'No, no. We don't need the sound of a radiator hissing. We need the sound of somebody jumping off a radiator.'"

One area in which cutting corners would have been seriously detrimental was the photography. "We were shooting in black-and-white," commented Jack Nance, "and it was going to be really good black-and-white," the best they could make it. "It was a very slow, time-consuming process. All of the lights had to be very meticulously placed."

The use of black-and-white was dictated more by choice than by necessity. (Lynch would make the same choice again seven years later when he began work on his first commercial feature, the $6 million *The Elephant Man*.) Why this preference for black-and-white? "I've been forced to think about this because people ask me," he said. He has come up with two reasons. "One, I think black-and-white makes things seem not so normal; because we're used to seeing in colour, it removes you one step from a normal feeling. It makes it easier to go into another world or to go back in time." And two, "it seems to me that it makes you see more clearly. To me, a frame in black-and-white is purer than a colour frame." The black-and-white image is more schematic, less chaotic. It allows the filmmaker far greater control, more unity within the film – there is less discontinuity between interiors and exteriors. "It's less distracting. You'd probably be more apt to see the character and hear the character in black-and-white."

"I learned a lot from David," asserted Fred Elmes. "I had done black-and-white films as a student, and always kind of looked down on it; we shot in black-and-white because we couldn't afford colour mostly. That's the way I looked at it. But with David I learned to really appreciate all the possibilities of black-and-white." Born in New Jersey, Elmes had studied still photography at the Rochester Institute of Technology, and then had gone on to the graduate film school at NYU, which had confirmed for him that he really wanted to be a cinematographer. While a student, he had shot things on the side – some documentary, some dramatic, occasionally working as a camera assistant. After a few more years in New York, he had decided to head for California and the AFI seemed like a safe way to make the transition: to be a student again. However, there was not much for him to shoot at the AFI; the older cameramen got most of the available work. But when it became apparent that Herb Cardwell would be leaving the *Eraserhead* crew before the film was finished – his commitments allowed him to work on it for only nine months – Tony Vellani introduced Elmes to Lynch.

"David came up," Elmes recalled, "a warm handshake, 'Hi, how are you?' And we chatted for a couple of minutes, then he took me in to see dailies. They had selected a couple of reels of film to give me a feel of what was happening, to see if I wanted to be involved. And they started with the real tame stuff; Henry in his room, walking outside and so on. And then they got to the baby, which–

they saved for the end and, god, I didn't know what to make of it. It was bizarre, but captivating at the same time. I just didn't know what I was getting involved in. But I really was hooked right from the beginning."

There was no difficulty in maintaining visual continuity. "In temperament they were very much the same," Lynch said of Cardwell and Elmes, "very reasonable and super professional. And Fred had plenty of time to talk with Herb. He saw a lot of the stuff we'd shot and he understood – Fred sort of segued in and took over for Herb."

"It wasn't difficult," Elmes affirmed, "because David had a real clear view of what he wanted. He had no trouble saying what it should look like. And I had done enough before to know how to get a certain look with black-and-white film. So it was a matter of carrying on the style that David had established."

That style, Lynch hoped, would capture something of the feeling of Billy Wilder's *Sunset Boulevard*, one of his favourite films, in which "the mood and the story, everything is welded together so beautifully." It was the only film he screened for the entire crew before production began. But Doreen Small also mentioned George Stevens' *A Place in the Sun*, "with Shelley Winters out on the lake with Montgomery Clift, where that lake is so black and so silvery at the same time, that kind of richness, that kind of deep satiny black."

Lynch would keep the actors waiting for hours in order to get a setup just right. "He didn't like to keep them waiting," said Small. "He would come out and talk to them, but he would do what he had to do. It was extraordinary; from the beginning they trusted him. He had a very, very clear idea; he knew exactly how he wanted it to look. The dailies would come back from CFI (the lab) and they'd say, 'Are you shooting this with one candle in a tunnel?' And David would send them back, saying, 'Not dark enough. I want this darker.'"

The results of this care have been called the best black-and-white cinematography to come out of America since the 1940s. Nevertheless, there was a great deal of trial and error involved; Lynch might know what he wanted something to look like, but he and his cinematographers often had to experiment before they found a way to achieve that look. Black-and-white photography presents some special difficulties. "It relies more on lighting than colour does," said Elmes. "In colour, the art direction fills in a lot because you have all this colour palette to play with." In black-and-white, the design of the lighting has to make up for that. "We did tests," Elmes continued. "We photographed gray walls, painted different shades of gray to see how dark is what gray." They shot makeup tests, tests for hairstyles. "There was a lot of feeling our way because David had not made exactly this kind of film before. We were both in sync as to what it should look like, but how to do it was a little bit new."

This applied particularly when it came to effects work. They had to learn as they did it. Elmes would find himself reading books on various effects techniques. They made contacts with key effects people at different studios whom they would call to ask for advice on specific problems. "And they would help," said Elmes. "They would give us little secrets and little tricks on how to do this and how to do that and how to save money doing it. And we would try these things and that's how the film was made. It was a little trial and error every step of the way. We knew what we wanted and we stayed with it." And that was part of the reason the film took four years to complete.

Along the way they had to rediscover such old techniques as fitting a frame of film into the camera viewfinder in order to line up a composite as precisely as possible. This was how they obtained the super seen early in the film, in which one of the "foetuses" emerges from Henry's mouth as he floats in space. More difficult was obtaining a sense of weightlessness. "Things that defy gravity require special handling," commented Elmes. "These aren't new tricks in the industry, but they were new to us at the time." They would obtain clues from their contacts, refine on them, shoot and shoot again. "I mean," Elmes continued, "no one gave us a book and said, 'Here's how you make the foetus float.'" They would shoot with the camera placed sideways, even upside down. For the opening shot of Henry floating against a star field, "we shot a couple of tests because we couldn't get him to float right. We knew where he was going to go in the shot, we knew what the move was, and how long and everything about it. We just didn't know how to get it. We shot it a couple of different ways, and ended up with him sitting upright and the camera sideways. We locked the camera off and he sat on the dolly and we just dollied him back and forth, bobbing up and down against a black background."

Another kind of floating was required for a scene cut from the final version of the film. When Mary leaves Henry, said Coulson, "there was this whole scene where she went into the bathroom to get her stuff and then she just roller skated through the room. You didn't know she was on roller skates; it was like she just flew through the room. We had this fan blowing so that it would blow her hair in a real unusual way. Things like that took a long time because David had never done them before."

Inevitably, the production encountered technical problems, and shooting in black-and-white was at the root of many of them. During most of that first year, they were lucky because at the same time Peter Bogdanovich was shooting *Paper Moon*; the lab, CFI, was processing black-and-white film every day and so there were tight quality controls in effect. But later, there was less demand for black-and-white processing. "They switched over to developing black-and-white twice a week," recalled Elmes, "which means that the machines weren't always run and they weren't always in great shape. We suffered little problems because of that. It was really a matter of staying in touch with them, communicating. A matter of letting them know that you know what you're doing. Because I think they try to get by with as little as possible. And unless you call them on that, and establish that from the beginning, you're off to a bad start. So we stayed close with them and we developed good relationships with a couple of people at the lab."

Occasionally, the film stock was not of the best quality. "We had bad trouble with the stock," said Lynch. "If you were to expose a gray, a dark gray especially, you'd see this 'breathing'. We didn't even know what to call it." This is particularly noticeable in one of the shots in which Henry appears against vast concrete backgrounds, or in muddy wastelands; there is an odd, fluid shifting in the grays. Luckily, rather than being detrimental, this instability actually adds to the uneasy mood evoked by the images. Also, there is a fluctuation in the shots of Henry walking to the X's house at night. This resulted from having relied on actual streetlamps for the lighting. With a sixty cycle per second pulse, the streetlamps were out of sync with the camera, producing the fluctuation. "But," said Lynch, "I really love that look."

More serious problems arose when there was something wrong with a camera. The shot early in the film in which the camera dollies in on the planet was, according to Fred Elmes, "a massive setup for our means at the time. It was a thirty foot dolly on an Elemack with a crane arm, a Mitchell camera going at high speed, and a model that had to move and coordinate." The star field was a black curtain about twenty feet high by sixty feet wide, with holes punched in it and lights behind for the stars. A large area was required to film the shot, which meant that it had to be done outside. "And it could only be done on a weekend," Elmes continued, "because the only area available was in the gardeners' setup down at the stables. There was no way we could interrupt their schedule, so Friday at four when they left, we moved in and hung the curtain and we put up the dolly track and started lighting it. It took us the whole weekend to do, so we actually shot it that Monday morning at about three. We had to work very quickly, grab the shot, then clean up real fast so we'd disappeared by the time the gardeners came in at seven in the morning." But the next day, when they viewed the dailies, "we found out that the high-speed camera was bad, that we had a very strange flickering." So they had to repeat the arduous process of building the setup, shooting, and quickly tearing it down again the next weekend, "regardless of the money we spent already. At the time all those problems were really earth-shattering because we didn't always have the money to re-shoot something and we hadn't had the years of experience to know exactly what it was that went wrong. So it was sort of trial and error to find out what the problem was, and then to solve it before we re-shot."

Those frantic weekend sessions had to be resorted to on any occasion when there was a particularly big setup to be filmed. One such was Henry's arrival at the X's house. "That was a set," said Elmes, "we built that. We started hauling in dirt at five o'clock on Friday. It was the craziest we'd ever tried, but we hauled in dirt, planted plants, built a sidewalk, built the facade of the house." That took all of Friday night. Saturday night they spent lighting the set, and Sunday night they filmed the scene, tore the set down and cleared it away before seven Monday morning. "I can't believe we did that," Elmes said with a kind of awe. "I still don't believe we did that.

"I don't know when I slept sometimes," he added. "We were on a night schedule, partly because a lot of it had to be shot at night and partly because David enjoyed working at night better. I would be up at AFI all day, working on other films or doing things around the classes, and then at five-thirty we'd watch dailies from the night before and then go down and start shooting, and shoot until three or four in the morning. Sometimes later. And then I'd get up at eight or nine and go to AFI or whatever other job I had, and then meet my friends and go horseback riding at seven on Saturday morning. And everyone did this. It just became a way of life. I used to live out in Topanga at the time and I sort of put the car on automatic pilot going back because there was no way I could manoeuver the hill by myself. It was a great time. I look back on it real fondly, but we really did work hard."

At one point, Doreen Small found it impossible to drive back and forth between her place in Topanga Canyon and the AFI in Beverly Hills; she was simply too tired. "So," she said, "I was living in Henry's room. But they said I was a fire hazard, so they actually threw me out."

One of the biggest setups of all involved the explosion of the planet. "We didn't know quite how we were going to do it," recalled Elmes. "David felt confident it could be done, and when he built that model of the planet, he built the nose section without any structure behind it so that it could pop out. It was planned right from the beginning that that was going to happen and we were going to move through and into the blackness. He had painted a white rim around it so that it would read right once it was broken away. It was all scored, so we had to be very careful not to bump it because it would fall apart. But when it came time to shoot it, we still really hadn't come up with a plan. Explosives were out of the question because there would be smoke and fire and that was not the effect we wanted. It just had to break up.

"So," Elmes continued, "Jack Nance and David came up with a plan to build a catapult. They were going to take these lead weights and put them on the catapult, underneath the planet, and on cue we were going to release it and these lead weights were going to spring out and explode it. I said, 'David, look, I'm sitting there with the camera ten feet in front of this; do you want me to just stand there?' David said, 'No. Maybe we'd better build you something.' So we built this enormously elaborate shield of four by eight foot plywood boards with holes in them which we covered with plexiglass. We had three cameras" – the only such shot in the film – "because we knew it could only be done once and we were going to get this shot no matter what." The high-speed cameras were set up, all running at different speeds so that Lynch could choose the most effective shot; the lighting was carefully rigged so that all the pieces would be visible, back-lit; the trajectory of the weights and the design of the lighting were such that the weights should not be visible in the shot. But unfortunately the catapult failed to work as planned. They tried a test shot, but the weight limped only a few feet. This was to be the last shot of the night; "it was five-thirty in the morning," said Elmes, "and the sun was coming up. We had to get this thing to break apart because the gardeners were coming in a couple of hours and all this had to disappear. So David, in a frenzy after finding the catapult wouldn't work, threw the thing halfway across the driveway, picked up the weights, and did it himself. So that shot was done with David under the planet, throwing the weights up through the nose and out at the camera."

One of these setups also involved the hiring of a couple of extra people, a rare occurrence on the film. For the scene in which Henry and his neighbour make love in a bed transformed into a pool of milky fluid, Lynch had part of Henry's room rebuilt outside in front of the stables at the AFI. The bed frame was set up around a big vat which was filled with water and milk. At the time, it happened to be cold for southern California and, according to Jack Nance, "we had a hell of a time heating it. It was like ice-water. I said to Judith (Roberts), 'It's a good thing this is just a movie; if it was real I wouldn't be any use to you right now!'"

"And just so that these people would not die," added Doreen Small, "David consented to hire a couple of extra people. Not that he worried about paying people; he just didn't want people around to see what he was doing." This necessitated the assuming of multiple functions on the part of the cast and crew. Jack Nance would help shift equipment and set up lights; Small would ride the dolly and operate the boom, simultaneously timing the shot, while Lynch himself pushed the dolly. Alan Splet recalled one night when "Herb Cardwell, our cameraman, was running sound. David was running the camera. And I was doing something else" – possibly operating the baby, a task usually taken by Small, who also worked the chicken which comes to life during the dinner scene at the X's. "But when the baby gets crazy, very hyperactive," said

Small, "it was Alan working it because he plays the cello and he has a certain kind of touch."

"David is very, very secretive," said Coulson. "He didn't want anybody judging his work before it was done." That desire for secrecy extended to his keeping the people at the AFI off the set. "The big boys up at AFI were dying to see the baby," recalled Small, but Lynch would not let them near it. "One day," Nance added, "Tony Vellani brought some people down to the set – guys in suits. Vellani asked if they could get in for a look. David said, 'No.' These were the guys putting up the money!"

The only people not involved with the production who were allowed to see the dailies were two projectionists at the AFI who, said Coulson, "were quite wonderful guys, and David still has some contact with them." But inevitably little rumours leaked out occasionally. "I used to hear stories about David from the AFI people who didn't realize how close we were," Coulson continued, "kind of wondering what was going on down there at the stables. But somebody must have known somewhere along the line that something good was going to come out of this. They harassed David to a certain degree, but for the most part they were indirectly supportive and pretty much stayed out of his hair." Although, recalled Small, "it was very difficult for me to get film out of them after a while," because officially the film was still not a full-length feature.

As the original grant ran low, the AFI did put more money into the project. But towards the end of the first year, Lynch recalled, "because we needed more and they'd given quite a bit, they said that they didn't want to stop it; they just said, 'We can only help you now in terms of equipment. You're going

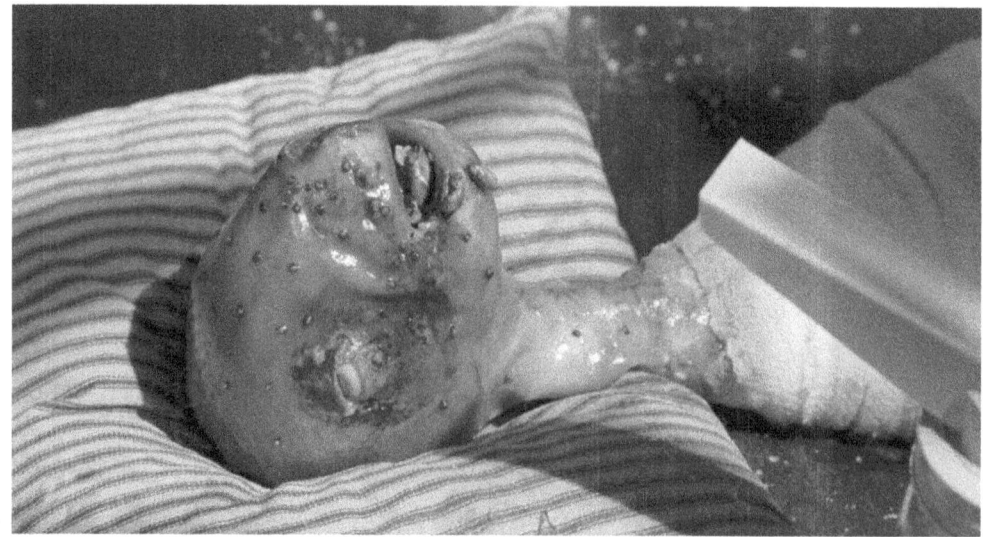

"Oh, you are sick!": Spike, the baby, falls ill.

to have to get the money somewhere else.'" And so in the Spring of 1973, the production came to a halt.

Lynch was used to temporary interruptions in the shooting. Simultaneous with shooting, they would work on major props and "when the thing was actually needed, I would really concentrate on finishing it up. A lot of things weren't finished until they were actually needed." Sometimes shooting had to stop until the props were ready.

In the Fall of 1972, shooting stopped for a couple of months while the planet and the giant baby head were completed. The planet was a major project; about ten feet in diameter, with enough room inside for someone to get in and move it for a shot (Jack Nance on at least one occasion), it was made from a combination of materials: plaster, fibreglass, polyester resin, wax. And, as already mentioned, it was built with a breakaway section for the explosion sequence.

The giant baby head, used at the film's climax, was built in Lynch's back yard. "Jack and I spent a lot of time that first Fall with David and Peggy," Coulson recalled, "while Jack and David built the giant baby head. They lived in this little house right in the centre of the city and on either side were these three-story apartment buildings. So people would look down into David's back yard where there was this giant thing – it was huge – which he had made out of a mold. The neighbours called it 'that big egg'. David and Jack would be sanding the head and little Jenny, who was four or five, learned how to mix cement and then give it to David, and they would put it on real fast. We were always waiting for the head to dry. That was the big thing. We sat around David's house and drank coffee and ate sandwiches and watched TV and waited for the head to dry for months, it seemed like. We were always waiting for something to dry. When David was in England doing *The Elephant Man*," she added, "I talked to him and he was waiting for *The Elephant Man* cast to dry at his house in England. I couldn't believe he was still waiting for things to dry!"

The plaster used for the giant baby head was quite gravelly and required a great deal of sanding "and they would sand down all their fingerprints," Coulson recalled. "So Jack and David were like criminals; they had no fingerprints left. And the neighbours said to me, 'What is that big egg there?' Then one day the big egg disappeared." Shooting had resumed.

But in the Spring of 1973, with no money left, the situation was different. Lynch began what was to become a very bad year. The project, said Lynch, "was just like an animal dying in the desert; at first the birds stay very far away, and then little by little they come in and start taking bites. And you're just too weak to get them off you. I really thought it was the end. They'd come down and take some piece of equipment, and it would be a horror. I'd wait for them;

they'd come down and take something else, and I'd say, 'You're going to bring it back?' And they'd say, 'Sure, we're going to bring it back.' They would never come back." At what must have been one of the lowest points in his career, Lynch "even thought at one time of building a little dummy Henry and stop-motioning all the parts in between what we had shot. Just to finish it. Because I couldn't do anything else until this was finished. I was caught in limbo."

Because the cast and crew had forged such close relationships during that first year, they remained in close touch now, even as they sought other work. Coulson worked in the grant program at the AFI and acted in a few plays, but also washed windows and became a waitress. "I worked in a restaurant," she recalled, "and David would come down in the afternoon and do some odd jobs for the people who owned the restaurant in exchange for a grilled cheese sandwich and fries. He was always doing odd jobs; we found him lots of things to do to support himself." Although shooting had stopped, Lynch and Splet cut together some of the material already filmed – in fact, the bulk of the film was already in the can, most of the principal photography completed. Coulson helped out, learning some basic editing skills, how to file trims and so on. Even Jack Nance found himself "running machines and matching up my own voice with my own lips and all of this stuff."

It was during this hiatus that Fred Elmes shot *The Killing of a Chinese Bookie* for John Cassavetes, taking Coulson along as his assistant. But Elmes too remained in close contact with Lynch. In fact, when production finally did resume, there was no problem in maintaining continuity because *Eraserhead* had managed to remain at the centre of their group life. "We talked about it a lot," recalled Elmes. "We didn't know quite how it was going to be possible – if we could get the right camera, if we could get all the lights we needed, if we could get the space if AFI needed us to move. There were a lot of 'ifs', but we talked about it all the time; it was just kind of assumed that it would be finished. One way or the other, the film was going to get finished.

"David and I used to live a block from each other," Elmes continued, "so we would go over and have coffee in the afternoon; even in the time we weren't shooting, we were planning. We would have so many napkins and place mats that had block diagrams and little storyboards written on them as to how we were going to do effects and what we would have to build in order to do the effect, and where we were going to get all this equipment from for free, and how long it was going to take. We really had that planned out and gone over so many times."

Eventually, as Lynch put it, "a lot of things came together. George Stevens, Jr, arranged a thing with CFI, the lab; at least they would develop the negative. We weren't even going to see workprint. But we did figure out a way to get enough money to see workprint." By a combination of deferments, money obtained from friends and relatives, and equipment loaned by the AFI, the production managed to get rolling again.

"Because he couldn't pay us," said Elmes, "David offered us a percentage of the profit of the film – if and when it should ever make money. I certainly wasn't in it for the money and we were all certain that it was not possible for the film to make any substantial amount of money. So it's a welcome surprise that there's some money coming back in for it." Coulson agreed: "There was a sense of collaboration, which is why David gave us all such a nice percentage of the film, something we did not even write down until after the film started making money. Which is a pretty impressive thing for a filmmaker to do. The reward artistically and emotionally was great, but to be able to also get some money back from it – a healthy cheque every quarter – is a real rarity in this particular business."

Shooting resumed on May 29, 1974, exactly two years after the camera first rolled on the set of the X's living room.

By this time, Lynch had separated from his first wife and had taken up residence in Henry's room at the AFI stables. "It was sort of illegal," he admitted, "but I found a way to camouflage the room to look like no one was in there." The main door was padlocked from the outside, while a secondary, plywood door was bolted from within. The set was draped with the sound blankets so that if anyone should manage to look in, nothing was visible. Said Coulson, "He never admitted that he lived there, and they never admitted that he lived there. But I think everybody kind of knew." But, said Lynch, "the parks department turned me in one time. They said people must be living there because there's garbage piling up. Of course, we were all eating there anyway. But they asked about it, and of course" he told them that no one was "living there. We were working down there."

When shooting resumed, it was on a piecemeal basis, with long intervals of planning and preparation between setups. Doreen Small had left the project when she moved to Santa Barbara, and Alan Splet had gone to Scotland. There was little live sound left to do, and what there was could be taken care of by remaining members of the crew, although on one occasion someone else was brought in to do it.

The first scene to be filmed after the long break was one involving the Lady in the Radiator. Laurel Near, who played the part, had been singing in a trio with her two sisters, Holly and Timi, the latter being a good friend of Coulson's. Near was introduced to Lynch, who, she said, "liked my smile," and he hired her for the part. She had never done film work before and "didn't know what I was getting into really."

The Lady in the Radiator's stage was built outside at the AFI and, according to Fred Elmes, "It just sat there for months and months and months until we could finally get around to shooting that scene." Lynch even made a stencil and hand-painted the pattern of squares on the stage. "We knew where all the black curtains were," Elmes continued, "and we'd made plans about how we would hang lights. But the problem was there was nothing up there to hang lights on." They had to build a scaffold and borrow a big extension ladder from the AFI, which they suspended above the stage as a rack for the lights.

The day would begin at five-thirty or six in the evening, with everyone gathering on the set. Elmes would ensure that all the lighting was correct – and then everything would have to wait while Lynch spent a couple of hours applying Near's makeup. Then shooting would begin. But sometime after midnight, Lynch would have to leave because now he had a job delivering the *Wall Street Journal*. He made $48.50 a week on a 210-paper route. His first night out, it had taken him about six hours to run the route in his VW, but eventually "I found shortcuts and studied a map, and I got this overview. I got it down to one hour."

While he was on the job, the others would take a break, eat, change the lighting for a new setup, or just get a bit of rest. "I know occasionally," recalled Elmes, "the *Wall Street Journal* didn't get delivered." And Coulson remembered running the route for Lynch on occasion; he taped it for her – "and now the orange house on the left, and then you turn right here ..."

Shooting would start again on Lynch's return and continue until dawn. Coulson recalled that "we seemed to get our best stuff right before dawn." During the first year "Alan would be listening to the sound and say, 'Wait, I hear birds.' We'd have to stop when we started to hear the birds." But later, said Elmes, "we started building canopies over things to keep the daylight out so that we could get one more last shot in before it was too light. I still look at shots in the film and think, 'That shot looks a little different.' And then I remember: everything was very subtly filled from the top by skylight because it was the last shot of the morning before we had to wrap it up."

Although Near found working with Lynch "a real treat; I love his sense of humour and he's real sincere," she did not realize how complicated a business it would be. "I thought I was just going to go and dance across the stage." What she actually got were some long, gruelling makeup sessions. She recalled that some of the materials used by Lynch were quite harsh. She went through five or six sessions and "it was real thick stuff that when you took it off it just sort of peeled your whole face off with it. My face hurt a lot after the sessions. But they took a lot of time and they were real sweet to me, they took care of me."

When it came time to film Near's musical number, it was shot synced to a pre-recorded tape of the song, "In Heaven". "I got the soundman at the AFI to teach me how to hook that up," Lynch said, "and I ran that setup myself." In the tradition of Bacall's number in *To Have and Have Not*, it was not actually Near's voice singing the song. New wave composer-performer Peter Ivers, who also wrote the music for the song, sings it in the film.

In keeping with Lynch's penchant for controlling all aspects of the production, he himself took on the makeup chores. "No one ever really taught me" the techniques, he said. He had developed a liking for casting people's heads while at art school, "and I'll cast anyone's head that'll let me." Jack Nance had to "go under" three times before Lynch managed to capture the requisite "Henry expression" for the Eraserhead dream sequence, in which Henry, having reached his Heaven, is decapitated and his head found by a young boy who sells it to a pencil factory where it is found to consist of top quality rubber, ideal for erasers. "Jack is the greatest, not only as an actor but as a person that will go through practically living hell for you – and for the film. A Henry expression is a subtle sort of thing and to hold that long enough for the mould to set is a real trick. He did it fantastically."

Coulson assisted in the making of the head and she recalled that it "was very strange for me because I was working on the plaster and filing it down. I was filing down the face of my husband."

Calls for advice to outside experts occasionally led to odd places. One of the film's effects contacts was Tim Baar, an Oscar-winner for *The Time Machine*, and he was able to put Lynch in touch with a man who could supply genuine human hair for the Eraserhead. "You better believe it's real," Lynch laughed.

Lynch dislikes standard makeup blood. "It looks too gray" in black-and-white, he said, "and it's always too thick. Real pig's blood would be the best thing to use, with maybe a little bit of darker colouring in it." But for Henry's nosebleed when he is cornered by the aggressive Mrs X, Lynch came up with a concoction of his own, the ingredients of which he no longer recalls, but "it was pretty toxic and it really burned the inside of Jack's nose."

Yet another person to suffer these discomforts for the film was good friend Jack Fisk, acclaimed art director and now a director in his own right with *Raggedy Man*. Fisk and his wife, actress Sissy Spacek, not only gave financial assistance to the film; they spent a day working on the production. While Spacek took on the task of continuity clerk, Fisk was transformed into the deformed Man in the Planet, the bizarre figure who sits at the controls of *Eraserhead*'s strange world. "I'd just started growing a beard," Fisk recalled, "and I'd had it about two weeks. David got this stuff and it was like a latex which he brushed on my face so it didn't look like I had a beard, but my skin was kind of deformed.

Then he built out my chest, like something was bulging out of my chest. When I went home after doing this, I was trying to get that stuff out of my beard, and it was impossible to get it out. Sissy didn't want me to shave my beard off, so I was in a tub of hot water, pulling it out a little piece at a time. I've never really forgiven David for that," he added with a laugh.

One of the more elaborate efforts in this area involved doing a body cast of Charlotte Stewart. Lynch was assisted in this by Doreen Small. "We had to get her undressed and cast her body," related Small, "and David's wife was there." But it went off without a hitch and they obtained a thin shell in the form of Stewart's torso. This was to be used in the scene in which Henry awakens to find Mary feverish in the bed beside him and begins to pull the "foetuses" from her body. "We cut a hole in Henry's bed," recalled Small, "and Charlotte would sort of settle in underneath it and we put this very thin shell of her body on top so there was a space between her actual body and the shell. Originally, Henry broke through that when he first found the foetuses." These "foetuses" were actually human umbilical cords which Catherine Coulson had obtained from a hospital – a half dozen or so of them. "Those were one of the things that we had in the refrigerator," Lynch commented.

For that particular scene, said Small, "I was under the bed to keep tension on the umbilicals – the 'billy cords' as Jack would call them. And Jack pulled and we sort of missed and one of them landed in his shoe. He got so grossed out that we had to stop filming for a couple of days." Jack Nance recalled having joked a number of times during the production: "Well, David, this is going to have them bolting for the fire exits. There ought to be a jail sentence for what this will do to them." In this instance, Nance himself became one of the film's earliest victims.

The use of the umbilicals illustrates Lynch's concern for authenticity in details; he has a passion for organic textures and, as he says, "There's nothing like the real thing." This is a part of his concern for proportions and relationships between the elements with which he works. "I'm going to tell you," he said, "about the duck. A duck is a shape that works because of the size and the texture of the parts. If you could make up rules out of a duck, if you could measure the beak and get the texture of the beak, and notice the relationship of the beak to the body, which has a fluffy texture; and then notice that the feet are bigger than the beak, but they're not quite as hard as the beak, yet they're the same colour; and then you have this 'S' curve of the neck – but then the eye of the duck is the neatest part; it's the littlest, but it's the most brilliant and the most intricate." The eye is what makes the whole thing come together and work. "I like in a scene something, one little thing that on its own would be nothing, but in the context and the balance of the things around it, it pops out and just gleams and it makes everything else work." Details like Henry searching his drawer for the torn picture of Mary, and pausing to flip a penny into a bowl of water which sits in the drawer; a peculiar moment which somehow gives a strange weight to the scene. "The timing does it," said Lynch. But details like that come from the "nowhere" of Lynch's subconscious: "I don't even know why I put that there. I can't even take credit for these things. It's not like I sat down and said, 'I'm going to make something that's mathematically right, like a duck.' You get an idea and you go with it and later on you find out that the proportions were correct, but it's happening so much out of your control. It's sort of a blessing to get an idea."

But if he trusts to fortune for that "duck's eye" detail, Lynch works extremely hard to create the right context for that detail to work in. He studies textures and uses them with great care. Jack Nance commented that Lynch was "the only man I've ever known that shaved a mouse." He also dissected a cat. He called a veterinarian and asked for a dead cat; soon after, the man called back and told Lynch to come on down. "And he said, 'Here it is,' and he put it in this box. It went in like a slinky. Just slinked in. And he said, 'Just do me one favour; will this cat be recognizable in your movie?' And I said, 'You would never recognize that cat.' So I took it home and I had my basement set up like an operating theatre. First I put the cat in formaldehyde in a bottle with a kind of narrow mouthed top. And it got *rigor mortis* in the jar and I could not get this cat out. It was like a boat you build in the basement; you cannot get it out of the door. But finally it popped out and I dissected the cat. It was an experience. I examined all parts of it, like membranes and hair and skin, and there are so many different textures that on one side are sort of gross, but just isolated in an abstract way are totally beautiful. It's the kind of thing where, if you don't name it, it's beautiful. But as soon as you name it, all kinds of associations become attached to it and people will be turned off. To me a lot of these things are really beautiful. And somehow I think other people feel that in *Eraserhead*: sort of finding beauty in something that was ugly, or could be ugly." Although Lynch commented of dissecting the cat that "I don't know what good it did me really," viewers who have seen the horrifying death of the film's baby will know the value of his explorations into the cat's textures.

The cat itself had been intended for a part in the film: "some kids had tied wire and did a cat in," said Lynch, "and Henry trips on the wire. It's just underneath the frame line where he walks through those oil tanks; the cat was there." Even though the cat just missed stardom when that moment was cut from the film, its story did not quite end there. "The shot where the camera goes over this puddle of black water," Lynch continued, "the cat went into that puddle. I came back a year or two later and fished the cat out; it was covered in oil and a sort of tar and it had preserved itself. I came back again a couple of years after that and there it still was, out in the dirt. I've got a photograph of this cat and it looks like it's coming out of the ground. It's earth-coloured and the earth, everything has been rained on and dried and heated – and it's pretty neat looking."

The quest for the organic would send Doreen Small and Catherine Coulson out in search of such substances as instant cream of wheat (a disturbing mixture in combination with the textures of a dissected cat), mashed potatoes, grape jelly. Coulson recalled going downtown one Saturday afternoon to film the scene in which the boy finds Henry's head in the Eraserhead dream sequence. "We had to stop at the market to buy some jellied consomme which we were going to use underneath the head. It had a kind of glistening texture that David wanted. I remember running in to buy it and thinking, 'Other people don't spend their Saturday afternoons doing this.'"

For another scene, which was later cut from the film, in which Henry goes to a drawer to find the vaporizer for the sick baby, Small and Coulson headed once more to the market. The vaporizer, recalled Coulson, "was in a drawer that was full of vanilla pudding and peas. So when Henry reached in he had to reach into the vanilla pudding and pull out the vaporizer which was then covered with peas and vanilla pudding. So the problem was how to make a drawerful of vanilla pudding. Doreen and I went out to the grocery store and we tried to figure out what kind of vanilla pudding would mix up the fastest. So we hand-beat instant vanilla pudding, filled this drawer with it, and then put these green peas on top of it."

Such labours were taken in stride by those for whom *Eraserhead*'s world had become a normal part of their existence.

The closeness of the group was not disrupted even when extra people had to be brought in – supplementary crew and actors to play small parts, who were needed only for a limited time. More often than not, these people were drawn from among the friends and relatives of the group. Many of them came to the film through Catherine Coulson. V. Phipps-Wilson, who portrayed Henry's landlady, a part later cut from the film, was a friend of Coulson's, as were Neil Moran, boss of the pencil factory, and Hal Landon, Jr, the operator of the pencil machine. That machine, incidentally, was designed by Lynch himself and built out of odds and ends of machinery although Lynch "never saw a real pencil machine; it was sort of like common sense."

The part of the boy who finds and sells Henry's head was played by Coulson's nephew, Tom Coulson. "Tom was a young teenager," said Coulson, "and just thrilled to be working on this. When he came to be interviewed, my brother and sister-in-law were there, and his seven brothers and sisters, and Jack

Earth and water: Eraserhead's *dank elements.*

and I; everybody was standing outside the stables like a cheering section when Tom went up for his interview. And David came back down the stairs and said, 'Well, Tom has the part.' Everybody cheered. Tom stayed with us for a while during the summer and helped David build a lot of sets. He was like David's young assistant."

Also among those who came to help were Jack Nance's brothers, who came in from Texas and stayed awhile when the crew were shooting the planet. Yet, according to Coulson, for all the closeness that the crew developed, the feeling of being a family involved in a special activity, "we didn't have too many clubby little things." Nance named the baby "Spike" and it stuck. He also gave a name to the hat rack which stands in a corner of Henry's room with an overcoat hanging from it: "Uncle Edgar." Nance kept his cigarettes in Uncle Edgar's pocket. On one occasion Coulson found some overalls at Standard Brands for $1.99 "and we were all wearing them for painting the set and David wrote *Eraserhead* on them – like you'd write 'Al's Garage'."

On at least one occasion Lynch felt a little awkward about inflicting this closely shared world on an "outsider". The X's kitchen was not a set but a location and the vegetative grandmother was played by the building's landlady, Jean Lange. "She was very, very nice," Lynch recalled, "but she didn't know what was going on. I felt kind of bad about that. I sort of felt like I was taking advantage of her, although she did have a very fun time."

The production's final major crisis occurred when the AFI told Lynch that he could no longer remain at the stables. Despite their wariness of features, the AFI had seemed, at least implicitly, to consent to *Eraserhead*'s expansion into a feature. "But then," Lynch asserted, "around that time, the unions told them, 'If you're going to have us come in and help you, give seminars and help bring these people along, we don't want you making films that are going to compete with our guys. You can't make feature films.'" So the AFI cut the production adrift, although they now receive a percentage of the profits in return for the services and equipment they provided during those years at the stables. Martin Brest, who went on to direct *Going In Style*, was not so lucky; his AFI-made feature *Hot Tomorrows*, started several years after Lynch began *Eraserhead*, was shelved with no possibility of distribution. "And every film that's made there now," said Lynch, "AFI owns lock, stock, and barrel – has all the rights, everything. I am a very lucky person," he added; he was able to retain the rights to his film.

"We kind of got kicked out of AFI," he recalled. "After two or three years of being down there, they suddenly gave us this unrealistic, ridiculous deadline." There was about thirty hours' worth of work left to do on the stable sets and they had to get it done in thirty straight hours of shooting, with the only break provided by Lynch's leaving to throw his paper route. What was left were Henry's scenes in the elevator. "We were totally exhausted," said Lynch, "but we got everything. But we weren't used to shooting like that, being under the gun like that. There are a lot of things that you might think of along the way if you have time, but we had to just race through that."

Lynch rented a little guest house joined to a double garage. The latter was transformed into a small post-production studio. It was there that he and Alan Splet would finally pull the film together. But there were still some major effects sequences left to shoot. These ended up being done for the most part in Fred Elmes' living room. "We did effects in every imaginable situation," Elmes recalled. "Most of the miniatures were actually done in my living room. We were given an animation stand for a little while; it was a horizontal job, twelve feet long, and I had it set up in my living room. We would rent special cameras to do pin-registered effects and things like that. We would build lots of things for weeks, and then shoot it in two or three days because that's the period of time we could afford to rent the camera for. We would rent it over the weekend because you could get two days for the price of one.

"What we would do," he continued, "is just build the effect, like the surface of the planet, bring it into the living room, mount a Mitchell camera – I think in that case it was sideways; it was actually shot sideways, trucking along this thing. We did tests. We tried it in real time and we tried it in slow motion, and it didn't work. It wasn't what we were looking for, so we ended up doing it stop-frame. Fortunately, the animation stand was rigged to time out things. The shot actually took us about two hours to film."

For something like the little worm which crawls across the planet's surface, growing bigger all the while, "it probably took a day to build it," said Elmes, "another day to do the test on it, and another day to shoot it."

"I love doing stuff like that," said Lynch. "Whatever you can think of, you can do. It's fun to try to think of solutions to problems and to do those things yourself. In every aspect of *Eraserhead*, it was just great fun." Whether it was devising the explosion of the planet, or just rigging a simple drip tube with holes punched in it to create the rain on Henry's window. "Then you find out that in Hollywood some of the fun is taken out of it because you're not the one doing it; there are people that specialize in this and people that specialize in that and it saves time," but a certain amount of control is lost, even when the technology filters through the director on its way into the film. Lynch would prefer to keep as much control over all the elements of a project as he possibly can.

On *The Elephant Man*, Lynch was initially to do Merrick's makeup himself but "what I did was a total flop. I was making this sort of skin and in theory it was a nifty idea; this skin would float over something, move and look like real skin." But the structure over which he placed this skin was too rigid. It was as if John Hurt "was working inside of a helmet, a diving mask." A large part of the film had been shot before Chris Tucker came to the rescue; it was another tense time for Lynch, but he still prefers to do as much as possible himself.

Elmes, like Lynch, sees effects in a purely functional light. He enjoys effects work – "I find it intriguing," he said. "You can make magic, you can make almost anything happen in movies." But for himself, he does not like the idea of effects specialization. He, like Lynch, does not want to become bound to any one particular approach to effects. "I have a grasp of what's possible, what's involved in photographing effects, how opticals work, how the laboratory treats them." But rather than approach a problem from a particular technical perspective, he feels most comfortable with just a general knowledge which permits him to look for whatever solution is the most straightforward and useful for that particular problem. A feeling he shares with Lynch.

It was partly this attitude which resulted in the almost complete absence of opticals in *Eraserhead*. The impracticality of opticals was partly due to the production's limited finances, partly due to a fear of the loss of control which would be involved in sending material to the lab. But also the quality to be gotten from mechanical effects better suited their needs on the film, emphasizing the density, the solidity of the images. "What we lacked in monetary resource," commented Elmes, "we had in time. We could take the time to build something right, and we could shoot a test, and if it didn't look right we'd go back to the drawing board and build it again."

Coulson, working as a camera assistant on *Star Trek II* in late 1981, found it interesting to watch the effects people photographing planet surfaces. "I'm thinking," she said, "how we photographed our planet surface. David just thought that all up, and Fred thought about how to light it. And we made a big black star field. That's the stuff that George Lucas and Industrial Light and Magic do now on a much more sophisticated scale, but in a way with the same kind of results." It is arguable that the technical superiority of what ILM achieves is not proportional to the vastly greater amounts of money available to them as compared with the budget of *Eraserhead*. The effects in Lynch's film are really remarkably good.

For his garage post-production facility, Lynch acquired a Moviola, "a real old-fashioned, totally black one with a magnifying glass on it. It was tremendously loud and it would really eat film if anything went wrong. I was kind of afraid to use it a lot, but it worked out real well. It did the job and I sold if after the film was finished," so the cost was negligible.

Somehow, through all the production troubles which culminated in the forced move from the AFI after some three years in residence there, no film was ever lost. Initially stored in the editing department at the AFI, it all ended up stacked on shelves in Lynch's garage "and it was not too well organized," Lynch recalled. After Doreen Small left the production, "we didn't really take great notes. A lot of times things wouldn't get quite organized. But I knew in my head where things were. I had to go by feel to find stuff, but it was sort of uncanny how you get to know your shelves and you feel where things are. And we shot quite a bit of film actually," he added. He estimates that they shot a ratio of "around ten-to-one."

When Alan Splet returned in the Summer of 1975 from two years in Scotland, he rejoined Lynch, actually moving into the garage facility. Lynch recalled with wry affection Splet's passion for oranges at that time. "Alan was eating oranges in those days," he said, "and there were orange peels everywhere. I'd come home and there'd be lines of orange peels on the chair arms. The whole place smelled like oranges. We had an orange tree in the yard, but Alan was bringing them home in these boxes."

They bought "quite a bit of equipment" for Splet and built a "pretty good console," all of which, like the Moviola, was resold after the job was done. "And we'd rent the odd thing that we couldn't afford," said Lynch, "for maybe a week or something. Alan had a real good setup."

They worked together on the massive job of creating the film's many sound effects. "That's when we really got into it," said Splet. He had come to have a feel for the way Lynch thought, for what he wanted. "I can recall one interesting instance," he said, "the opening sound where there's a sort of presence and it kind of widens out as you move in on the planet. David and I were talking about it and really weren't sure what to do, and I just took this one presence that we had in the library, called 'early morning presence', and while we were sitting there I was sort of fiddling around with it and I just stuck it through this one-third octave graphic equalizer that I had and I started to open it up, push it open. And the sound started to open out and we said, 'My god, that's it.' You don't know how something like that happens – was it conscious? was it a lucky accident or what? But it was the right sound."

"It starts off in space," said Lynch, "and we wanted this open sound. So we got this sound, then it changes subtly as you go in and in, and those changes are all equalized. Then when you come in on the next cut it's lower, and you're roaring along, and then there's a kind of a segue – and one by one we got all those till they felt right. It just started like that." Lynch uses the sound, the flow of sounds, to draw the viewer in. And once held, the viewer is subjected to a continuous, finely modulated pattern of sound which amounts almost to an emotional and psychological assault. Lynch's technique gives the viewer no breathing space; the film becomes a mental roller coaster which leaves one exhausted and drained, yet nonetheless exhilarated from the ride.

The sound forcefully enhances the lifelessness of the film's world. There is an almost constant machine ambience underlining the bleak images, a lack of living sounds. Even thunder sounds like the rumble of rolling stock in a freight yard. The only animals seen in the film are a bitch with her puppies; the sound of their suckling is oddly off-centre, like the squealing of rats. The effect is of Henry being trapped in a great machine, intensely claustrophobic.

Splet, an inveterate collector of sounds, had acquired a huge library of effects to work with. Even now he will sometimes collect with Lynch in mind. "Sometimes I find sounds that I know David's going to like," he said. "There's a low sound in *The Elephant Man*; I discovered that sound about a year before and just sort of kept it away on ice. Then when David and I finally got together to work on *The Elephant Man*, one of the first things I did was, I said, 'David, I've got this low note for you that I think you're going to love.' So I played him some of this stuff and he flipped out over it. I knew he would."

As Lynch cut the picture together and locked in each sequence, Splet cut in the sound. They worked from the Summer of 1975 through to the Spring of 1976. Towards the end of that period, recalled Splet, "we had a real push because we thought we could possibly get it into the Cannes film festival. I remember at some very late date, David and I finally agreed to do it, and it meant really working almost around the clock. I was sleeping in the same room that I was editing in. So for about a month and a half I would work 'til like three in the morning, then I'd crash right away, get up the next morning, eat breakfast, go right back in and cut again. And we actually got most of the film done very quickly to screen for them."

"The mix only took seven days," Lynch recalled. "To me, there's no reason for a mix to take a real long time because Alan has sort of spoiled me. He knows all the tracks since he cut them himself and he was doing the mixing. We talked so much about every single thing that it seems like it took us a long time at a week."

As for the prospect of a Cannes screening, Lynch picked up the story: "The film was rough cut," he said, "but they said that they would take a rough cut. I was kind of sick at the time with a cold. I got this money to go to New York; it was part of the *Eraserhead* money. It would cost a fortune to go. And I got a shopping cart from Farmer's Market; the owner let me have the cart to take the film to New York and back. I had twenty-four reels; twelve of sound and twelve of picture. I took it to New York and I was so sick and I screened it for these people, but I never saw their faces. There were supposed to be three heavy-duty Cannes guys in this little screening room in some weird place in New York. All day I waited for my turn to show *Eraserhead*. And then I wondered about it: it seemed like the movie was five million years long. Then I got it back and I left, and I found out later that the Cannes guys had gone back the day before. I had flown all the way to New York and there wasn't anybody in the room – there was some guy in there, but I don't know who he was. Obviously I didn't get into the film festival."

Lynch also tried to enter the film in the New York film festival. This time he simply sent the rough cut; it was turned down. Later, the film now completed, Lynch tried once more to get *Eraserhead* seen. "I thought," he recalled, "there's no way I'm even going to get into festivals with this." His second wife, Mary, the sister of best friend Jack Fisk, "talked me into trying Filmex. It was the last day of applications and she said, 'We're going to get right in the car and drive over there, and you're going to turn it in. You've got to give it a try.' And I said, 'Well, yeah, I'll just go over and get rejected again.' So I went in and set the film down, and I said, 'Look, this has been rejected from Cannes, it's been rejected from New York; you guys take a look at it.' And I thought he'd say, 'Well, we'll probably reject it too.' But he said, 'We don't care where it's been rejected from. We're our own people. We're going to look at it and we'll let you know.'"

As it turned out, *Eraserhead* was accepted for Filmex. In fact, the festival people were "really excited" about their find.

The film's unofficial premiere was a screening at the AFI, mostly for cast, crew, and friends. It ran about one hour and fifty minutes and, recalled Doreen Small, "it was very long. It was unremitting. Just didn't give you a break. There's the roaring in the sound effects, and it gets a little loud and it gets a little difficult."

"Nobody knew what to think," said Catherine Coulson. "They came out kind of quiet. David was real depressed, because people really didn't respond – they didn't know what to say."

"The theatre was so quiet after the screening," added Fred Elmes, "it was a little bit spooky. No one knew quite what to say. It was really completely different. No one had seen it except for the couple of close people, nobody had seen the whole movie together. And it was sort of different, I think, than anyone had imagined it to be. It was really a shock. It does take your breath away at the end and it's hard to know how to respond to it. Which I think depressed David a bit because he was kind of expecting some response."

This was the version that was screened at Filmex. Lynch knew that the film was too long; he knew that scenes should be cut, but he liked each individual scene. Yet "the pacing is slow anyway in *Eraserhead* – and that's great, I love the feel of it – but I think these scenes were dragging it down to where the pacing was painful. It was pushing you out of the film. I stayed out of the room at Filmex, but I could feel that it was too long. Fred was in there and people weren't reacting; it was like lead, it was just too long. So that night I made a decision; in my heart, I knew that these scenes had to go. I'd never been able to quite do it, but when you feel an audience not reacting, then you can do it. Because it's way better than suffering through that. So out they came."

Jack Nance had a much more positive memory of the Filmex screening. "That was the first time that I saw it in toto," he recalled. "All of these bits and pieces that I'd seen ten thousand times all of a sudden ran from beginning to end, all together – and hell, I was ecstatic. I loved it. To finally get an audience reaction like we got was a big kick. At the end of the screening there was complete dead silence. And I knew that it worked. I said to Lynch, 'You see, I told you it would turn them into zombies.' People were stunned, and there was this long, shocked silence. Then a huge burst of applause. It was beautiful. I'd been waiting five years for that applause. It was great."

Applause or not, Lynch set about tightening the film up. Those cuts were extensive, amounting to about twenty minutes of screen time. They included: a scene in which the Xs bring Mary home from the hospital with the baby; a phone call that Henry receives; a fit that Mary has in Henry's apartment. The scene for which Catherine Coulson had originally been hired, in which the Xs pick Mary up at the hospital and a disgusted nurse (Coulson) hands them the baby, was not actually filmed; by the time they got around to that scene, late in the production when finances were very tight, Coulson suggested that the scene was not critical and therefore should be dropped – "one of the hardest things I had to do," she said. However, she did act in another scene, one of those now cut by Lynch.

"It's just down the hall from Henry's room," she said. "There are some women who are in a room with a very strange man who has this black box. My friend Phipps-Wilson and I were lying on this bed. Now, somehow it didn't seem at all sexual, but we were bound by these kind of battery cables. And the guy had this black box and he was just kind of walking toward us with these prongs. I remember wearing this slip and some pearls. It wasn't sexy really; it was David's sexy, which is always kind of pristine in a way. And what happened was, Henry hears these strange noises and he walks down the hall. He opens the door a crack, and this is his vision of what he sees. The women kind of look at him and then he shuts the door real fast."

The single largest excision was a lengthy sequence, the tail end of which is still seen in the release version. On a rainy, windy night Henry looks down from his window and in the windswept gloom of the alley sees two men fighting, an apparent murder. When he looks again a little later, there is nothing down there. This brief disturbing moment was originally preceded by what Lynch calls the "digging for dimes" sequence.

"Henry hears this sort of calling," Lynch said, "and he looks out his window. It's daytime out there, the wind is blowing dust, and there's this little kid out in the alley. His little friends have run off and he's left alone. You see his little friends go and then he comes up. So he's standing there in this wind and there's an oil puddle there, a pipe, and he's kicking the dirt. Just being alone. Suddenly he sees this shiny thing in the dirt, and he gets down and starts digging and he finds all these rows of dimes. So he really starts digging and Henry sees this and he's going crazy. He runs out of the room, but the baby starts crying immediately; but he's got a good run going and he makes it to the elevator and he's pushing the button, but the elevator won't come. So he runs down the stairs. He runs into the lobby and we see the elevator door is propped open with a mop; there's a mop bucket in there and the landlady has been cleaning; that's why he couldn't get the elevator. But because the door's open, the baby's crying is real loud and echoing all through the elevator shaft. So Henry gets frustrated and kicks this couch in the lobby, and the landlady (V. Phipps-Wilson) comes and says, 'Don't you kick my wood.' She gives him this business; she's cracked and she starts into this landlady-tenant thing. So Henry leaves her and goes back upstairs. He looks out the window, and meanwhile more people have come and they're digging and the dust is blowing. By night there's just sort of fighting going on out there." But all that was left of this after Lynch

Henry's ambivalent attraction to Mary.

cut the film down was that brief glimpse of fighting. He left that in because "it has the right feeling for the night, for Henry's world."

"It wasn't like an overall trim," Lynch said of the cut. "I lifted out whole scenes. I always felt they were too long, but I always wanted to fool myself that they could be there. After the premiere I knew that they couldn't." Luckily, because he chose this approach, the sound did not require re-mixing: "it just needed that twenty-frame pull up here and there." But because the cuts were made in the final composite print there are, in the release prints, characters and actors listed in the credits who no longer appear in the film.

Coulson was sorry to see some of the material go; she regrets now that she did not appear as an actress in the film. "I think it would be fun to say I acted in *Eraserhead*. When I say now what I did on it, nobody really believes me because it was so many different things that in a way it's almost too much. It's like too many excuses; you kind of don't believe any of them." But also, like Lynch, she feels that in themselves the scenes which were deleted are good ones. "I wish that sometime David would show those scenes that he cut."

Filmex was the big break for David Lynch and *Eraserhead*. Because of the festival screening, the film found a distributor, a man who knew just the right way to sell it: Ben Barenholtz of Libra Films in New York. Somebody who had seen the film at Filmex mentioned it to Barenholtz, who then called Lynch and had a print shipped to New York. Barenholtz was the man who pioneered midnight screenings at his Elgin Theatre in New York, turning films like *El Topo*, *Pink Flamingos*, and *The Harder They Come* into midnight hits, films which would never survive a regular theatre run. He was immediately impressed by *Eraserhead*. "It was so original," he said, "there was so much in it and I just thought I could do something with it. I was in my screening room with somebody who was working for me at the time and about halfway through the film I told him to get on the phone and make a deal for the film. I liked it."

Nursing a film through to midnight success is a long, slow process. It relies on what Barenholtz calls "a discovery aspect." The audience must find the film for itself and appreciate it without the aid of established publicity mechanisms. Because the film has appeal to only a limited audience, the investment involved in promoting it through the usual channels is simply not economically feasible. "Many limited audience films," said Barenholtz, "are killed if you go through the normal process."

Barenholtz, said Lynch, "learned through experience about releasing a film with no money and just word-of-mouth, letting it ride these ups and downs that they go through." Patience is the chief requirement; to give the film time to grow. *Eraserhead* took more than four years to make; Lynch would just have to wait a while longer. He described the process involved: "The major studios will put a film out for a week and if it doesn't do so many dollars they'll pull it forever. It's gone. Well, Ben would put a film out and just kind of water it and just watch it. First, the real weirdos would see it; they'll see anything if it's running at midnight. And if it clicks with them, it'll enter the next phase, which is a slightly bigger group of people." The film goes through a number of these "levels", the audience pyramiding out and, one hopes, stabilizing; this type of film depends for a long life on a faithful repeat audience, not a constant turnover of new people. "And these transition areas," Lynch continued, "are critical. But you can't tell how long it will take for the word to spread and for people to respond." So you just wait. "The first night in New York there were twenty-five people in the theatre. I think it went down to twenty-four the next night. But the next weekend it got more and more people. And went from there." It was given a little assistance by a plug from John Waters, himself creator of several midnight classics, including *Pink Flamingos*. "He was real good to me," said Lynch, "because when *Eraserhead* opened, his film *Desperate Living* was opening in New York at the same time and at a personal appearance, he told the audience that his favourite film was *Eraserhead*, and he recommended that everyone see it. So he really helped the film out."

But the process was so slow, the response so long in growing that, according to Doreen Small, Lynch "doubted himself for a while; things were getting a little bleak. David was going to give it up and teach meditation. But all of us, the close circle, weren't going to let him go. If he didn't stick with it, it would have almost invalidated a whole bunch of our lives."

In the years since the film's release, it has been shown at a number of festivals, including Edinburgh and Avoriaz in France. Word has filtered back to Lynch that *Eraserhead* is a favourite with a number of directors besides John Waters, among them Stanley Kubrick and William Friedkin, who was on the panel at Avoriaz which awarded the film the Golden Antenna award and the Jurors' Choice award. Lynch finds the admiration of other filmmakers very gratifying after the long hard years of effort he put into the film. *Eraserhead* continues to play steadily, "'as strong now," according to Barenholtz, "as it was four years ago." It has opened in about a dozen countries from Europe to Australia, Mexico to Japan, repeating the kind of success achieved in the U.S. whenever it has been handled carefully. Hardly a day passes without the film being screened at least once somewhere in the world. In both France and Japan, it was given a more general release, but although the initial response looked quite good, Barenholtz was not optimistic about the possibility of achieving success by that route.

Despite Lynch's less than favourable opinion of television – he has said that he wants to make films that can only be seen in a theatre – he personally supervised the transferring of *Eraserhead* to videotape late in 1981 for a pay-TV showing on New Year's Eve. "The bad part about it," he said, "is that *Eraserhead* works best when you run the mix on magnetic with a brand new print off the original negative on a huge screen. That's the way it should be seen. That's the way every film should be seen. If it can't be that way, you're always going to miss something. The worst thing about TV is the sound. So much will be lost for those people; they'll think they saw *Eraserhead* but they haven't seen it. You can't really experience it on TV. You can only go into the world a little bit. Right outside the TV is your rug, and the dog, and that window – it's so simple to escape with just a nod. It's not the same experience at all." Nonetheless, he felt that the transfer job was as good as it could be, and he made a point of taking the sound from the original mag tape. But the film was never shot with TV in mind; the extreme darkness of many of the images was a problem from the video point of view. However, the film was quite well received on TV and following its New Year's Eve broadcast, it reopened at Los Angeles' Nuart Theatre for another midnight run.

By the time *Eraserhead* had been completed, said Lynch, "film had really gotten in my blood." Although he still possesses a love of painting, making films is what he wants to do most. "Sound and picture: there are two senses involved.

It can really do something. It covers so many different things; you can't get the same feeling from any other art form. And no one has really figured out even yet how powerful it is. I don't ever want to figure it out so it's like a mathematical thing, but I really want to explore it in a 'feeling' way, really learn about this business of pacing and what goes next to what, and think in terms of sound and picture real close together." Ironically, despite the technical achievement of his first feature, *Eraserhead* could almost be said to have been an obstacle to the furthering of Lynch's career: first, being a limited audience film released on the midnight circuit meant that few people in a position to put up money for movies were likely to see it; and second, the few who did see it were likely to find it too strange to consider its director a likely prospect for more commercial enterprises. The midnight circuit is essentially a small ghetto off to the side of the mainstream film industry.

So, as *Eraserhead* began its slow climb to cult fame, Lynch remarried, sold the sound and editing equipment he had bought, and converted the garage into a workshop. "I built sheds," he said. "And I built one very good shed. Mostly out of found wood." His "dream world is going into my little back yard and having my saw all set up and everything, feeling that California sun on the back of my neck, and running wood through the saw."

One of those who discovered Lynch's film in its early days was Stuart Cornfeld, who would eventually be executive producer on *The Elephant Man*. A friend at the AFI had mentioned the film to him and he went along to the premiere showing at the Nuart in L.A. where there were about twenty-five people in the audience. "And," recalled Cornfeld, "I looked at this friend of mine who I went with and I said, 'Jesus, I've never seen anything like this before.' I thought it was the best film I'd ever seen and certainly the most unique. The guy did so many things that had never even been tried before, let alone executed." The following Monday Cornfeld called the AFI, obtained Lynch's phone number, and called the director. "I said, 'Listen, I just wanted to tell you I thought your film was incredible.' He thanked me and I asked him what he was doing, and he said he was repairing roofs; that the initial reception that the film had had a year before was somewhat disappointing and that he hadn't received any offers to do anything." Lynch and Cornfeld got together and became good friends.

Lynch wrote a new screenplay around that time: *Ronnie Rocket*, a film which would, he said, "cost a lot of money to do." Set in an *Eraserhead*-like world, all he is willing to say about the story is that "Ronnie Rocket is a small person with red hair and physical problems. The movie is also about sixty-cycle electricity – sixty-cycle alternating current electricity." It is, said Cornfeld, "much stranger than *Eraserhead* – I don't like to use the word strange; let's just say more things happen in *Ronnie Rocket* than happened in *Eraserhead*."

Together, they attempted to get the project off the ground, but, said Cornfeld, "nobody was very interested in it."

"I think it will be commercial," asserted Lynch, "but other people who have track records for predicting this or that say they don't think it will be commercial. And how are you going to argue with them?" No interest was forthcoming; Lynch was still an unknown, even though "toward the end of the two years it would be possible to mention *Eraserhead* to ten people and have one of them have heard about it – they hadn't seen it, but they'd heard about it. But, in terms of the industry, they were the last people to hear about it – and by then I'd gotten *The Elephant Man*."

There came a point when, desperate to be working again, Lynch decided that he should consider directing someone else's script. He mentioned this to Cornfeld, who thought it a good idea. A few weeks later, Jonathan Sanger, who owned the rights to the Chris DeVore-Eric Bergren *Elephant Man* script, gave it to Cornfeld. "I read it," Cornfeld recalled, "and said, 'I know the guy to direct this.'" Cornfeld thought of Lynch "basically because of his ability to deliver a character as being sympathetic even if they're 'different'. It was also the tone of the piece, seemingly bleak yet ultimately transcendent, which is where I think that David has his greatest strength."

At Cornfeld's suggestion, Sanger went to see *Eraserhead*. Fascinated, he asked to meet Lynch. "He was not at all what I had expected he would be," recalled Sanger, echoing a reaction common among those who meet Lynch only after having seen the film. "We just started talking about the script, and everything I felt about it he felt about it too. We had really good discussions, and I had a very good feeling about him right from the start. When I saw *Eraserhead* initially, it was the kind of movie where just his use of film technique to me was astonishing for somebody who'd never had very much film experience before. And when I saw *The Grandmother*, I said, 'Jesus, he's not a flash in the pan. This is somebody who has a real consistency of vision.'"

For Lynch's part, he said that as soon as Cornfeld said "elephant man", the words "made a little noise in my head. And I knew I was going to do it, I knew I was going to do that film." Even though he had at that time never even heard the name John Merrick, let alone the story of the man's life.

But despite the trio's enthusiasm, they could not interest the major companies. "The response was not negative," said Sanger, "but it wasn't positive either." A film about a grotesquely deformed Victorian, with a producer who had not actually produced a feature before and an unknown director with only a bizarre midnight cult film to his credit: the package did not sound very commercial. Then the Broadway play appeared and the chances for the independently written screenplay seemed to fade away entirely. Until the script found its way to Mel Brooks, for whom Cornfeld was working as associate producer on *History of the World - Part One*. Brooks liked the script; he was looking for projects for his Brooksfilms company to take on. He met Lynch and, said Cornfeld, was impressed. When he saw *Eraserhead*, Brooks said, he was "flabbergasted. It's very clear. It's beautiful and it's clear. It's like Beckett, it's like Ionesco. And it's very moving. And very, very well done; really kind of Max Reinhardt expressionist filmmaking." He was also impressed by *The Grandmother*. "I thought that was lovely, touching, and weird and beautiful." With Brooks' enthusiasm and influence, backing was finally arranged for the film. The Chris DeVore-Eric Bergren script was rewritten, with Lynch now collaborating with the two original authors. And eventually the film went on to garner several Academy Award nominations and resulted in Lynch's being offered the *Dune* project by Dino De Laurentiis.

The Elephant Man bears the imprint of Lynch's distinctive style; the careful, moody photography, the expressionistic use of sound. But here the narrative is far more prominent; and the story is not Lynch's own. Though visually powerful, many of the images lack the intensity and resonance possessed by the images of *Eraserhead*. The necessities of telling the story seem to have brought Lynch closer to the surface of the material here than he had to be in the previous film. "It goes back," he said, "to personal films and films that aren't your own. I am really happy with *The Elephant Man*. I think I did the best job I could've done. And I didn't sell out - I may have sold out in a couple of instances, but I could've sold out in so many more. But when you compare it to *Eraserhead* - I had control over so much more of *Eraserhead*."

Interestingly, while *The Elephant Man* depicts a world which is like a prelude to the dead, industrial wasteland of *Eraserhead*, the film is much more optimistic than *Eraserhead*. Henry is lost and helpless, completely ineffectual in his trap; but Merrick is able to assert his identity and affect the seemingly unfeeling world around him. As dark as Merrick's Victorian world is, that little bit of light represented by the Lady in the Radiator seems to have grown stronger.

With his reputation now firmly established, the offers come to Lynch in great numbers. Though no one is offering him the kinds of films he would really like to do, films set in the Forties, "a dark sort of film noir kind of thing," or the Fifties, a time "just like my woodpeckers and bobby socks and wild fins and plastic," or the Sixties, "kind of dreamy and the girl next door and sidewalks.

"I like diners," Lynch continued. "I don't like dark places. I like light places with Formica and metal and nice shiny silver; metal, mugs, glasses, a good Coca Cola machine. So I'm looking for stories or a script in the Fifties, you know, detectives and that kind of thing, diner stuff."

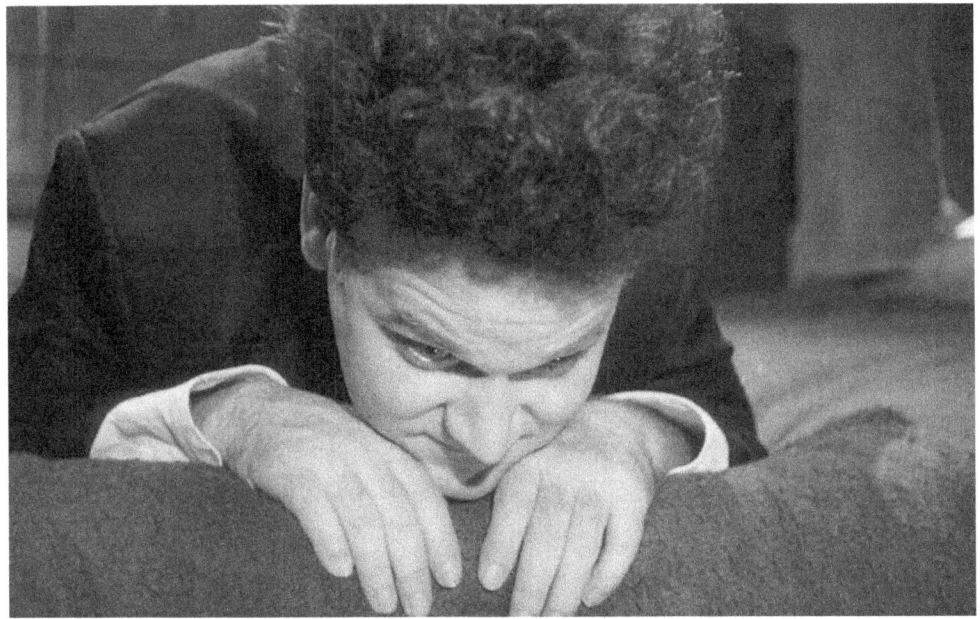

Henry Spencer (Jack Nance): Everyman as blank slate.

A successful career would seem to be virtually certain for Lynch now. He already has another project lined up to follow *Dune*, a story of multiple murder called *Red Dragon*. But *Eraserhead* is likely to remain his most distinctive, purely Lynchian film until he has the box office power to create and control his own projects; at which time he may at last be able to give life to his pet project – *Ronnie Rocket*.

For those who worked so hard with Lynch to make his vision a reality, the creation of *Eraserhead* remains a very special period in their lives; they forged strong friendships during those years, friendships which still remain strong today although they have all gone on to other things. Their admiration for Lynch is combined with an almost fiercely protective loyalty. They trusted what amounted to several years of their lives to the belief that what he was doing was worthwhile. The film's success has vindicated that belief, and confirmed and strengthened their admiration for Lynch. As Doreen Small put it, "We were all hand-maidens to genius."

Yet while they worked, it seemed that none believed – or dared to believe – that the film would actually find an audience. "One of the things we used to talk about," recalled Catherine Coulson, "was 'wouldn't it be fun if this film were really successful.' We used to joke about people wearing their hair like Henry Spencer. And now I understand people do that," she laughed. "It's so amazing. It really does happen."

What counted, as Fred Elmes said, was that "if it was going to be done at all, it was going to be done the right way." As for finding an audience, "we thought it was a real long shot. It was really a surprise when David told us that he had a distributor and he was going to sign a contract with him. It was such a dream come true because none of us had ever imagined that there would be an audience out there for it. It was so nice to see David happy, that it was all for some good. We used to buy New York papers and find reviews of it, see how people liked it and what the responses were. And we'd get reports from the distributor: it just opened in Cleveland, it just opened here, and it just opened there. It was great. We're all still close now. And," he added with a touch of amazement, "we have a movie. A movie came out of all that."

For his part, Jack Nance considers *Eraserhead* his most rewarding filmmaking experience. He "got an appreciation for the movies" out of it, "what a monumental task making a film really is. I used to think, here they've got all these dozens, hundreds of people working on these movies, and, here's one guy to move this wire and another guy to do this and another guy to do that. But really there's a lot of work involved. It's hard work and I got a real appreciation for that. I really like having had the experience of being behind the camera, but I wouldn't want to do that stuff because everything is heavy in movies. Little bitty boxes weigh five hundred pounds and you have to carry them up. There's a lot of schlepping. It's hard work. I don't envy those guys their job, but it was neat to do it."

Catherine Coulson remembered it as a "richly rewarding" time. "We had the opportunity to work things through and then see them happen. And to actually see them on film and to have it be good was so wonderfully rewarding. I'm very happy I had that experience." It was for her the start of a completely new career and "every once in a while when I'm on the bridge of the Enterprise pulling focus and being in charge of several cameras, I think back on that time when Herb Cardwell said, 'You pull this knob faster the closer he gets to the camera.'

"We became like a family," she continued. "I got to know David better and better and we became really good friends; basically Jack's and my home life became *Eraserhead* and oftentimes after we were through shooting, David would come over and we would all eat pancakes at our house. We spent a lot of time that first Fall with David and Peggy while Jack and David built the giant baby head in David's back yard. We're all still real good friends. Peggy and Jenny used to come down to the stables and Jenny would ask David if she could go play with the baby. I remember spending New Year's Eve at the stables. We were all drinking champagne and Jack gave Jenny, who was about four, a couple of sips of champagne so she would go to sleep. We all listened to music and had a real nice time in our little home away from home."

"The old gang," said Alan Splet, "we still all know each other. That *Eraserhead* period spawned all these friendships. I've just got to say one thing: it was a really unusual way to make a film. It's too bad most films can't be made this way. It was a real group experience where everybody really shared. It was like a family for a while; everybody shared everybody's problems. We shot a film, but there were all sorts of other dramas going on too that we all shared in. It was really an exciting time, and it's sad that other films aren't made that way. Most films are such a mechanical process; they come, they work on it, and they leave. It was a very rare moment in filmmaking. It was good to be a part of it."

This small group of people, fired by the vision of David Lynch, managed to create, on a minute budget, one of the greatest films ever made.

Doreen Small summed it up for all those involved: "I think it never gets any better than *Eraserhead* got. Maybe it'll feel as good, but I don't think it can feel better than that. So committed to something, so proud of something."

ACKNOWLEDGEMENTS: I would like to thank the following for taking the time to speak to me during the preparation of this article: Ben Barenholtz, Jeanne Bates, Mel Brooks, Stuart Cornfeld, Catherine Coulson, Fred Elmes, Jack Fisk, Peter Ivers, Jack Nance, Laurel Near, Jonathan Sanger, Doreen Small, and Alan Splet. Thanks also to Steve Martin, David Lynch's former assistant, for his help; and to my friend Tim Kulchyski for all those long post-midnight-screening talks which helped me to get a grip on *Eraserhead*. And thanks most of all to David Lynch himself, who showed not only patience and courtesy, but also an enthusiastic interest in this project from the start. Kenneth George Godwin.

Interviews

The interview transcripts presented here have not been edited, merely tidied up for readability, with some trimming of repetitions and verbal tics; what follows here is everything I had available when I originally wrote the article for *Cinefantastique*.

David Lynch

Kenneth George Godwin with David Lynch at Universal Studios, December 1981. [Photo by the author]

In December 1981, I had two lengthy sessions with David Lynch in his office at Universal Studios, where he was working on the script for *Dune* (at that time, in collaboration with Chris DeVore and Eric Bergren, who had written *The Elephant Man*; later, they left the project and he produced the final shooting script by himself). These sessions were not interviews in any formal sense (I didn't know enough about what I was doing to manage that!), but rather conversations which ranged over a number of subjects, following whatever threads arose. Later in the week, I did a follow-up by phone from my hotel, and then again in February by phone from Winnipeg, after I had transcribed all my tapes and begun the first draft of my article.

David Lynch in his office at Universal Studios, December 1981.
[Photo by the author]

December 8, 1981

Kenneth George Godwin: I ought to get some background. *Eraserhead* doesn't just spring from nowhere – so what interests led you into it?

David Lynch: What led me into *Eraserhead*?

KGG: Well, into film first of all.

DL: Okay. Well I was wanting to be a painter. I still do, you know, I paint and I still do drawings. And I never really was a film buff and I – I went to films, but I wasn't into it at all, never thought about making films. And I just, you know, wanted to be a painter. And in high school I would go on weekends to Corcoran School of Art. I lived in Virginia, and I'd go over to Corcoran in D.C. and study painting. And then I went to the Boston Museum school for a year after high school. And also during high school I had my own studio and I shared the studio with my best friend Jack Fisk, who's now my brother-in-law and married to Sissy Spacek. And so – I went to the Boston Museum school but I didn't really like it there. And then I went to Europe and I was going to stay for three years – and I came back in fifteen days.

KGG: Was there any particular reason?

DL: Well, yeah, a lot of reasons. I didn't take to Europe. It just – like if I'd just gone to see it and just to, you know – but I was all the time thinking "This is where I'm going to be painting." And there was no inspiration for the kind of work I wanted to do there at all. And so I came right back. And then I was sort of cut off financially. I didn't really want to go to school and my family didn't want to give me any money. So I kind of went to work – printing blueprints, and then I worked in an art store, and then I worked in a frame shop. And I kept getting fired from these jobs because I couldn't get up in the morning. And so finally I really hit – I scratched this frame. I was working for this guy named Michelangelo, and I scratched this frame and he fired me. And so he rehired me as a janitor. So my job was – you know, he had a bell installed, he was the manager of the building and he had a bell installed in my apartment that he could ring and wake me up in the morning. And –

KGG: Is that where you got the idea for –

DL: Well, no – I don't know. But anyway, I worked fine for him and instead of paying me, he would give me money for food, but then he would make me show him my food. Because he didn't want me spending it on just paint, and not eating. Well, I wasn't going to do that. I mean, I was hungry. So I'd have to show him this peanut butter and this bread and milk and whatever I'd got. But, no, mostly what I'd got. So that went on for a while – and then my friend Jack had gone up to Philadelphia and started school work at the Pennsylvania Academy of the Fine Arts. And he came down and we – the reason he came down – his name used to be Luton, and we were Luton-Lynch – I followed him in the alphabet – and we were called at the same time for our draft physical. And because we were in art school – you know, out of school and in art school, you're not in school, no matter what. Art school didn't hold any weight. So we were called in. And so he really saved me because he got me up at 4:30 in the morning. I didn't know he was even coming down, you know, and I never would have woken up for my physical. So we got up and went over and had donuts and got on this bus. And on the bus ride to this physical, he was telling me about the Academy in Philadelphia. So I got all worked up about it and in about a week or so I got my portfolio together. My father sent me enough money to get up to Philadelphia in a bus and I enrolled in the school. I got in okay and I started – well, the last of 1965, it was. And that really started everything rolling. I kind of got a feeling for things in terms of painting. And my own style kind of clicked in. A lot of things started clicking. It was a great, great time to be at the Academy. Schools, as you know, have waves and it just happened that I hit on a really rising giant wave and there were so many good people at the school. It was real exciting. And a lot of people that went there during those years have gone on and really, you know, done neat work. And Philadelphia itself was a place I never wanted to go to – ever. And it was really a frightening city.

KGG: In what way?

DL: Well, there's an atmosphere, you know, in every place that you go. And it's hard to imagine the atmosphere, but it's like once you're set in it you say, "Oh, I see what you're talking about." And it's mainly an atmosphere of fear. It's just all-pervading fear. And I lived there for five years and this was, in a way, good because it was before the hippie times. And we were kind of like art students – we were really hippies, you know. We lived in strange ways and strange parts of town, but because there wasn't any of this thing between the police and hippies – that's what I mean, it's like – one time I was walking around at night with this stick with nails driven through it, you know, and a cop car, squad car pulls up alongside of me, and he says, "What have you got there?" And I showed him this stick with nails driven through it. He said, "Good for you, bud." And took off. So this is the kind of neighbourhood I lived in. I lived in an industrial area. After five o'clock, there was no one there. One or two people. Very quiet, very dark. Little narrow streets. Tall buildings, but no light in them. Brick, you know, black windows, soot. Once in a while a car would come through, but you'd kind of like hear it – you could hear people walking quite a ways away, and then under-passes and railroad things – but not too much. I lived kitty-corner from the city morgue. And I lived just a few blocks from where Edgar Allen Poe worked, where he lived for a while.

KGG: Sounds like a morbid atmosphere.

DL: Yeah, yeah, it was. I mean, it was a weird place. Like, next door was this diner, Pop's Diner, and Pop was an old guy and he had a son, Andy, and then there was another guy that lived there too, and they had little dogs. And the dogs were like – you know how ticks fill up with blood? These were totally ready to burst, the little dogs. You know, like water balloons with legs. The whole – everybody in Philadelphia that, really, that were the people that lived there were, especially in these areas, were extremely strange. And all this started taking its toll. And that's why I say that *Eraserhead* is the real *Philadelphia Story*. And all – I met my first wife in Philadelphia and my daughter Jennifer was born in Philadelphia. And we lived in this strange area of town. And, you know, that I'm sure – see, with me I don't think of making a movie about something. I mean, I work the other way around. And if an idea comes, that's it. And these ideas started coming, you know, for this movie. They came for other movies too, but through this series of events *Eraserhead* was the one that I made. I mean, I made two short movies in Philadelphia before *Eraserhead*, before I came out here, but somewhere along the line in the painting I wanted to do an animated film. And there was this contest at school called the experimental painting and sculpture thing, at the end of the year, and a lot of people would do some strange work, you know, and then enter it in that. And there were some nifty things, like, the year before this I made a thing where you drop a ball-bearing in this little hole and the ball-bearing would roll around and fall down these pipes and come out and hit this hair trigger and it would release a match up a little ramp and light it and then there was a firecracker waiting for it, right, and when all this was happening then this ball-bearing would roll back and fall onto a trough and the weight of it going along the trough would contact these two microswitches and it would light a red light and open this woman's mouth and there would be a scream when the firecracker went off. So that's what I made the year before. And then this time I was going to do an animated film that would repeat itself over and over, and then I had a loop of a siren going and then there would be six figures. Three of them were three dimensional with film overlapping them and then the other three were just film figures. But all the figures – there were eighteen or twenty things working, animating, you know – it was more like a painting. And these figures all got fire and headaches and their bodies and stomachs grew and they all got sick. And then it started over again, right, with this siren going. Anyway, this guy – that was going to be the end of my filmmaking experience because that cost me two-hundred dollars to do, and that was just too expensive. The sculptured screen itself cost a hundred dollars and the movie – to get the camera – I shopped around for cameras because I thought all 16mm cameras were the same. I thought when you said 16mm, that was a certain kind of camera and I was amazed at the varying prices I was getting, right? And so I finally found a place that sounded more reasonable, you know, and it was a weird little bitty camera with a cassette, a fifty-foot cassette in it. But it had a little turret and it had a real nice little Cook lens and it had stop-motion. It had to have stop-motion, I told the guy, right. So he said come on down. I didn't even know how to run it. He sort of showed me – he didn't know how to run it really. And I said, "Well, how am I going to light this business?" So he gave me these two photofloods and he said, "Put them at forty-five degree angles to the …" – and I was working on a big board, this animation thing – "and it will bounce the light right into your camera, right, and you won't get any – look out for glares," and he said, "Set them just right so you don't get glare from anywhere." And so I set the screen, the big board at a radiator – it was the seventh floor of this old hotel in downtown Philadelphia where they had part of the school, but up in the seventh floor there was these rooms that hadn't been used for a long time, a lot of furniture stored in the hallway, and it was a great place to work. It was real quiet. So I set this thing on this radiator and I glued the camera down to a dresser that I drug in and I figured it wouldn't move around and I marked every place, you know, on the floor. And I taped this camera down and I set my lights up and I went to work, you know, animating this thing. But it didn't have reflex viewing, so I wanted to get back far enough so I know I'd get the board in, right. Well, I got back so far that I got a lot of the wall and the radiator. So I had to hang the sculptured screen in the middle of the stage and let the radiator and all the wall fall back into the background and it worked out great, but like I said, there were so many problems with it that I figured, well, it was much nicer to paint than to make these movies. And also I wasn't ever interested making "movie" movies. I mean, like I figured every painting had an idea but it was more like, not even a theme, it was just a little bit of mood, you know, like maybe if a painting can move, it can move from here to here, but not go into other rooms or something. It would just be right there and there would be some sound that would go with it. But not a big world, not a big thing. And so these movies that I'd got were little bitty things. They weren't movie stories at all. But anyway, this guy – this was one of these things, you know, where you can't – it's a crossroads sort of thing, where you say, well that's the end of it, but then something happens and you say, no that's not the end of it. Because this guy came along and he said, "I want one of these for my house." And so he gave me close to a thousand dollars. I bought a new camera and I started working on this thing for him. He wanted exactly the same thing – a sculptured screen he'd hang up, and we'd mount a projector, get an old projector, and get a loop going some way, and just screw the projector down to his room. He was a millionaire, you know, he could just set it anywhere he wanted it. It could be just sort of like a piece of sculpture and then this thing on the wall, and turn this movie on and have a moving painting any time he wanted it. So, it was a great idea and he was excited about it, and so I went to work. And I was animating for two months, this little bit that would go, and I took it down to be developed and I was real excited – you know how when you get your pictures back and all this – I came home and I'd waited till I got back, I think, to look at it and I opened it up, and I just quickly kind of like held it up to the light to see some frames and stuff and it was totally – there weren't even any frame lines. It was just a blur. The entire thing was a streak of blur. And the camera I'd bought, although a really good Bolex, had a broken take-up spool or something, and it was not pulling, it was just sort of sliding the film through and not going on a frame-by-frame. And it was totally ruined. So I called Barda and I told him, I said, "I've ruined this, you know, it's no good and I've been working all this time ..." And he said, "Look, take the rest of the money and do whatever you want." And so I did, and I made this little film called *The Alphabet*. And I got some money from my father to finish that up and he said, "I don't care if it's a sculptured screen or anything, just – whatever you do, give me a print of it." And so, he just got a thirty dollar print of this four-minute film and I've got this four-minute film myself, you know. We got two prints made, one for him and one for me. And so, if the other one had turned out, I daresay there again that would have been the end of it, but now I had this little film and this guy told me about the American Film Institute. And he said, "You ought to apply for a grant. Just, all you have to do is write a script for a film you want to do and send them previous work." Well, I had the previous work and I wrote out this script, and it was like the script was very weird because I'd never written anything. And, well, it was just little images and stuff. And it was sort of like shorthand and poetry and it wasn't even – it was sort of a story in a way. But I sent this off and I sort of forgot about it. And I had this job printing engravings and stuff. And I wasn't – we were really poor. This was when I was married and real poor, in Philadelphia. And one – I got a thing in the mail that said the first group of grants had been awarded, the very first group that they ever gave. And they sent me the list of the people that had won.

KGG: This was in, what, the late '60s?

DL: This was '68. I think it was probably, yeah, early '68. And Jordan Belson was on there, and Stan Vanderbeek. And these names that I, they were all like a lot older than I was, and they said what these people had done. And I said, "Man, I am so embarrassed that I even applied to this place. This is ridiculous." And I just knew I was never going to win and I forgot about it right then. I was, like – I just wanted them to send my stuff back and that would be the end of it. So, it was about – they gave them away every quarter of a year – and I was printing and Roger said, "You've got a phone call." So I went and I answered the telephone and it was this guy, it was George Stevens Jr and Tony Vellani from the American Film Institute, saying that – I had asked for seven-thousand-one-hundred-and-eighteen dollars – and they said, "Can you do it for five thousand?" And I said – I would have said I could have done it for, you know, five dollars. But anyway, I said, "You got it." And then later on George told me a nice story, that they put films into categories, and after they got through putting piles here, piles there, and piles here, they had this little film in its own little pile and they said, "We gotta give this guy a grant." So that was how I got it. And so then I went to work making *The Grandmother*. And that is thirty-four minutes long. And I made that in Philadelphia and I needed more money to complete it because I budgeted for seven-thousand-one-hundred-and-eighteen or nineteen dollars and they gave me another two thousand, no two-thousand-two-hundred – it was seven-thousand-two-hundred dollars it had cost. So that's a very good budget.

KGG: Was this all live action?

DL: Live action and animation. Yeah. In fact, we'll show you. I think Steve's gonna show you. So, let's see – when Tony Vellani came up to see it, we were – another thing, right before, on *The Alphabet*, I went to this lab, Calvin Defreyn. It's sort of a – was a branch outfit from this Calvin lab in Kansas City that does a lot of industrial films. And Calvin Defreyn was a little lab in Philadelphia, but a real good little lab. They did industrial films and I went over there for *The Alphabet*, to have this guy cut the sound effects. I rented a Nagra – no, I didn't, I rented a little Uher tape recorder – and the tape recorder was broken even. But because it was broken it made certain sounds that it never would have made if it was working. And so they gave it to me for free, but I kept all the sounds I made and I used them in *The Alphabet*. But I needed somebody to cut them and, you know, sync them to the picture because I didn't know how to do it and I didn't have the equipment to do it. And then the mix as well. So I worked with this guy Bob MacDonald and Bob Collom at Calvin. Those guys, bless their hearts, are great guys but they're not – well, on *The Alphabet* I guess they did do what they did. Bob MacDonald cut the sound effects on *The Alphabet* for me. And Bob Collom mixed *The Alphabet*. But when it came time to do *The Grandmother*, I wanted to work with Bob Collom again. But Bob said, "Fine, you know, and when you get your stuff together come on by," and I was making a lot of effects. But I really wanted to work with him and make more effects there and use their library and stuff like that. So, I went over to talk to Bob and Bob met me at the door to the sound department and said, "I'm sorry, David, but I'm not going to be able to work with you this time, but my assistant, Alan Splet, will be working with you." I thought, oh brother – you know, I said, oh man, I'm being shunted off to this assistant. And so there's Alan – so Alan is, he's very very thin, and I remember he had, you know, he was a strange looking guy because he was this little sort of – synthetic black suit and real short hair and sort of a strange look to him, and I shook his hand and I felt all his bones shaking in his arm. And I thought, oh brother, this guy is an oddball. And I'm working with this guy who's, you know, the squarest guy I've ever seen in my life and we're going to try to make nifty sound effects. And I just said this isn't going to work, you know. So I talked to him for a little while, told him that I wanted to work with the library and use those effects as sort of raw material and alter them and, you know, start working through the library and all. And he said fine and he'd kind of gather some things together maybe, and if we talked, and helped me and then we'd, you know, go from there. So I said, well okay, and then we made an appointment to start a couple of weeks later and when that day came around and I went in and we started at nine o'clock in the morning and we worked until seven or eight at night. And we worked that day and then we worked for sixty-three more days straight through. And we got along so well, it was unbelievable. And we were making effects – we had, we really did a lot of, we made up our own effects, say ninety percent, and then some were altered from the library and this and that. But we were recording and making effects all day long, and Alan was cutting them in. And we had four or five tracks, that's all. But by the time we got finished cutting them in they were solid brown. At first they were white leader, then by the time we finished, solid brown. And one night, about halfway through, Alan just put the four tracks up and we just, for this one scene – and he said, "Well, we'll just open up all the pots and let them run and see what happens." And it blew us away. It was just, just the greatest experience. We were high as a kite. So we brought Tony up from AFI down in D.C. to show him and to try to get more money. And he came up and he loved what he saw and he got us the extra money and he told me then about this Centre for Advanced Film Studies at AFI out here, which had been set up – again I didn't get, I was in the second group of grants and then I was in the second year at AFI. And so, with *The Grandmother*, I applied to the American Film Institute and went out, came out here in 1970. And because of *The Grandmother* Alan got the job as head of the sound department at AFI. And because of *The Grandmother*, Jack Fisk came out to California. Jack and I were going to work together, but –

KGG: He worked on *The Grandmother* as well?

DL: No, Jack didn't work on it at all, but Jack, he wanted to get into movies and – but Jack came out and started art directing pictures for Roger Corman. And then he finally art directed on BADLANDS and he met Sissy on that and then he art directed more and now he's just directed his first feature. So, we all came out in the same truck. So, it was just one of those things that was meant to be. And that's another thing: after every film that I did, even that little bitty one, something would happen and it would open the door for the next one. And because I never really - it's not - while I was working, I was really working hard, but afterwards I never really - I thought, well that's enough, you know. But something would happen, and I'd be back at it again. And when I came out here I worked for the first whole year on a script called *Gardenback*. But they wanted me to do it into a feature. I could've gotten the money from this producer at 20th Century Fox, but it wasn't a film that was really meant to blow up - or I couldn't think in a regular enough way, with like regular dialogue to make it work for them. And a lot of people tried to help me, but to me it - the bits that I liked started floating further apart, you know, and in between was the stuff I didn't like. And so I got real upset and I was going to quit. And I walked and Alan walked.

KGG: Was this a narrative film?

DL: *Gardenback*? More than any - they all got more and more and more, you know - like *The Grandmother* you'll see has no dialogue at all. And *Eraserhead* has a bit of dialogue, but *Gardenback* had more than *Eraserhead*, but less when I first wrote it. Then it got more but it wasn't right. It just - I couldn't find the, this kind of dialogue that fit these kind of images. But in *Eraserhead* I did more, and then in *Ronnie Rocket*, which has never been made, I really got it, I really was writing dialogue like crazy. My kind of dialogue, you know. I was really in it. I was onto it. But now no one wants to make that movie.

KGG: What was *Gardenback* about?

DL: *Gardenback* was a story of adultery. It was like, you know, when you look at a girl, right? Something crosses from her to you ... you dig what I'm saying, George? And in this story, that something was an insect which grew in this man's attic, which was like his mind, right. And the house was like a head. Well, it didn't look like a head, but it was that way. And the thing grew and metamorphosized into this monster which overtook him. But it influenced him; he didn't become it, but he had to like deal with it. And it drove him to completely ruining his home, and going madly for this, you know, this woman.

KGG: Sounds quite interesting.

DL: It was pretty interesting. It got, um, it got ... you know, like I say, bogged down in the expanding it. But I learned an awful lot expanding it, but it sort of killed it to me ... I worked on it for so long. I didn't really understand reality that much, you know, and so like to do realistic things was so hard and they just were sort of, you know, it just didn't work. It was not ... it wasn't ready to go.

KGG: What sort of things were you trying to put into that?

DL: I was trying to put in more realistic dialogue and a couple of scenes with ... that were more realistic, you know, just among these people that lived next door to one another, so there would be a realistic level to the story and this, you know, abstract level. And it sort of was working, but it wasn't ... like I said, I'd worked on it so long it sort of killed the spark for me.

KGG: Was *Eraserhead* written before?

DL: Well, I ... you know how when you are told you have to do something your mind immediately goes to something else? Under the pressure of *Gardenback* I would sort of sneak off and write down ideas for *Eraserhead*, and I was getting ideas that I knew weren't working for *Gardenback*, but were still really, you know, kind of exciting to me. In fact, in *Gardenback* the main characters are Henry and Mary and I transferred them from there to *Eraserhead*. And all of a sudden *Eraserhead* was becoming much more interesting to me than *Gardenback*. And so when these things happened at AFI, I ... you know, when I was going to quit, they asked me what I truly wanted to do and I told them and that was it. I had enough to show them ...

KGG: So *Eraserhead* was a way of doing *Gardenback* without all the ...

DL: I also realized ... now, see, this is another thing ... I don't know what's going to happen, but I don't like films that are a one-thing film, and since the theme of *Gardenback* was adultery, all the scenes had to be tailored so that that theme could be, you know, explored. You know what I mean?

KGG: Yeah.

DL: Well, life isn't that way to me, right? And, see, *Eraserhead* had to do with adultery too, but it was one part of it.

KGG: Yeah, there's lots of other things going on too ...

DL: And that's the kind of thing I really like, and I don't know if it's possible to do that in a commercial way. Most films are like a one-line joke to me. They explore one thing, and even then it's not really true because nothing is ever that isolated and builds to a climax and all this, it just isn't that way. It just seems wrong. But I don't know what to do about it really, because whenever you write something they say, well, it's scattered or ... you know what I'm talking about.

KGG: Yeah.

DL: So *Gardenback* was more of a one-thing thing. I was excited about *Eraserhead* because it had the same ... you know, it had something to do with what *Gardenback* had something to do with, but it was much more. And so, let's see – when I came out here – then I got upset and I walked and I went in and told Alan, and Alan said, "That's it," you know, and he was fed up, so we both walked. And we walked down the street to this restaurant, ate a big meal, and then we walked back to my house and the phone was ringing. My wife was saying they were calling, won't I please come back and at least talk to them. And so I went back and they said, "Okay, you know, everybody's gotten upset but you've been very good and calm and reasonable. Now if you're upset we must be doing something wrong. Now what do you want to do?" And so I said, "Well, I don't want to do this. This is ruined, you know. And I don't want to do that. I want to do this thing called *Eraserhead.*" They said, "Go ahead and do it." And, you know, I said okay. And so I had to – I started pre-production on *Eraserhead*. I had written a script and it was a twenty-one page script. And so they said the movie will be twenty-one minutes long. (laughs) So I said, "I think it's going to be a bit longer than that." And they said, "Well, okay. Forty-two minutes." It would be forty-two minutes long. And I said okay. And so I started doing this pre-production, and we started shooting May 29th – I think it was May 29th, 1972. And little did we know that we were going to be shooting still into '76. And I'd already done a lot of work before, you know, we started shooting. So, we had a real ideal situation, that we had tons of equipment from the American Film Institute, we had these cameras – we had two CM-3, Eclair CM-3 cameras, and we had – Alan was head of the sound department. And we had, down below the American Film Institute, they had – Doheny's mansion was the main part of the AFI, down below were the stables. And the stables were horse stables, car garages, quarters for maids and mechanics and whatever, and a huge hay loft. Plus quite a big bunch of garages and a greenhouse and the ground around it. It was like a complex, really great. And the one drawback was, it was used by the park department, the Beverly Hills park department, during the day, and they were like noisy. They had trucks, and dragging equipment around. But we switched totally over to working at night. And just about the time they were driving out, we'd be driving in. And we'd have dinner or breakfast or whatever it was, you know, and then we'd start working. And we had about five or six rooms and this giant loft, attic, and we had a miniature little soundstage and studio, set thing, with the hall, and then we had the attic where all the other sets were built. And when one was finished, we would tear that down and use the same stuff. And I'd gotten, for a hundred dollars, a lot of flats from a studio that was going out of business. And so all those flats were used over and over and we were using a lot of *papier mache*. And, you know, it's like *papier mache*, wallpapered *papier mache* looks like it could be forty feet thick wall, but it's, you know, a sixteenth of an inch thick. And that's what I loved about the whole *Eraserhead* thing; it's like faking stuff and – but still taking the time to get it right and get the mood and everything, but literally, you know, like most sets if they cost thirty or thirty-five dollars, it was a huge amount of money, but it would take forever to do them. And, too, there were only five of us working most of the time. And little by little we slipped into this world and really kind of like lived in that world for four or five years.

KGG: You weren't shooting continuously?

DL: No, no, no, we weren't. In fact, we shot for a full year and then stopped – and we stopped for a full year. And, although I lived at the stables and – but little by little by little it looked like I was going to lose everything. And they'd come down and take some piece of equipment, and it would be a horror, you know. And then I'd kind of like wait for them – they'd come down and take something else. And I'd say, "Well, you're going to bring it back?" And they said, "Oh, sure, we're going to bring it back." They would never come back, you know. And then finally we got – a lot of things came together. George Stevens Jr arranged a thing with Sid Solo at CFI, a lab, where we could – let's see – at least he would develop the negative. We weren't even going to see workprint. And he was going to defer some things. And – I'm not sure – I think we did figure out a way – we got enough money to see workprint. But he was going to defer some things – I forget exactly the nature of it, but with that and some money that we raised, we were able to start back again. The equipment came back and we really were on a roll. And that was almost a year after we stopped.

KGG: Did you have any trouble maintaining the continuity?

DL: Well, everybody asks that, you know, and it was – there wasn't any trouble at all.

KGG: It seems odd – with something that dense and coherent you would lose the feeling.

DL: Yeah. I think because we really got into it so heavy the first year, that it was like – everybody that worked on it sort of knew, knew it, and it was real easy to tell when you were doing something wrong. Because the rules were so strong and the world was so real that it was just, you know, it was pretty easy to get back. Henry went through probably the hardest, next to me, because he had his hair, you know – it was like he was really in, had to hold on to Henry for all this time, you know. You'll meet Jack tomorrow. He's a great guy. And really I could talk for a long time about Jack. You'll love Jack.

KGG: I can't really envision what he'll really be like.

DL: He's the greatest, but Jack was – we shot then like two or three weeks at a time, stop, build another set, get all geared up and then shoot again. And we did that until it was finished. And toward the end it was like, Fred and I were working – see, Herb Cardwell actually started shooting the film and Herb was a really good friend of Alan's from Calvin in Philadelphia, and Herb had done a lot of industrial films, but he'd always wanted to get into, you know, just shoot – being a director of photography. But he – let's see, how did that work? – Herb had to get a certain amount of money a week. He was the highest paid guy on the film. And that sort of helped deplete our – the salaries were so small, but each week they had to be paid out. And so Herb could only go for nine months, that was it. And he said he had to have, you know, he had to do something else, he couldn't hold on. And so Fred was a cinematographer fellow at AFI and he came recommended by Tony who was also out here by then, Tony Vellani. And so I met with Fred. Fred came in and Fred sort of segued in and took over for Herb. And -

KGG: Did you have any trouble matching?

DL: No. Again it was like they were - in temperament they were very much the same. And very very reasonable and super-professional. And Fred understood the whole bit and had plenty of time to talk with Herb. And Fred saw a lot of the stuff and just, it was very smooth. So Herb - although Herb shot more of the actual footage of the film, that's in the film, Fred worked for three-and-a-half years, whereas Herb only worked for nine months. And so Fred - Herb told Fred that he should get, you know, the top billing because he did much more work really. But toward the end Fred and I were just shooting like special effects things and a lot of times it would be in Fred's living room or in my garage - I lived in a garage but I sort of had part of it for shooting, you know. And we'd build some rig and then, you know, shoot and then kind of work out something else and - like that. And, sort of, it was - there was - I don't even remember the day we were actually finished everything, but - then Alan and I started working on sounds, and then Alan - once we got all the sounds made, then Alan started cutting in once I'd locked the picture and all of that. And that was all done in half my garage. And Alan was staying at my house, and he was actually living in the part we were working on and Alan was eating oranges in those days. And there were orange peels everywhere and he was also - he had bad teeth, so he would dig into his teeth with these toothpicks, right, and then after Alan left I found thousands of toothpicks that had fallen down into chairs. And I'd come home and there'd be like lines of orange peels on the chair arms, you know. And the whole place smelled like oranges. And we had an orange tree in the yard, but he was bringing them home in these boxes. And then he'd make these salads too. And he made these giant salads and put a lot of oil and vinegar on them. And then he'd leave these bowls around and there'd be this putrid oil and vinegar sitting in the bottom of it - oh, it was horrible. Anyway, although I really love Alan, it was good, you know, that he left (laughs) finally when we had the film finished.

KGG: Did you work closely with him doing the sound?

DL: Oh, yeah. We - pretty much everything, every effect, we'd work on together. And even if it's altering some effect - Alan by this time had developed, you know, quite a huge library. And because he'd worked for - well, he'd got a hold of tons of library effects and developed a huge huge library. And so - but we were both against synthesized sounds, you know, like electronic stuff. But a lot of sounds we called like organic sounds, were raw material type sounds, were fed through lots of electronics to arrive at the thing. And so we'd – Alan is the engineer, I mean he's like, he's fantastic. And so what we would do is like put in a sound, start fiddling with it – Alan said, "You like this? You like this?" You know, once we got something that was right, I would write down the equalization, all the little tidbits – I don't even know if we'd transfer it then or what – we might, or he might make a note of it – transfer it to quarter-inch and then he would take it up to AFI to transfer a bunch of stuff and just start collecting. And then we went over to Warner Brothers and this other friend of mine was telling me that they threw out a lot of sound stock at studios. And to them it's really nothing, but to us it was pure solid gold. And we were going around in the trash at Warner Brothers and we got my Volkswagen filled with raw stock. And Alan went through and got it all into nice big reels with very few splices in them – and it wouldn't matter if there were splices in them anyway, except if it happened in music or – you know, even then it may not matter. And he degaussed them all and we had all the raw stock we needed. And so we worked on all the effects together, but then once we got those all made Alan cut them all in himself. And in a lot of cases that was very intricate cutting, and that's – Alan loves cutting little bits, you know, and like taking just a half a frame of this sound and cutting it in here and putting this little – and just getting them so they sync in and feel just right, and all this painstaking stuff – I mean way more than most people would even hear. But he just, you know, really goes with it.

KGG: Did you have a definite concept of the sound when you started or was it something that you gradually built up?

DL: Well, the way – you see, we had, sort of had now, because of *The Grandmother*, and then even before *Eraserhead* we were making a lot of effects for *Eraserhead*. We had a way of working and I don't even know exactly how – it's, the main part of it is that picture dictates sound. And it's sounds that – it's like, it's not a mathematical kind of thing as you know; it's all on feeling but in a way it is sort of mathematical. If you have – you have so many possibilities, but really you only have one sound that's right for that scene. And when you hear it, you really know it. Then before you hear it, you at least know that it's not this – it's a sound that kind of does this, and it's low or it's like a whistle, or it's like something that starts off rough and then smoothes out and then it goes up and comes over here like this. And a lot of times I do little drawings and – but even that, it was like an under-the-surface kind of knowing that was the whole thing. And Alan, you can – people tune into things and I think *Eraserhead* was a real good example of how different people can tune into something even if it's strange, you know what it is you're looking for. And it just, it was like a sort of a very smooth thing. We started right at the beginning, and started making effects. And it starts off in space and we wanted this open sound and so we got this sound, then sort of like it changes subtly as you go in and in and those changes are all, you know, equalized and then when you come in on the next cut it's lower and you're in a very – roaring along, and then there's a kind of a segue and it changes in – and just one by one we got those till they felt right and it just started like that. And –

KGG: Did you ever consider sound in any way before you started working in films?

DL: No, I never – no, see, the thing is that's what I discovered. I just love working in sound. And I really want to do an album with Alan, of sound effects that are a lot like music.

KGG: The thing that struck me with *Eraserhead* when I started thinking about it was that where sound effects usually are part – just to help the picture, it's to go along with the thing you're seeing – in *Eraserhead*, the sound is used more like music than like sound effects –

DL: Exactly.

KGG: Which is why the music itself in *Eraserhead* doesn't even sound like music, it's just another effect.

DL: That's exactly right. That's right, and I – it's – that's what happened on *The Grandmother*, the same thing. They had a, they knew that I was there with Alan week after week after week, and they were keeping records of how long Alan was working on this thing. But they also had an in-house rate of two-hundred-and-fifty dollars per sound effects reel, which was a ten-minute reel. And usually, Alan explained to me, that's like five effects: a car door slam, you know, the engine starts, maybe some – a door close, a horn honk, and a step. Something like this. And that's on one reel that they have to cut in. And a vast majority of the stuff is music. Well, they – bless their hearts – they gave me the whole thing for seven-hundred-and-fifty dollars. That was seven weeks, nine hours or ten hours a day for Alan's work, because they didn't need Alan at that time for anything else. So they let him go. Alan was drawing his salary, but the money that Calvin really made was, at least for those sound effects, for all his cutting work was seven-hundred-and-fifty bucks. That's it. So that was an awful good deal. Otherwise it would have been thousands of dollars. But it's like music I guess – that's why it was – I don't know – there's a – it's just like when something is brittle and it goes on the way to liquid, it comes into this area where it sort of stretches, you know, on the way toward liquid. Well, I guess these sound effects are – if music is brittle, and most effects are just liquid, we're getting real close to this stretchy in-between thing. And even toward brittle, but we haven't really gone into music. But I think we could, and I really want to try working with Alan in something that, even that gets closer to music. It would be real neat.

KGG: When you were working on *Eraserhead*, was there anybody who came in and looked at what you were doing while you were doing it, or were you entirely free –

DL: Because of the – there was a lot of, you know, how, like – I don't know, everything relates, you know, everything all relates, but because AFI was the way it was, I was able to make *Eraserhead* and part of it was they were busy up there on the hill. And so part of it was because I had gotten upset and they said, well just go do it. That was kind of – they were letting me do it. And then they got busy on other things, lots of other problems, and I was not – I was out of sight, out of mind. And I was down there and they didn't see me. And I was working at night. Well, the first day, the first night we shot – the very first shot was when Henry sits down on the couch with Mary and Mrs X. And that was scene 1-A, take one. And we did it one take. And so, they came down just before we started shooting and kind of peeped in and sort of smiled. And then they left. And all the big guys at AFI came down and – Frank Daniel, Tony Vellani, and, I think, a few other people. But then the first dailies they saw, then they never said anything about either one. They thought everything was under control. And really, because Herb had shot so much and, you know, Alan had done so much with sound and we were, you know, building sets – not too many people built sets – they had been built before, but this was kind of a complete set, and it was – Alan and I had built these sound blankets and so we had, all the walls that were not in the shot covered with these – what do you call it? insulation? – fibreglass insulation in burlap bags to absorb all the sound. And we had a lot of real nice equipment and it just looked like we were really rolling. And we were. And so they thought everything was fine and they'd just leave us alone. But they didn't really realize till much later that – how this was expanding into a bigger film than this forty-two minute one they had thought about. And they did put in more money in the film, and there was finally at the end of the year, because we needed more and they'd given quite a bit, that they said that they didn't want to stop it – they just said, "We can only help you now in terms of equipment. And that's it. You're going to have to get the money somewhere else." Well, also, another good thing in our favour was that, when *Eraserhead* was getting near to being finished, they had never made a feature film. And they had sort of consented in a way to let me expand this thing out, but then around that time the unions told them, "Look, if you're going to have us come in and help you, and give seminars and do all this stuff and, you know, help bring these people along, we're not going to – we don't want you making films that are going to compete with our guys. You know, our guys get this much money, you're cutting them out of jobs and getting films out. You can't make feature films." But *Eraserhead* was just this side of that line. And so they really didn't want to have any part of it, because it had already - I mean, it could cause trouble. So they in effect really sort of gave it over to me. And when, I don't know if you know Martin Brest - he made *Sunshine Boys*, and *Hot Tomorrows* was his short film. I mean it was a feature.

KGG: *Going In Style*.

DL: *Going In Style*. Yeah, that's what - *Going In Style*. *Going In Style* - I mean, *Hot Tomorrows* was made at AFI. And Marty was on the other side of the line. And they wouldn't let him distribute his film, even though he could have got distribution. They said no way and they kept all control over his film. And every film that's made there now, AFI owns lock, stock, and barrel, has all the rights, everything. But I was on, you know, the old way. And so it was just -

KGG: Sheer luck.

DL: Sheer luck. So they never - until, like I say, when we started running out of money, during that year we were trying to hold on, they would come down. It was just like an animal dying in the desert; you know, at first the birds stay very far away, and then little by little they come in and start taking bites. And you're just too weak to get them off you. And I really thought it was the end. And it was - I even thought at one time of building a little dummy Henry and animating, stop-motioning all the little parts, you know, in between what we had shot. Just to finish this. Because I couldn't do anything else until this was finished. This was like - so, I was caught in limbo. And I knew that nothing would happen for me unless I had something to show that was finished. And I just couldn't get it finished. It was really a nightmare for a lot of the time. But it all worked out.

KGG: What was the reaction when, once completed, people who had put money into it, saw it?

DL: Well, all the people connected with it, and the people, you know, that put money into it - it was a very favourable reaction. But they were so close to it really, and it wasn't a fair, objective thing at all. It was - some indications were, along the way - one day we took Henry down to these tanks, these oil tanks, which is a little scene, a shot in the film, and we had - he was all dressed up as Henry and we'd gotten his hair up and all that, and put him in the back seat of this car. And we were driving him down to the location. And as he was getting in the car, some secretaries came by and saw him. And we were just, you know, we were so used to him that it was nothing, but when I saw the looks on these girls' faces, it kind of made me think back to when we'd first, you know, done Henry, right. And so that, and then let's see - Oh, this one guy we were trying to get money from saw some of *Eraserhead* and he got real upset, and he started like giving me and Tony a lecture on filmmaking. And he was screaming that people don't act like this, you know, and he just gave us a lecture and didn't put any money into it at all. And so there were indications that things weren't going to be – it was not going to be a blockbuster, and that a lot of people weren't going to be able to relate to it. But we sort of knew that and like there was no, oh let's hurry and finish it so we can release it and make some money or anything like that. It was never even – I mean, there might have been some joking about it, you know, at the end of the day or something – maybe someday people seeing it, right. But it wasn't ever made for that reason. And it wasn't – the idea of a lot of people seeing it was like a total fantasy. It was not based on any kind of realism. And we just knew it wasn't going to happen. It was that way. And I got – one time, the film was rough cut and I wanted to enter it in the Cannes film festival. And they said that they would take a rough cut. And then by the time the festival came around we thought we could get done; if we got accepted, we'd put the rush on, really try to get it done. And I was kind of sick at the time with a cold. And I got this money to go to New York, and it was like part of the *Eraserhead* money. And it would cost a fortune to go. And I got a shopping cart from Farmer's Market and the guy, the owner of the whole shopping thing, let me have the cart, to take to New York and to come back with, you know, to hold all this film. I had twenty-four reels – twelve of sound and twelve of picture. And I took it to New York and I was so sick and I screened it for these people, but I never saw their faces. And I – there were supposed to be three heavy duty Cannes guys in this little screening room in some weird place in New York. And all day I waited for my turn to show *Eraserhead*. And then I wondered about it, and it seemed like it was five million years long, the movie, you know. And then I got it back and I left, and I found out later that they had gone back the day before. And I had flown all the way to New York and there wasn't anybody in the room. There was some guy in there, but I don't know who he was. And I got – you know, obviously I didn't get into the festival – and then I got turned down from the New York film festival. And I thought, you know, there's no way I'm even going to get into festivals with this. And my wife Mary talked me into trying Filmex. She said – it was the last day of applications – she said, you know, "We're going to get right in the car and drive over there and you're going to turn it in. You've got to give it a try." And I said, "Well, yeah, I'll just go over and get rejected again, right." So I went in and set the film down, and I said, "Look," I said, "this has been rejected from Cannes, it's been rejected from New York, you know, you guys take a look at it." He said, "Well –" and I thought he'd say, "Well, you know, we'll probably reject it too." He said, "We don't care where it's been rejected from. We're our own people. And we're going to look at it, and we'll let you know." I thought that was really great. And –

KGG: Did you get to show it to anyone from the New York festival?

DL: Yeah, it was sent to somebody. Again, it was rough cut. For Filmex it was a composite print. And so Filmex – apparently they flipped out, you know, and it was like one of their films they were really excited about for the festival. And because of that, word got to Libra Films in New York and Ben – Ben Barenholz – wanted to see it. And Ben saw it and, I guess right when he saw it he didn't know whether he wanted to release it or not. But he couldn't stop thinking about it for the next twenty-four hours. And he said that he had to do it, you know, 'cause if it stuck with him that way – and so he's sort of like called the grandfather of midnight films because he started *El Topo* in New York. He owned the Elgin theatre in New York City, and he started running *El Topo* at midnight and he learned through experience about releasing a film with no money and just word-of-mouth. And letting it ride these ups and downs that they go through. And he told me, he said, "Look, you've spent five years making this film, now you've got to just hold on and continue to have patience because it's going to take a long time. And if it's got word-of-mouth eventually good things will happen. But if it doesn't have good word-of-mouth, you'll know pretty soon and it'll just dry up. But if it's got word-of-mouth it'll go, but it'll go slow." And that's exactly the way – it went so slow you couldn't believe it. But it kept growing. And apparently if someone could make a study of how films work – like the major studios, they will put a film out for a week and if it doesn't do so many dollars they'll pull it forever. And there it's gone. Well, Ben would put a film out and just kind of like water it, you know, and just watch it. And it would come down – first, the real weirdos would see it, they'll see anything, right. And if it's running at midnight you're going to get – you've got them. And then, if it clicks with them, it'll enter the next phase, which is a bigger group of people, but they're still the – I mean, such a minority, right. And then if it clicks with them, it'll enter another bunch – and if it keeps entering this next bunch, this next bigger bunch, and if it gets good word-of-mouth, it'll keep going. And it'll pyramid out to a huge audience. And it's critical – these transition areas are sort of critical. And you can't tell – if someone tells so-and-so, and how long will it take him to hear it and then make the decision to go see it and then for him to tell his people, you know, and then they'll all go. It's a weird thing. But it happened. And the first night in New York there was twenty-four people – or twenty-five – in the theatre on opening night. And then the next night, I think it went down, I think it went to twenty-four the next night. But the next weekend it got more and more people. So it ran in New York, when it opened it ran Friday and Saturday night at midnight at the Cinema Village. And went from there.

KGG: How widely has it been distributed now?

DL: How widely? Steve has got a list of the theatres for this record company that wanted to know, and the countries. He can give you that. It's really gone out there now. And it's going to be on the Z Channel, on television, and then Select TV's got it. And I think On TV wants it.

KGG: How do you feel about that considering your quote in Rolling Stone about wanting to make movies you can only see in a theatre?

DL: Well, see, the thing is, like we transferred *Eraserhead* the other night to videotape and on the monitor in the transfer room, I was amazed at how good it looked. And the bad part about it is, in a way *Eraserhead* – there are – to me, it works best when it's a magnetic track – you know, it's like you run the mix on magnetic film on a huge screen with a brand new print off the original negative. That's the way it should be seen. That's the way every film should be seen. But if it can't be that way, you're always going to miss something. Like, the horrible thing about TV is – I think the worst thing is the sound. And so much will be lost for those people and they'll think they saw *Eraserhead* but they haven't seen it, they haven't – it's not – you can see it and hear it, but you can't really experience it. You can only go into the world a little bit. Right outside the TV is your rug, and the dog, and that window that you see all – I mean, it's so simple to escape with just a nod, you know. At least there's no commercials, but it's not the same experience at all. But what can you do? I mean, it looked pretty good on the monitor, and we were running, we were transferring the mag tape with it. And for video I think it's a real good job. But it's – I mean, it could be worse, but it's certainly not, you know, the way it's supposed to be seen. Even in the theatres it's not the way it's supposed to be seen. Because by the time – a few times they run the print, although a lot of the theatres, the midnight theatres, they really do keep the prints up nice and they're not run that often if they're run only once a week at midnight. But there's always something wrong.

KGG: A break here, or scratches –

DL: Yeah. And that's just the way things are. It's a horrible thing. On *The Elephant Man* we had giant problems. Giant problems. The film, because black and white is so – we had more problems – I don't know why it happened, but the film would vibrate in the gate, because it's thinner, I think. Black and white's thinner than colour stock. And it would keep going out of focus. And because it's thinner, it breaks easier. And so when they put them on these big plates in these three-plexes and quad-plexes or whatever, and the tension is great enough so that it will pop the black and white film. And so they would like – in one case, I mean probably way worse in others, but I never heard about them – but one print they were running was missing a whole scene. It just broke and they just took the whole scene out rather than try to fix it. They just cut the whole scene out of the movie. And stuff like that. And so here you are, you've got Dolby stereo, wide screen, perfect quality on the original – and off their first print, Dolby stereo, in a good theatre it's beautiful. Here you've got Dolby stereo in a mono theatre, and now in a mono theatre Dolby stereo is worse than mono, because it has to be turned up even to equal mono and if they don't turn it up then it's worse. Well, they never turn it up of course. So here it is, a little bitty sound when it should be bigger than mono, it's littler. And the film is flapping in and out of focus and they've got scenes missing or scratches and it's horrible.

KGG: Depressing.

DL: It's horribly depressing. And it's just - we're in a time when a lot of theatres are going out of business, so there's these new little bitty theatres, right, so it's almost like watching TV in there. And really what they, I think, want to see happen is get better TVs at home, you know, great sound, big screen at home. But then if you do go out for a movie, you've got a giant screen, unbelievable sound, and a real experience. That would be the way to do it. But they're not really getting it together right now.

KGG: How close is the final *Eraserhead* to what you envisioned when you wrote it?

DL: Real close. Real close.

KGG: Did it change at all while you were -

DL: Yeah, it did, but the main thing that changed was the Lady in the Radiator. And you may have, you know, I've said this before but it was - to me, the Lady in the Radiator is real light in this dark world. And the film was totally dark, you know, without her. And I, one day I was sitting in the food room and I just drew this little lady and little, like little fetuses were falling out of her. And I wrote this song, you know, the lyrics for the song "In Heaven". And I thought that she would live in the radiator, where it's nice and warm, and this would be a real comfort to Henry. And so I thought, gee, and I went running into this set which was just across the hall and I looked at the radiator and, lo and behold, there was this little - it was a certain kind of radiator that had that little square in it. And it was perfect. And not only that, but we had shot scenes with Henry two different times looking at the radiator. And, I don't know, there was no loss and there was nothing else we had to shoot - it was just like something that fit in perfectly.

KGG: There was nothing like her in the original concept?

DL: No. Not at all. Not at all.

KGG: How would it have ended then?

DL: He would have just done the baby in and that was it.

KGG: But it seems so essential -

DL: Yeah. Well, it was like - that's why - I mean, it's like in a way a film isn't done till it's done. And it doesn't matter if an idea comes at the very last second, it's - you know that it's complete and you feel it's complete. And even if, a lot of films people juggle one scene over here and this scene and this guy or this cut and this cut, and you could say, "Well, gee, that makes it totally different." But the thing is it's not done, you know. And a lot of ideas, well not a lot of ideas, but some ideas came during the shooting. A lot of them were done in the beginning. But like the sets, those are like real close to the picture in my head before I ever started working on the film. And I remember standing in the X's living room and, like I could – you can remember, say like you're going to picture your grandmother's house before you ever go visit her; and then when you get there it's totally different, right. Then you try to remember what your picture was and it's hard to remember that because you're standing right in this other picture. But I closed my eyes in the X's and I remembered what the picture was for this set and I opened my eyes and I'd be in this same picture. It was weird. And, I mean, it's a little bit of difference, but the layout, the blocking and everything was pretty nearly exactly the way it was pictured. And I think that's part of these rules; you know it's like if you try to stick close to that original thing, unless it really starts feeling, you know – then it's – because that idea came with some power to it and you just try to be true to that. You'd be closer to the truth of something if you try to be true to those things. But – I don't know. A lot of films it's hard to do, but *Eraserhead* it wasn't. No one was fiddling with it. It was – we were working in a real safe way.

KGG: Were there any things that you shot that –
DL: Weren't in it?
KGG: – were dropped?
DL: Oh yeah, there's a lot of stuff that's dropped. And a lot of scenes that I really love never made it to the final version. But – there's a landlady scene that I really love and a phone call that Henry gets that I love. And the X's bring Mary home, and I like that scene. And those three are the ones that I was – and there's a couple of other things I was sorry to see go really. Mary has a fit in Henry's apartment when they're living together that I liked. But like they say, you can like something but it's killing the film. And they have to be pulled out.
KGG: A matter of pacing.
DL: Yeah. It was – just the film – the pacing is slow anyway in *Eraserhead*. And that's great. I love the feel of it. Now –
KGG: Well, that's one of the things that draws you into it.
DL: I think so.
KGG: If it goes too fast, you always remain on the surface.
DL: Exactly right. But when you have that pacing, the film – I think these scenes were dragging it down to where the pacing was, you know, painful. And you weren't – it was pushing you out of the film.

KGG: Are the release prints the way you did the final cut or were there changes made for distribution?

DL: No, they're exactly the same.

KGG: There's something that puzzles me – I'm sure there are a few characters listed in the credits –

DL: Oh, that aren't in there. That's right. Yeah. They –

KGG: What happened?

DL: Well, that's where at Filmex there was a composite print shown, Filmex and that was the long version. And it was during the Filmex screening, I stayed out of the room, but I could feel – I was just outside – and I could feel that it was too long. And Fred was in there and people weren't reacting – it was like lead, it was just too long. And so that night I made this decision to, you know – just, I kind of in my heart, I knew that these scenes that had to go, that I'd never been able to quite do it. But when you sit, or you feel an audience not – then you can do it. Because it's way better than suffering through that. And so, out they came.

KGG: What was it that you cut out?

DL: Well, those are those – the landlady is mentioned in the credits, so that landlady scene is out. Then there's a scene in the alley out in back – there's – you can hardly see this cut now – there's two figures fighting. Well, that's the ending part of a sequence that – where this little kid – Henry hears this sort of calling, and he looks out his window and it's daytime out there. The wind is – this sort of dust is blowing by and there's this little kid out in this alley, and his little friends have run off and he's left alone and you see his little friends go, and then you kind of see him come up. And so he's standing there in this kind of wind and there's this oil puddle there, kind of this pipe and he's kind of kicking the dirt. And kind of just like being alone. And suddenly he sees this shiny thing in the dirt, and he gets down and he starts digging and he finds all these rows of dimes. And so he really starts digging and Henry's seeing this and he's going crazy. And he runs out of the room, but the baby starts crying immediately, but he's got a good run going and he makes it to the elevator and he's pushing the button, but the elevator won't come. So he runs down the stairs. And then we see in the lobby, him running into the lobby, and the elevator door is propped open with a mop – there's a mop bucket in there, and the landlady has been cleaning. And that's why he couldn't get the elevator. But because the door's open, the baby crying is just real loud and echoing all through that elevator shaft. And so Henry – he gets frustrated, goes and kicks this couch in the lobby. And the landlady comes and says, "Don't you kick my wood," she says. And she gives him this business. Well, she's cracked and she starts into this sort of landlady-tenant thing. And so Henry kind of leaves her and goes back upstairs. And meanwhile – he looks out the window, and meanwhile more people have come and they're digging and the dust is blowing. And so it's kind of gone into – by night there's just sort of fighting going on out there.

KGG: Why, if you cut that out, why did you decide to leave that little bit of –

DL: Little bit of fighting?

KGG: – where you see what appears to be a murder?

DL: Yeah, well, it has the right feeling for a night – his world, outside his –

KGG: It never even occurred to me that this was part of a –

DL: Yeah, I know--

KGG: It seems complete in itself.

DL: Yeah. Well, that's one of those things where it's complete but even though there is something else there, that's what ended up in the thing. But there's a lot of scenes that are gone, that I really wanted, but they just, finally just didn't work.

KGG: How much longer was the original cut?

DL: Well, I think I probably took out twenty minutes. Yeah, it was about an hour-fifty. But those twenty minutes were really, really bogging it down. And it felt much better after they were out. By themselves, these other scenes I really like, if I could just run them, you know, just on their own, but in the context of the whole they were killing it.

KGG: Were there any particular influences on –

DL: On the film?

KGG: On the visual design or –

DL: No. This is part of what I kind of got on to in Philadelphia. *Eraserhead* is – the real influence was, you know, Philadelphia and my stay there. And it's – there are people, there are films that I really like and that are – and most of the films that I really like are in black and white. But how much they influence you is hard to say. Because, like I don't have any – I guess, if I had thought, well okay I love Fellini and I want to make a film, I want to kind of like tune into Fellini's style and do this, I wasn't – *Eraserhead* just kind of came out of something. Like, it wasn't the other way around. And so I'm sure there are influences, but they've gone in and then they've been absorbed and come out – yeah, exactly. And that's, I think, the way – if that can be the way to make a film, that's the ideal way. And that's like *Ronnie Rocket*, to me, is the same kind of thing. I just sat in my room and wrote that, and I made myself write ten pages a day. And that's what – I could go into that world, I could just sit there and go right back into the world, you know, the next day and continue the thing along. And I had a list of ideas that I'd gotten, and sometimes the sequence of the ideas that I wrote down worked great and I'd know exactly where I was going. But then sometimes it was totally wrong and I'd jump to this one. And these would fall away or they'd find another place. And that's the way it was. And it just felt just right. It was all feeling and that's another thing about being from painting, to go into a script conference with people from a studio, you know, they are smart and they're great and they know what they're doing for themselves, but they'll never make a film like *Ronnie Rocket*, they'll never do it.

KGG: Is this a fantasy?

DL: Yeah. I mean, it's more like *Eraserhead* than anything else. But it's - they would like, probably they'd worry about losing their job if someone up higher knew they were doing this kind of thing. And it's something that - and so there's a huge world, probably, of filmmakers out there who would know what I was talking about. And it's not like saying, "Well, they don't want to do my stuff, and so I must be doing something really way ahead of its time." It's not that. It's just that it's - you're doing something that's - it's just different. And they just - it doesn't fit into this kind of thing. They go by certain kind of rules and they, I think they get more and more strict, these kind of Hollywood rules. And it's a hard thing.

KGG: Do you find it more difficult now that you're doing major features?

DL: Well, I've been lucky because I've been working with good people who understood what I was doing. On *Elephant Man*, there was Mel Brooks who was very supportive. And Jonathan was protecting me. And it was not this normal studio thing. Now, with *Dune*, it's not really a studio picture either. It's Dino's. But, you know, Mel and Dino both are real strong people. And I mean if they don't like what you're doing, you've got a problem. So, you either have to alter what you're doing or stop the whole thing. But -

KGG: Did you have to adjust on *Elephant Man*?

DL: No. Really it was so - it was almost like a paradise. Everything sort of fell into place in a weird way on *Elephant Man*, and the film - everyone sort of felt the film was sort of blessed. And it was horrible rough times on the film, it was - it was a lot of things were - it was the hardest thing I've ever been through in my life. And I reached some real lows on that film, but all in all, I made the film that I really wanted to make. And I learned a tremendous amount about making a film with other people. And it was a great experience. And Mel really kept if from being a film that would have been taken away from me. And there were things that were different from my original concept of the film in *Elephant Man*, way more than in *Eraserhead*. But I don't think it's possible, you know, to do a film with so many people involved, with that kind of schedule, where you don't have to be more flexible. And it's like - it's not that - you still have control, but you have to - this is the way it is today and this is the things that you've got to work with and you've got to make it work with these ingredients and here we go. You know, we're going. And so you kind of act and react real fast. And - whereas *Eraserhead*, it was a plodding sort of thing, and it was like much more exact, because we had way more time. But in a way that was bad as well. We could have had a little faster pace, maybe, and got the same things.

KGG: Is the final *Elephant Man* much different from the script you originally saw?

DL: I haven't even – I've forgotten, seriously, the original script in *Elephant Man* and *Eraserhead*. I know that there are things that got cut out of both films. And, you know, Chris and Eric, who I'm working with on *Dune*, who I worked with on *Elephant Man*, and they wrote the original *Elephant Man* script – they had to adapt much more than I did. And I think it was harder on them. And they take things, you know – they see things one way and if they're not that way it upsets them. And I think they had to give up much more than I did. When I came along, they had to change – you know, Mel had input, Mel always tempered it with, like, "You don't have to listen to me, but if it's a good idea, we want you to find a way to go and do it." And so it was a real kind of experience for them, that way. And then what I did with the film probably was a lot different than what they wanted. But ultimately they were real happy with it. But, you know, it's like – there again, it was like three minds working on this script rather than just one, and then when the director can take it and do what he wants with it, it's going to be different than what you want. But, you know, that's the way it goes.

KGG: Is it deliberately similar to *Eraserhead*? I mean, a lot of the visual elements – there seems to be a direct relationship.

DL: Well, it's deliberately, in a way – I mean people have a style, I guess, and that style kind of came out in *Elephant Man*. But to me, it's a lot different. But some of it, the dream things are the same. And a feeling of industry is sort of there.

KGG: That's what I was thinking. It seems sort of like a prologue, in a way – that this is what *Eraserhead* developed out of.

DL: Oh, huh? Uh-huh, that's right.

KGG: I wondered if *Elephant Man* indicated that you were less – not depressed – I can't think of any other way to put it –

DL: Less dark.

KGG: There's a lot more optimism in *Elephant Man* than –

DL: Yeah, well, see, I – well, yeah, I mean I'm a lot more optimistic than I was, I think when I made *Eraserhead*. And – like the Lady in the Radiator coming along was an indication of that. And *Elephant Man* was, to me, a real uplifting story. Not to say that – see, every film is different and like, if you tune into that film and do that then – it doesn't mean, although you still put a lot of yourself in, so – but I am more optimistic. But still, that was the film too. I could have gotten a film that was, you know, a real dark film again. But I – putting in some of myself, you can't help but getting that into the film some way, I mean it kind of creeps in there. But I'm doing this film after *Dune* called *Red Dragon*. It's this book that's just coming out, and it's a pretty horrific story about this mass killer. And I worry about it because it's such a great, you know, it's a great read, the book, it will be a real fascinating film, but it's still a sick thing. And, you know, it's - you've got to - it's hard to figure out what's the right thing to do in cases like that. It's weird what you're doing to people. But, we'll see what happens.

KGG: There's one thing that - I personally, you know, I - you may throw me out, but I wasn't as happy with *Elephant Man* as I was with *Eraserhead* as -
DL: As a film.
KGG: - as an entity. Like *Eraserhead*, I was totally into, but *Elephant Man*, there were points when something would click and I couldn't accept something.
DL: Yeah.
KGG: The key comes in that last sequence, in the theatre. And I wondered why you did it that way, with him visible and the audience cheering and everything - which struck me as not entirely believable.
DL: Yeah, well, there's things in it, there's - the only thing I can say about it is, it's - the feeling of a scene is more important than the actuality of the scene.
KGG: Yeah - but with that, for me, what it mainly did was bring out the point that - it sets up a sort of class thing there, that he's become accepted and cheered by these people who are essentially middle class and upper class, which immediately makes you think of how inhuman the sort of lower classes are, which, even though they're brutalized - it's a sort of denial of the way that Merrick himself can become sensitive and human even though he's the most brutalized of all. It seemed false even in terms of the film.
DL: Uh-huh. Well, see, I'm not going to argue with you because I know what you're talking about. But I'm just saying that in terms of - and also, I'm not that political a person - and, you know, it's like, a lot of people have gotten onto this lower class and upper class business. And the lower class, he lived around them because he was deformed and the lower class people, you know, were the ones that ran the freak shows and all this kind of stuff, and the lower class people - a lot of them were the people that went to these places because they were in those neighbourhoods. But even so, the nurses were lower class, and they were very nice to him. A lot of the people at the freak shows were upper class and took advantage of the - there's, you know, good people everywhere and bad people everywhere, and it doesn't - this class business, it's not just black and white in that film.
KGG: No, I agree with that. But it sort of sets up that idea.
DL: Yeah, well - what I'm talking about, in terms of the way the film starts, and in the growth of John Merrick, the last - that standing up and that, is more

like a certain kind of thing that he overcame. And – I mean, he stands up three times, you know, in front of people in the film. Once when Treves comes, and once in the doctors' place – and he gets applauded in two of them, but it's all – it's very different.

KGG: Yeah, I picked up on that, the total sort of balance of opposites with the lecture and the final scene.

DL: Right.

KGG: I mean, the lecture is his sort of lowest point in the film, totally demeaned.

DL: Yeah. But I still see the dishonesty of it too because in reality, he went to the theatre but he was completely clothed and he was sitting in the back rows.

KGG: Hidden away.

DL: Right. But this is like – I don't know, it's not to me breaking a rule, but it's really stretching it, a rule.

KGG: It was more a sort of personal preference. I would have preferred the sort of quieter thing, that he'd made these friends, there were people who care and that he'd been made happy rather than a sort of overall acceptance.

DL: Yeah. But then there's also something about, if you accept yourself, you exude that feeling and that can turn the tide on how other people see you. And he did finally stand up for himself, and this scene follows that. And it's a kind of a growth and a new sort of level. And even though it has that feeling which I agree with you on, it has another kind of thing that in terms of this whole thing for just him, that culminates in just – it feels right for that part of it. And even though it's using things that are not really obeying the rules, it has the right feeling for that growth and that sort of celebrating thing that he – See, that's the horrible thing about making a film sometimes, it's like you can see it's too late to do anything about a lot of things anyway, right, and then you can see other people's points of view. But that's part of what you've got to take. But, see *Elephant Man* – I mean, *Eraserhead*, in a way it's more flattering, you know, to me that you like – because that's like more totally my thing and the thing that I really like. Even though the films could get lighter, have more light in them, there's a certain kind of humour and a certain kind of thing, an absurdity sort of thing that I like that's in *Eraserhead* more than in anything that I'll do probably until I can do *Ronnie Rocket*. Or something else that I write completely on my own. And, I mean I did write this thing called *Blue Velvet*, that was – but it didn't have – it was more normal story, and it does have, you know, problems and stuff. It's not going to get done, but – I don't know. I know what you're talking about in other words.

KGG: It's sort of interesting, though, if you see it as a sort of prologue to *Eraserhead*, that you now –

DL: But I made it after--

KGG: - that now -

DL: Oh, prologue. Yeah--

KGG: - you see a possibility of escaping from what you see as sort of total in *Eraserhead*. There's no way for Henry to escape from the way things are in *Eraserhead*, except, you know, by sort of dying or something, whereas Merrick just through force of will and just being himself manages to overcome the dehumanizing influences.

DL: Right.

KGG: That's why it seems a much more optimistic film than *Eraserhead*.

DL: Right, for sure. Except--

KGG: Even the death at the end is not a sort of negative -

DL: No, no--

KGG: It's a simple assertion of being human.

DL: Right. But, see, the thing is like in a way - and you can't - the feeling here is different, but the - more intellectually *Eraserhead* is a happy ending. But the feeling is still heavy. It's that most, ninety-nine percent of the film is very dark; even though it ends in white light, the balance is so far in the other direction that it can't bring it up. But you can see, intellectually, he's in happiness. His own idea of happiness.

KGG: How - considering that your first feature was that distinctive, that accomplished - how does it affect the way that you think about each new thing? I mean, I would think that it would be easier for somebody to start with something that's promising, and build, whereas you seem to have started with something -

DL: Yeah, well a lot of people think that, you know, that's the way *Eraserhead* is, that it's promising but it's not - but see, I mean I think *Eraserhead* is a whole thing, and it's - but see, one reason it's got this whole thing is that I had plenty of time to fashion it and to think about it, and work with it. And a lot of times - number one, people don't care about much more than the surface level of a film anyway. And they're making films - everybody's making films for different reasons. Most of them are commercial reasons. And if a film escapes every now and again that's got some depth, they can always say, "Well, it's also commercial." Otherwise, you couldn't just go to a producer and say, look that film you made was really great, but he'd say to you, "Yeah, but it didn't make a nickel." Every one that doesn't make a nickel is fuel for them. And so, once - the thing I worry about is making films that have some depth to them and have room for me to, you know, to go off and get into some nifty areas. And then eventually reach a point where I can - not just financially - but just sort of settle back into where I know that a lot of people are not going to really kind of go for what I'm doing but I'm very happy in my world, you know, doing these things. But the thing is I need to find somebody that can help, can back these films because – like *Ronnie Rocket* for instance: it will cost a lot of money to do it. I cannot do it on my own. And I think it will be commercial, but other people who, you know, who have track records for predicting this or that say they don't think it will be commercial. And how are you going to argue with them? But there's always that new film that comes along that proves them wrong. And I just – whether it makes a lot of money or not – I feel, if it came out by somebody else, I'd want to see it. And I feel that there are other people like me. I'm not totally wacko. And it's just, it's a film that would be really fun to see.

KGG: It's much lighter than *Eraserhead*, is it?

DL: Well, it's lighter in some areas. It's got a lot of comedy in it. But *Eraserhead* has got comedy in the first half. But it's got some dark, scary things in it as well. But it happens in a lot of the same world as *Eraserhead*. And it's this world that I'd like to keep going back into, you know. It's sort of like Philadelphia, but it's just this side of Philadelphia.

KGG: What were you doing between *Eraserhead* and *Elephant Man*? Did anybody come to you after *Eraserhead* and ask if you'd like to do anything?

DL: No. No, they never came. I wrote *Ronnie Rocket* and I got remarried. And I built sheds. And I built one very good shed. And that just about took me up to *Elephant Man*.

KGG: There weren't any other projects in between?

DL: No. *Ronnie Rocket* – I very much tried to get something happening with that. And all during that time *Eraserhead* was growing in popularity. Toward the end of the two years it would be possible to mention *Eraserhead* to like ten people and have one of them have heard about it – they hadn't seen it, but they'd heard about it. And that was real growth. But, in terms of the industry, in a way, they were the last people to hear about it – even though it was a movie and they were in the movie business. Other people had heard about it before them, but they hear one type of movie business story and that's it. And so when they finally heard about it, it helped me, but by then I'd kind of gotten *The Elephant Man*. And there was a point where Mel had to see *Eraserhead*, and that was my big test. But he flipped out, he loved it. So that worked.

KGG: How did *The Elephant Man* project come to you?

DL: Well, Stuart Cornfeld worked for Mel Brooks, and Stuart loved *Eraserhead*. And Stuart called me and we'd get together every now and again, have coffee and talk about stuff, and he became a friend of mine. But he couldn't help me, really, you know – we'd just talk about this and that. And he liked *Ronnie Rocket* as well, and wanted to be involved with it in some way, but there was no one – you know, there was nothing we could do. But one day I asked

Stuart if he knew of any projects around that I could direct, other than *Ronnie Rocket*, because I'd reached a point where I just had to work. I didn't now care whether it was *Ronnie Rocket* or anything. I just had to work. It was better than not working at all – making any kind of film. And there would be something about any film that I could get into some –

KGG: So by the end of *Eraserhead* you'd decided that film was something you really wanted to do?

DL: Well, yeah, and it was – all this time I was drawing and painting, but – yeah, film really has gotten in my blood, you know, and I really like it. And there's – one thing I really learned on *Elephant Man*, though, is that this kind of filmmaking is tremendous pressure and you wonder, like, in the middle of a film why you're doing it. And it's not worth any amount of money in a way. And you're longing for more time and less pressure to really kind of create something. And it's not there. And it's like a steam roller just – it just rolls. And you've got to be on it, you know. So anyway I wanted to make films and I asked Stuart and he mentioned two or three things, and I remember sort of thinking as he mentioned them, "Oh no, that's not it at all. That's not right. Maybe I should keep working on *Ronnie Rocket*," you know, because this is – I just couldn't do that, even if they gave me all the money and – just not it.

KGG: What sort of things were they?

DL: Well, I forget what they were really, but maybe like – I don't know, I forget the names. Just the titles didn't, you know – turn me off. And then he said "*Elephant Man*" and that word – just "*The Elephant Man*" – made a little noise in my head. And it's just like I knew I was going to do it, I knew I was going to do that film.

KGG: Did you know Merrick's story before?

DL: I didn't know the story at all. Stuart told me right then. And the script had been written, like I said, by Chris and Eric, and Jonathan Sanger had optioned their script. So, there was Chris and Eric, there was the future producer, and here was the future executive producer, and here was the future director – and we all got together at Bob's on Santa Monica. I got together with Jonathan first and he said, "Yes, I would like you to direct *The Elephant Man*. I have the option on it." So Stuart and Jonathan and I went to different studios. Promptly got turned down. And I hadn't met Chris and Eric yet, but then – and I don't know how this happened, but if you talk to Jonathan on your trip here, he can tell you the rest of it – but somehow, I don't know whether Anne Bancroft read it first or Mel read it first, but they both flipped out over the script and Mel wanted his company to do it. So Mel worked things out with Jonathan, and then there was two tests for me: one, to see if I was going to be directing it, and to see if I was going to be writing it. And so Mel saw *Eraserhead* and, like I've said this part before, but he came running out of the theatre yelling, "You're a madman and I love you." And so he was tickled and he really liked the feel of *Eraserhead* when he thought about the person who made it directing *The Elephant Man*. He thought it would go real well. And Mel is a real fan of kind of German expressionism and this kind of thing. And so – also, Mel being a comedian, no one ever sees this other side of Mel, this really serious, really artistic savvy, sharp side of him. He's a real heavyweight, and he really knows the score. And so then he said, "Well, look, you write with Chris and Eric and we'll see how it goes and if it goes well, you can do that too." He liked the way things were going, so I got in on that. And Chris and Eric wrote this screenplay that sparked everybody, but there were things wrong with it – mainly in terms of structure, just because they were true to Merrick's life. Merrick's life was bad then very happy. It was like one-third bad, two-thirds happy, and it was like a very boring sort of story in a way. So mainly we restructured everything and then wrote in, you know, quite a few new things as well, but saved a lot of their original scenes. But we got along famously. And it was part of what I was saying, the feeling of the film was in so many ways – it was sort of effortless. And then in other ways it was the hardest thing ever.

KGG: How tough was it to go to England, into a totally new environment?

DL: It was – I may end up there again on *Dune*. It's hard enough making a feature film, but then when you go to a foreign country and you're working with all new people, and you're trying – you're an American making a Victorian drama, and they don't let you forget that – and like, who are you to be doing this? It's not – no one ever really said that, but I mean it's like, certainly they must think about it. I would think about somebody coming here. Like Milos Forman, you know – I mean he's got a lot going against him. To me, he pulled it off fantastically on *Ragtime*, but – I loved it. I love the movie. I think he's a great director. But it's the same sort of thing. And sometimes you can come in with new eyes and see something, and I think that – I don't know even if I did that, but I didn't really know, it scared me, you know, that part of it. But we went to this hospital, where we shot part of the film, and the atmosphere in that hospital was what really – I knew what it was like in Victorian times. I just knew it, and I knew it as much as they did, having lived there. I mean, to me, I really felt it. And so – and then they – you have so much help too, because there's people like who have studied, like the set decorator, you know, he knows this thing is 1880 and this thing is 1881. And he knows all these different things. And so you have all these people to rely on for little details. But the atmosphere you can pick up from the place, because everything in England is, as you know – still a lot of it is right there.

KGG: How intimidating was it to start working with a cast like that?

DL: It was like Freddie Francis says, you've got to, at some point or another, get thrown in the deep end. And that's just exactly the way it was. It's either going to work out okay and you'll, you know, survive, or it's going to just devastate you. And it's heavy duty, I'm telling you.

KGG: I don't know how you deal with actors. Do you -

DL: Talk with them?

KGG: Do you direct them a lot?

DL: Yeah, well, I like to. I like to. You know, it's like every actor is different and I like an actor that I can talk to and get what I want from. And I don't want to force - I don't want to say, "My way," or I'm not listening to anybody else's point of view. If somebody does something that is super and it works, I hope I'll be able to see it, you know, and that would be great. But if they're doing something that doesn't work, to me, and I know the rest of the film and the way it's going and this is wrong, they've got to be able to, with their great talent, do it so it's right. And that's the whole bit. Otherwise you just turn them loose. And I, especially on *Eraserhead*, well Jack will tell you, we worked things out to the nth degree. And in *The Elephant Man*, we did a lot of rehearsing, and on *The Elephant Man* the difference was, by the time we were through rehearsing, it felt right. Even though it was different from maybe my original concept. But I still say, if it feels right, that's it. And with John Hurt it was magically right. Whatever - I really almost believe he was like tuning into the real Elephant Man. And it felt so right, it was really always just on one take. And he was - there was no directing him really. Because he was so truthful and honest and it was just right.

KGG: How long did it take to film *Elephant Man*?

DL: It took about - I think overall we were working on it sixteen weeks, four months of filming.

KGG: The things like the street scenes, the slums, was that studio work?

DL: Well, some - most of the street scenes were on location. And some of the interiors were on location. Some of the street scenes - well, a couple of places might have been in a studio and then - well, really what it was was fifty-fifty on the whole film. Fifty percent of the film was on location. And the rest was at Lee International film studios in Wembley, and then we did about a week or two weeks of shooting at Shepperton, and then did all the post-production and mixing at Shepperton.

KGG: Are you happy with the final result?

DL: Oh, yeah. I mean, it's like - I don't know. It's like - it's hard to say. I think - I don't want to, you know - I am really happy with it, but it's - it goes back to what you were talking about, of personal films and films that aren't your own. And I think I did the best job I could've done. And I'm real happy with that. And I didn't sell out – I may have sold out in a couple instances. But I could've sold out in so many more, you know, I didn't. And I'm real happy about that. And so, basically, I really am happy with it. But, I mean, as far as when you compare it to *Eraserhead* – *Eraserhead* I had control over so much more of it. But, sometimes when you have a lot of input things get better. And so that's always a possibility too.

KGG: How did you come to *Dune* after *Elephant Man*? It seems so –

DL: Well, it's a weird thing. I got tons of offers, you know, for films after *Elephant Man*, but there was nothing that I wanted to do. And along came *Dune*, and I'd read the book, and I love the book. And here again, it's not my story. But there's so many things, if I'm able – I say, if I am – if we are, you know, able to write this thing the way we want to, and to do it, I think it could be a great film. And there's tons of areas – I mean, the film could have great depth. And it could be so powerful on lots of different levels. And there's different visual feelings in the film that could be great. And the biggest problem with it is it's an awful lot to put into one film.

KGG: That's probably one reason why all the projects have fallen through.

DL: That's right. Well, there's different reasons, yeah. That's right. And if you're going to do it, you should do it right. And we're right in the middle of trying to see if that's possible. And I think it is, you know. But we'll see how it goes.

KGG: Does it make it difficult that most of the science fiction and big films made now don't really have much content? I mean, is the atmosphere against making *Dune* with a lot of depth?

DL: Well, probably. I mean, a producer can't help but think about how much *Star Wars* had made, although George openly admits he ripped *Dune* off like crazy. And a lot – and other things as well. But one thing that *Dune* – no one's ripped off about *Dune*, is the depth to it – and that's what people love, why people love the book. And if you don't have that, you don't have a movie. And if you just take the surface things, then you've got *Star Wars* and people have already seen that. It's a tricky thing. You can't – this will only be successful if you have that depth and deal with that, and have characters that you can relate to and that you care about. And that's one of the things, you know, like – well, Chris and Eric particularly are – they are sort of un-science fiction to the max. And I think that so far we've been going in the other direction, you know, and we've been neglecting the surface of the thing. So we have to kind of come back a little bit. But it's going pretty good and we've got some real nifty things in it. But it's still – like I say, we're still working on it.

KGG: How big is it going to be? have you tried to get it all in?

DL: It's still big. It's still real big. It could be a three-hour movie.

KGG: Even then you're still –

DL: We're cutting stuff out. Yeah. Right now it would be four-and-a-half hours. What we've got.

KGG: We haven't even talked about the *Eraserhead* effects. It's hard to deal with it without referring to the effects at all. Did you do the stop-motion yourself?

DL: What stop-motion?

KGG: That little worm that –

DL: Yeah, yeah. Well, I did it with Fred Elmes. Yeah, that was stop-motion there, the little worm.

KGG: Do you find you like that?

DL: Oh, I love doing stuff like that. It's like – whatever you can think of, you can do, right. And it's – one thing about – it's fun to try to think of solutions to problems. And it's fun to kind of do those things yourself. And in every aspect of *Eraserhead* was – it was just great fun. And it's just like this feeling if, just like I said, if you can think of it, you can think of a way to do it. And so you just, you know, just do it. And then you find out that in Hollywood, like in a way it takes some of the fun out of it because you're not the one doing that, and there are people that specialize in this and there are people that specialize in this and people that specialize in this and it saves time, but what you've got to try to do is let them filter through you and not not filter through you, so something gets in the film, that hasn't filtered through you. And it's a whole 'nother kind of experience, but in *Eraserhead*, you know, we did everything ourselves. And there were no experts, we were all just figuring things out and just doing them. But it was great, yeah.

KGG: And you're not going to say how you did the baby?

DL: No. But I – Steve said he'd sort of told you – see, like *Cinefantastique* is, they'll have pictures and they'll tell you how – you know, you go behind the scenes, right. And that's – it's interesting, but it's just like a magic act. As soon as you see how it's done, you say, "Oh brother, of course that's how they did it, you know, that's so simple." And it's not that it's so spectacular or anything, or it's some sort of huge secret. It's just that you can't help but put that in your computer and have it alter your experience of the film. And, man, I hate knowing how something was done before I see the movie. And I don't really care about how it's done – it's all logic and common sense anyway. And sometimes it's, you know, someone's great talent pulling something off, but it's one of these things – it's curiosity, and as soon as they're satisfied they're chewing on something else again. And I just can't stand it. And there's just certain things that I don't think people should talk about. It takes away so much magic from movies, not just *Eraserhead* but every movie.

KGG: It is amazingly life-like. That's what got me the first time I saw it – it's hard to believe it's not real. Did you design the baby yourself?

DL: See, you're talking about the baby.

KGG: Yeah. I meant the look of the child, as a creature –

DL: Well, in a way, like, nobody designs anything, because, you know, all these shapes are sort of found in nature. And –

KGG: Okay.

DL: But there's something about the shape of the baby, and it's – there's something like archetypes, you know, and like things that everyone can relate to even if they can't intellectualize why. And somehow a lot of these things are in *Eraserhead*. And I wasn't – it's even a surprise to me, because I wasn't intellectually trying to put them in to manipulate anyone or to try to stir up their subconscious. I was just getting ideas and I was trying to put them on to film. And so I'm surprised sometimes when I see – gee, there's a repetition of a shape, or that relates to that. And because it's so sort of like life, once you start getting on to seeing something a certain way, you say, "Holy smokes, this guy saw that a long time ago, and I'm just seeing it now." Or, "This really reminds me of this," and things start relating, and you sort of see something going on and it's like – I'm going to tell you the story about the duck sometime. It's like a duck is a shape and – but it works because of the size and the texture of the parts. And if you could make up rules out of a duck, like if you could measure the beak, and get the texture of the beak, and notice the relationship of the beak to the body, which is a fluffy texture. And then notice that the feet are bigger than the beak, but they're not quite as hard as the beak, but they're the same colour, you know. And then to have this "S" curve with a round, you know, coming up. But then the eye of the duck is the neatest – it's the littlest, but it's the most brilliant and the most intricate, right. And so it's like – I always say, like, well if I'm working on something, I may have like the feet and the body and all this, but if you can get the eye of the duck, then you really are cooking. And it's a little something, but it's – it works because of the other stuff around it. And that's why I like, in a scene, say, something, one little thing on its own would be nothing, but in the context of the things around it and the balance of the things around it, it pops out and just gleams and it makes everything else work. And anyway there's something about this duck and the proportions of a duck, that if you could know about that, you could maybe make a scene or make another – art, something – sculpture or something and it would work, because it works, you know, in nature – you know, it teaches these things.

KGG: Do you think in these terms when you're setting up a scene?

DL: Well, see the thing is, like, I've got this problem – I mean, it's a good problem in a way, but it's a problem just the same. It's like I can't talk about things so well, it's like – to take a feeling that you feel and then to put it into words, somehow it's very difficult, you know – something gets lost or it's – and everybody must have this, this –

KGG: Well, I can tell you – you've read that essay that I wrote, which I hate –

DL: You do hate that?

KGG: – because it's destroyed the film for me.

DL: Oh, yeah.

KGG: I totally intellectualized it. I've seen *Eraserhead* once since I wrote it and I sat there and I – "Oh my god, what have I done?"

DL: But see – well, now, that's okay because it's still the best thing that's ever been written on it. And it's – somebody has got to intellectualize stuff and put things into words. And, you know, there's – and if you do it well, then that's peachy keen. And if you could – just like putting $E=MC^2$, I mean somebody's got to, you know, got to do it. But when you just – like you say, you don't know what's gone into your machine sort of, but when you come down to working it – all that plays a part. But you don't have to write it out into words, it's just a feeling and you say, "Well, I think that you should be more like this in this case," but maybe you don't even have to get to why, maybe they say, "Oh, okay," or they say, "Yeah, I see what you mean," and you haven't said anything. It's another kind of talking, it's – you get the message across, but it's not, if you typed out what you say, or how you figured it out, it would – you'd sound probably like an idiot and yet it works, something happens. But there's a process going on but it's not in words. In fact, if you – if *Eraserhead* had to be put into words more than it did, I think a lot of it would have been killed. It was only because it could be floating like that in this lower, or higher or whatever realm that it kind of stayed pure and stayed fun, you know. And that's what I mean about Hollywood – things come out and they get so crystallized – I mean, it's ridiculous.

KGG: That's – do you know the work of Peter Weir?

DL: Peter Weir? I haven't seen any of his films but I know I'd love –

KGG: In these terms, *Picnic at Hanging Rock* is a good example, which I think is one of the most beautiful, graceful films I've ever seen.

DL: I've heard of it.

KGG: Yet every criticism I've read of it is always how it's very stylish and everything, but it's very frustrating because the mystery remains unexplained at the end. But it doesn't. If you watch the film, there's no mystery at all.

DL: Really?

KGG: It's about mystery, but the mystery is not something that has to be solved. But everybody wanted an explanation put into words – and because they're waiting for that, they've missed all these beautiful things that he's doing all the way through it.

DL: Yeah.

KGG: **I prefer to get something through the feeling.**

DL: Yeah, me too.

KGG: **Which is why I like film, because there's nothing else that can do it like film.**

DL: No kidding. No kidding. Well, I think certain writing can do it.

KGG: **But again, writing – the whole verbal thing has still got that sort of intellectual filter.**

DL: I guess that's true, but if you just sit down and you read something – well, see, I don't read that much, but I've had that feeling come through.

KGG: **It tends to be pretty rare though.**

DL: Yeah. Film can do it, and sound and picture – there's two senses in all this – boy, it can really do something. And no one has really figured out even yet how powerful it is. It's like – you know, I don't ever want to figure it out so it's like a mathematical thing. But I really want to explore it in a feeling way and just really learn about this business of, like you say, pacing and what goes next to what and think in terms of sound and picture, real close together. And it's a great thing. And then what's – another thing, the problem is that you get onto a film, some films don't allow you to really explore that, just the nature of the film, I mean, it just doesn't allow you to go into those areas that deeply. Well, *Dune* will allow me to go some place, and explore those things if I can do it the way I want to do it. And I don't know if *Red Dragon* is not that kind of film really, but there's still some – it's another kind of thing. But if I can do *Ronnie Rocket*, that's a real feeling film and a real sound-and-picture-barrelling-along-together film.

KGG: **In *Eraserhead* there are lots of little details that I – like the tub of water in the drawer – I mean, where do these come from?**

DL: I don't know. I don't even know why I put that there. It wasn't like I saw that and I said, "I've got to put that in my movie." It's not a good answer for you, but it's one of those things where – it's an idea, you know, it just comes along and you say, "I'm going to put this bowl of water in the drawer. And where he keeps all these pennies floating in this water." And it –

KGG: **It's sort of like what you said before about the proportions that make it right –**

DL: Yeah.

KGG: **There's something about looking through the drawer and then picking up the penny –**

DL: And the timing does it.

KGG: **– and the whole thing just seems right.**

DL: Yeah. And it's like, I can't even take credit for these things because, if I sat down and said, "I'm going to make something that's mathematically right, like a duck, that would be something, but when you get an idea and you go with it and later on you find out that the proportions were correct and stuff like – you can't really take credit for it. It's – because it's happening so much out of your control, really, it's sort of a blessing to get an idea, you know. And if you let them flow, they flow. And you get them when you need them. And you can open up this channel, and you get those kind of ideas. Or you can open up that channel, and get those kind of ideas. And that's one thing about people, it's like they can tune into real good things or real evil things. And it's up to each person really.

KGG: It's sort of a minor point, but the fact that Henry sticks his right foot in a puddle and takes off his left wet sock – is that purely accidental?

DL: Well [laughs] that's accidental. Yeah, but see the thing is like both socks were wet, but we couldn't remember which shoe went in the puddle. [laughs]

KGG: It's something everybody notices.

DL: I know.

KGG: They think they've found something significant: what is it?

DL: Yeah, right. It's like, I know that – you know, it's hard to believe that someone looks at your films so closely. But then I turn around and I look at other people's films so closely. And it's like, it's hard to realize exactly what a viewer is going to see because you see the behind-the-scenes, and this and this and you never actually – it's hard to be as objective as the viewer. And that's why I want to have someone invent a pill that they give – for a director – and you cut your film and you cut your sound and you are given this pill. And it blocks off your memory. And you're told you're going to go see a film, but you don't know the film from anything and you just sit down and you watch a film and you fill out a card and you just say what you liked and what you didn't like and what was wrong with the picture. And then the drug wears off and you read that and I'll bet you'd be totally amazed.

KGG: But I think *Eraserhead* does it more than a lot of films because there is that feeling to the film, that you start looking for all these things and wonder, "Is this significant? Does it mean something?"

DL: Uh-huh, yeah. Sometimes I think that in a foreign world you look more closely.

KGG: That's the thing. You don't know this world at all –

DL: That's right.

KGG: – and you're trying to pick up something that'll give you some indication.

DL: That's right. But in – but the world is really very familiar. And that's what I like. Well, I – here we're making *Dune*, but I don't really like science fiction. I don't like going to another planet so much as I like being right here – but just on – but if you could just go to Philadelphia, and it's sort of like the twilight zone – you know, you just, you go there and you just step over to this side of Philadelphia, and there you are: it's Philadelphia, but it's a little bit of a different world. And you – because it's a little bit different, you're never quite sure what's going to happen. But you have to be very careful with the rules, because if you don't obey those rules then you've done even worse than just being in Philadelphia, because people say, "Oh, you know, you're trying to be weird for weird's sake and it's just" – they just turn off a hundred percent. You've got to really love that world and respect it, and do it right.

KGG: There's one other point – I feel like a fool mentioning this, but somebody else I know has also seen it –

DL: What's that?

KGG: There's a certain thing in some of the shots in *Eraserhead*, that – where the image itself seems to waver, it's unstable. Like the big concrete walls when Henry's walking towards them. The concrete itself seems sort of semi-fluid.

DL: [laughs] Bad stock.

KGG: Is it?

DL: Bad stock.

KGG: It gives it a really good feeling, you know it's got that –

DL: Yeah.

KGG: Also the floor in the lobby.

DL: The design of it, huh?

KGG: The design seems to shift.

DL: Uh-huh. Well, it's not done on purpose. But I do – I made that rug myself and I love that rug. And we had bad trouble with the stock. And if you were to expose a gray, a dark gray especially, you'd see this "breathing". We didn't even know really kind of what to call it – it was sort of a fluctuation and a breathing, in the gray, dark gray. And the film was dark, so a lot of times you see this. Now when Henry walks over to Mary's house, after he, you know, gets the message, there – those were – that scene was lit by street lamps, and they were pulsing – you know, they're on a sixty-cycle pulse, and so the –

KGG: It was out of sync with –

DL: Yeah, it was out of sync with the film and it's fluctuating up and down – but I really love that look.

KGG: I've got a friend who swears it only does it when he's outside his apartment, and the world is sort of threatening.

DL: Uh-huh. (laughs) Well –

KGG: It does add a lot to the effect, that whole sort of disturbing feeling that the film gives.

DL: Yeah. Well that's –

KGG: I guess it's another lucky fluke.

DL: Yeah, exactly. Now, let's see, that's another thing: I am a really lucky person. Because I've lucked out in *The Elephant Man* and *Eraserhead* on so many things that just came my way, that you could never get if you went out and tried to find them. Like Henry, for instance. Jack is the only guy that could be Henry, to me, in the whole world. And he was a dream to work with. And his hair stays up in the air, if you comb it up that way. How many people's hair would do that? And really, like it was a – I wanted Henry to have short on the sides, tall on the top. But when I was saying and thinking tall on the top, I wasn't thinking like five or six inches tall on the top. I was thinking like two or three inches, you know, just up. And we cut Henry's hair, we cut Jack's hair and it was two weeks before we started shooting, so it had time to grow out a bit. And the first night, Charlotte Stewart teased Jack's hair, and it went up in the air. And I was in the other room, she was working on it, and I came in. And they were all laughing and they thought it was totally ridiculous, no one could – that obviously was going to have to be cut down, right. And I sort of looked at it and I said, "By god, you know, that is it." And they said, "No, no, no, you can't do that!" And I said, "No, we've got to do this, this is unbelievable." And so that's how it happened and we just happened to have Jack whose hair, you know, really did that. And then, like everything else, in a couple of hours literally it became so ordinary. And you just – human beings can adapt to anything. And the whole world became very ordinary. But it was a fun world. And everybody had a lot of humour about different things, but it was pretty commonplace, everything. I think it was – I think that for everybody it was a real great experience, you know. And for the few of us that worked through the whole thing it was a real good time in our lives. I hope they'll say those things.

David Lynch at Universal Studios with "the boys" – Chucko, Buster, Pete, Bob and Dan. [Photo by the author]

December 9, 1981

DL: Okay. Did you think of some more questions?

KGG: Well, it's mostly scattered points. One thing I did want to know: do you have any copies of the scripts that you did for *Eraserhead* **and** *The Grandmother***?**

DL: Even if I did, I wouldn't want them out. Because they're not really, to me, they're not really a script. And, you know, it's just they wouldn't be, it wouldn't mean much at all.

KGG: I'd like to know how you described *The Grandmother* **before you shot it.**

DL: Well, actually, you know, it's hard because – it's what we were talking about yesterday. I really don't know how I got the grant. It wasn't on the basis of a script. It was – it's just one of those freaks of nature. I just scooted through.

KGG: A great film.

DL: Oh great. I'm glad you liked it, George, yeah.

KGG: It's sort of surprising considering – I mean, *Eraserhead* **was sort of surprising because it's so well done and everything and it was your first feature. I mean, it's just amazing because you really hadn't done anything before that. One thing I did want, I mean, I'd like to talk about meanings in the films if that's possible.**

DL: Uh-huh.

KGG: You - in both films there's a, I mean, the family is a big thing in them.
DL: Uh-huh, yeah.
KGG: Is there any particular thing about families that you -
DL: Well, actually, see the thing is when my parents saw *The Grandmother*, they were very upset because they didn't know where this came from. And I had like a, sort of like a golden childhood, I mean, extremely happy family. And very very very happy memories. And I remember blue skies, red flowers, and white picket fences and green grass and birds chirping in the trees, and a plane droning overhead. And just a feeling of happiness. And, I mean, it was like I had little naps in the afternoon and I'd be able to watch the red ants crawling on the cherry tree. And I - my parents never argued and I had a brother and sister, but, you know, we were all happy. And I had toys that were like real shiny paint and kind of new and I had nice clean little corduroy pants and stuff. And like all my grandparents were, you know, everyone got along and they would come and visit and bring little treats and stuff and drove nice Buicks and stuff. And I think what happened was that I went to a big city and it scared me. And I think that was what did some stuff. I started sensing that the real world, or a lot of it, wasn't the way my world was. You know what I mean? And it was real frightening. And, I mean, if there's any kind of reason for those things that - I think they hit me harder. Someone brought up in the city is used to this sort of thing and to them it would be very surprising to know there were forests, you know, and trees. And that would like be mind-boggling to them and - but to me it was sort of the opposite.

KGG: One thing I'm wondering is what kind of painting do you do?
DL: Oh.
KGG: Considering your films, I mean, what sort of -
DL: Well, like I - now, this is not a painting. This is like a - these here are some drawings. These are "Ricky boards". And this is a modular Ricky board that I invented. I'll show it to you.
KGG: I was going to ask about that.
DL: You see, it's got square blocks and you can arrange them in different patterns. And it's got seven rows of nine, my Ricky board is fine; nine rows of seven, with my Ricky I'm in Heaven. And all the Rickies are named. You know, no matter what pattern you - you can put white glue on those blocks, see, and do rubbings. And then, so you can do patterns, you know, groupings of Rickies. Then you name each Ricky and then you make a little hole and a little stain, and a letter - each of those things - and then you put your fingerprint on it and you've got a Ricky. And so these are real Ricky drawings. I've done some test Rickies, but then I built my board and now I'm rolling. But I do other things, like

these industrial symphony kind of drawings, but these are not really those kind of things – these, but real big, and there's a lot of more action in them than this. Then I do – but I've got several different kind of styles. I do a lot of figures in kind of quiet rooms, but sort of strange feeling thing. But more realistic than these. And I do a lot of abstract. I did – I like to do action painting, where it's sort of like hard edge and action painting combined. Like to have a big brush dipped in like jet black paint and like take about a fifteen foot run and whack the canvas, right. And then do some hard edged things, you know, floating in this sort of spray. And stuff like that. But I really like figure painting and drawing as well. And, let's see – I don't have any example of those. I've got a lot of drawings at home. I could show you some of those. But this stuff here is more abstract. And then this room – the reason this room is the way it is is because I came in and there were many many little holes in the wall, and so I brought some spackle in and I started spackling them. And my brother-in-law was finishing his picture here on the lot and he came over and he says, "You're going to paint your office, aren't you?" And I said, "Yes." And he says, "You haven't asked anyone, have you?" And I said, "No." Because at Zoetrope I'd tried to paint my office and they wouldn't let me, and so I said, "I'm not going to tell anyone because I want to be able to do it, right." And he said, "Don't do it. Because you'll get in, you know, real big trouble. And you could hurt the film as well." So I said, "Well, okay." So I had the spackle already on. And so I figured, well that's kind of an interesting – there's so many holes and so the little white dots of spackle were all over and I thought I would number those and mark them, right. And then I started going with other things and then I got this thing going. Then I bought the boys there because I needed a transition from the wall to the black vinyl. And so they sort of fit the bill.

KGG: What were their names again?
DL: Chucko, Buster, Pete, Bob, and Dan.
KGG: Actually what I thought of when I came in, considering you're working on *Dune* and everything, it looks really like a star field –
DL: Oh, yeah –
KGG: A star map.
DL: Well, some people think that it's – I've – it's a strange storyboard, you know, that I've mapped out different scenes and stuff.

KGG: Yeah, one thing – you were at the AFI for several years obviously. Did you actually study their actual program?
DL: Study – well, in a way. You know how some people don't believe in schools, even though they're kind of fun places to be because of the inspiration of other painters or other filmmakers. I really believe it's possible to learn

a tremendous amount about film and there are people that can really teach you a lot of things. And then there's a tremendous amount that you can't learn. And one thing good about AFI, their independent grant program allows you to learn by doing, right, and you go off and you just do it, you make your own mistakes and, you know, they give you this responsibility. They give you the money. You do your budget, your picture. And get it together and do it. And so, because they give you that responsibility, they're not treating you like an idiot, you know, you kind of – or at least I did, I felt that, and I tried to do a good job, you know. And not just throw the money away. And then at AFI, at the Centre here, their program is good – at least it was when I was there. It was good because you could see lots of different films, you could go to seminars where people in the industry would come and speak and give you some things from their experience, teach you from their experience. And you could go to some classes on – say, like they have – an acting teacher would come in and you'd maybe work out some little scenes or something like this. Or you could go to the film analysis class. Now, for me, film analysis class was the best class. And Frank Daniel, who used to be dean of the Czechoslovakian film school, came to AFI, was dean of AFI during most of the years I was there, and he – you would see a film and break it all up into sound, editing, camera, acting, you know, all those different things and each person would have one of those, a different one each week, and you would really watch the film from the editing point of view, or watch it from the sound point of view, or watch it from the music point of view or whatever. And then kind of give your idea of how the guy thought about music and how he used music and how it fit in or it didn't fit in with the story and all this kind of stuff. And then Frank would kind of sum up or add his two cents' worth which was beautiful. And then we'd talk about structure, about a three-part structure as, you know, most films fall into. And then – and kind of like – it helped me so much because I was coming from being a painter. I never – all these things kind of like registered. And it really gave me something to think about. And I – something happened because of that particular class that helped me out a whole lot. And even though I never really thought about it so much, like with *Eraserhead*, I think that a lot of this stuff sunk in and I'm glad I went to those classes. I didn't go to too many seminars, but I don't – the ones I went to were pretty interesting but I didn't really learn a lot, I mean, they're sort of like – a lot of filmmaking to me is like common sense and, I mean, sometimes it's interesting to hear about people's experiences and there's neat stories and stuff, but how much do you learn? And I figured you learn mainly by doing and that's – at the Centre they let you make a film. And so it's kind of like both things. But once you start into work on a film, you can't go to those seminars, you can't go to see those movies and so you have to make a choice;

either you're going to make a film or you're going to go to all that. And now they have – now I'm on the board of directors up there – and the school is completely different. And it's much more organized and, like I told you yesterday, no one has the opportunity to make a feature film, but they do a lot more with video and apparently they have – Sony is helping AFI a whole lot with all this sophisticated video equipment – and so they can like see things very fast and really experiment and learn. But – and then the second year certain people are allowed to make a film. And so it's good, but it's – there's more people up there and it's more regimented. And one – I would never have been able to make *Eraserhead* in the school the way it is now. But I still – I figure you could really learn a lot, but I'm – I wasn't really a school kind of like person. I'm thankful that I went when it was more loose and you could kind of – if you wanted to learn something, somebody would be around to tell you about somebody that knew that or you could drop in on a class if you wanted to, but you could do a lot of your own work. And so it was – what – I even forget what your question was.

KGG: I forget.

DL: Yeah. Frank Daniel was one of the best people for me, for that. But – like in painting, I never – the instructors were like the smallest part of the school. And the people that I went to school with were doing such great painting – it was so inspiring, the atmosphere was way more important to me than anything else. I mean, I liked the school building itself, and the smell of oil paint just drives me crazy. I love it. And it was a whole, the art life, you know, is what it was all about.

KGG: Getting back to what I was saying about meaning – you can't really work, I wouldn't think, for five years on something without –

DL: No –

KGG: – considering exactly what you're saying with it.

DL: Yes, you can.

KGG: Can you?

DL: Yeah. Because – now we're going back to what we talked about yesterday. It's like an intuitive feeling about what you're doing is, to me, where the meaning of *Eraserhead* lies. It doesn't so much ever bob up to the surface and get put into words. And because I was working at American Film Institute, I never had to articulate into words what *Eraserhead* meant –

KGG: Not even to the people you were making the film with?

DL: Well, I could do it enough – now, I don't know what Jack told you, you know, but I don't think anybody knew as much about the film as I did. About – or – and it didn't matter. About, at least they didn't know what my interpretation was. You can do a whole lot of stuff scene by scene, if a thing has got, if it has resonance in different levels, you can talk mainly on this level and if it's true, it'll do this one too. But you don't ever have to really talk about this. It just feels right. And there was something else - I don't know how it happened but, like I say, everybody seemed to tune into what it was that we were doing and we never really sat down and did any heavy kind of intellectualizing, you know. And like what Jack says - we'll leave that to the smart guys back East.

KGG: The thing with that is, considering what I wrote, how valid is -

DL: Okay. Now see, you were the - you leaned real heavy on a sort of a sexual thing.

KGG: Yeah, that's true.

DL: But now, that's - I mean, that is definitely there and what you wrote, to me, is the best thing I've ever read on *Eraserhead*. And it was, you know, like the ins and the outs of the story and a sort of a confusion and a sort of a - like these archetypal things and this feeling of a sexual thing running through and all these different things that you talked about are real true. But it's just like - I don't know. It's just like in life there's so many symbols and there's so many things that you could see, you know, and some people just don't see them. And it seems to me that you saw a whole lot more than most people see, and your interpretation is one of the best. But I still say that everybody's interpretation is valid because, like I said before, it's a real abstract thing. And, like with Jack - you know, we were just talking, it's like one of those inkblot tests. And, so that it's just peachy keen, each person's interpretation is real good, really, but - and I have my own feelings about the way things are. Like you said, I had to have them and had to be real sure about them because in order to make the next thing work, this one had to be a certain way and that one had to be a certain way to be, like I say, be honest. And it's just - it doesn't really matter what my interpretation is because it's like I wasn't really intellectualizing, like I say, and I was just getting ideas, so it's not really, wasn't really - I learned more about what it was all about more like after the film was done. And all this other stuff was happening like under the surface during the making of it. And that's - maybe I said it yesterday, but that's where the powerful stuff is. And that's why I don't think the way Hollywood is - I'm real thankful that, you know, it's - the people are making films and they all love films, but it's a certain type of film that gets made and the others, you know, they just can't be done because as soon as you start talking about them and picking them apart before you even get rolling - and if more than one person is really involved in making the story, it's got to bob up close to the surface, if not right on the surface, start dissolving.

KGG: The strange thing with *Eraserhead* and *The Grandmother* is that sense that it is from the unconscious sort of directly coming up rather than

– because if you do see movies that sort of deal with dreams and so on, they usually intellectualize, or make literary or something –

DL: Yeah, exactly.

KGG: – but somehow you got that sort of direct contact with it which, I would have thought, was very difficult to do on film because of the simple working situation.

DL: Uh-huh. See, the thing is, it's like, sort of like a primitive painter, you know, they just – like Rousseau, right. He's just out there painting, he's sort of a – I don't know if he was – he wasn't an intellectual, he was sort of a simpleton, but when it came time for painting, the guy was clued into something. I mean, you just can't – it's just incredible. And that's what we're saying: there's so many different things you can tune into, but once you tune into a certain thing, then you – that means that you, for that project, you can't tune in over here. You've got to keep the tuning in right here and you'll be all right. But it wasn't – I never thought about – now when I saw *The Grandmother* after several years, I saw it again, and it was number one like I never even made it. And I was amazed at – some of the things in it, I really loved. And I was amazed at some of the innocence about it. And it was – I mean, I really liked it, I liked it when I saw it after all those years, but it was like, still it was innocent and sort of primitive. But it, like you say, it had something, you know, it was – something was happening.

KGG: As you say, most of your favourite films are black and white and so on – how much sort of German expressionist stuff have you seen? because I kept seeing things in *The Grandmother* which sort of looked like something German.

DL: Well, I haven't really seen any. I saw, after *The Grandmother* and I don't know if it was after *Eraserhead* or something, but I saw *M* and *Metropolis* and I've seen *Cabinet of Dr Caligari* and – but that's, you know, that's it for Germans, really. Although one of my favourite films is *Sunset Boulevard*, Billy Wilder's – so Billy Wilder's German. And I love – I think I really – *Metropolis*, I think is really nifty – and *M*, some of the things; just that window display in *M* drives me crazy. And some of those dark street scenes and things. And in *Sunset Boulevard* the mood and the story and the way everything was welded together so beautifully. I – it was really banging on all cylinders, you know. And, let's see. I like Bergman – *Hour of the Wolf* and *Persona*, I like those two films of his a lot.

KGG: I haven't seen those.

DL: You haven't seen those, huh? And –

KGG: My favourite Bergman is *Virgin Spring*.

DL: *Virgin Spring*, yeah. You'd like *Hour of the Wolf* and *Persona*. You should see those. And I like *8 1/2* and I like *I Vitelloni* – did you ever see that?

KGG: No.

DL: And I like *La Strada*.

KGG: That's my favourite Fellini.

DL: Yeah. *La Strada* is just a beautiful film. And I like Jacques Tati. Jacques Tati. You like -

KGG: I'm not a big fan of his.

DL: You're not?

KGG: At moments, I really get off on him, but I can't take too much of him.

DL: No kidding? Huh? I found - I just think he's like brilliant. And I just, I think he's one of the greatest. Let's see. There's - I know I'm missing some - I know I would like Peter Weir's films, but I haven't seen them.

KGG: If you ever get the chance - I think he's one of the great directors.

DL: Yeah, absolutely. Yeah -

KGG: I've seen everything he's done as far as I know -

DL: Incredible. Yeah, yeah.

KGG: I did wonder - what is *Ronnie Rocket* about?

DL: Oh -

KGG: You told me a lot about it, but -

DL: Oh yeah. Sorry. Well, I can't really tell you too much about it. But it's a character. *Ronnie Rocket* is a little - he's a little person. And he has been somehow very very very badly deformed through some - not some accident or even birth, but no one - not even known how. Almost unrecognizable as a human. And he's been - he's been rebuilt by these two doctors who sort of have - they - they're not very good doctors. And so they both have the same girlfriend, right. And so they kind of like have a family now. And - but he is very badly, you know, even after they rebuild him, he's got an awful lot of problems. And he - he's got electrical appliances that kind of keep him running. And meanwhile there's a sort of a search by a detective that's happening in another, you know, unbeknownst to the doctors, there's a search deep into the city for something concerning Ronnie. And - but what happens is they finally, they can't really determine how old he is, but they figure because he has such bad acne that he's high school age. And so he gets - one way or another, he gets into high school and, since he has to plug himself in every fifteen minutes or so, he interacts with some rock band and makes a strange sound. And from then on is exploited in this rock world, see. And becomes like a superstar. And - but that's, you know, part of it. There's another whole world with the detective. And it's a - it's, like I was telling you, a comedy but it's also - it's also frightening in places.

KGG: It sounds pretty strange. I don't know if you're - do you ever read any fantasy or science fiction?

DL: Science fiction?

KGG: Have you ever come across Brian Aldiss?

DL: No.

KGG: He did a very strange short novel called *Brothers of the Head*, which is about Siamese twins who hate each other's guts and become successful punk rockers, which – the tone is very much like what you've just described.

DL: Oh.

KGG: Why are you so fascinated with this sort of – I mean –

DL: What sort of thing?

KGG: Well, sort of very bizarre, mutated, deformed people.

DL: I don't know. It's like there's plenty of normal people around, but they are not normal. And the more you really get to know someone, the more abnormal they seem to get. At least that's been my experience. You see quirks and strange habits and – and like they become very interesting. And then in Philadelphia, I met so many people that were even more, you know, more strange. And I just – what happens is they spark my imagination and like a little world develops around them that may or may not be true, but it gets me going. And I can go off into these worlds. And then I'm real happy in these worlds, you know. And so I – I don't know. It's just that happiness is what does it.

KGG: Seeing that you make films, do you have any sort of concept of what the function or purpose of film is, or do you just like to make your –

DL: Well, that's a real good – it's – at the opening of the American Film Institute this year they talked about responsibility of filmmakers. And I really do think that film is a powerful medium and, although they say that film is not so powerful that it could really, really change things – but I think that all the films – I don't know what comes first, you know, the chicken or the egg. I don't know if films reflect what's happening or if what's happening is caused by, you know, films. But I think that films reflect what's happening. And that you – but you still have a responsibility. If enough people made more uplifting, good films, I think it would have an effect. And if everybody made like exploitative superviolent films of a real negative nature, that would have the opposite effect. And it would have effect – a big effect on people. And it's just like on the news, if you hear about murders enough and you see them and they – you can't – each time you hear it it lessens the impact. And it kind of dulls you out, you know, for those things, and they're not so shocking. And it would seem to me that it would take an awful lot of that to turn a regular person into a murderer. But if a person was on the edge, it maybe could drive him over. I mean, it maybe could make it be – it could take away whatever was holding him back. It could erode that maybe. But I still think – I sort of like – I'm going to do this movie about this mass murderer, right. And like I really worried about it and so did Richard Roth, the producer, and we decided that, well, the Pope was shot and we said, "Well, that does it." And because the world has got too much violence and to make a movie about it is, you know, it's just not right anyway. But then I heard on the radio this cardinal talking about this violence and he said, you know, we cannot run from it, we have to face it. And it's out there and it's powerful and it has to be faced. And you have to deal with it. And in a way this movie *Red Dragon* is about a guy who – he has a gift for thinking like a murderer really. I mean he's a detective, and they want him to come back. He's a retired FBI guy. They want him to come back and help find this guy. He's killed two families. And he could just say, "Well, I – look, I – you know, that's too bad. I'm too – I'm retired. I have a family now. I've got to – you know, I want to – I've done it, you know." But, I don't know, it's sort of like you've got to, you just can't pretend it's not there. And that's what this film is about. And that's sort of how we rationalized being able to work on it. And if we – and another thing about this movie *Red Dragon* is that you feel this killer's battle between good and evil. I mean, it's powerful. And it's the first time I've ever felt – the first time I've ever sort of been inside a killer's head where that was that powerful. And I think that somebody who was right on the edge could, if they felt other people feeling that and battling it, I mean it could even make them stronger, you know, to see the futility of it and the horror of it and it could end up being a good movie, if it's not exploitative and it's like an honest picture. And – but I don't know. It's a tricky – it's a tricky thing. But I think that it's pretty powerful, movies are pretty powerful – I mean, you have a responsibility, you've got to think about it at least. And like, then on the other hand there's another kind of a thing; if you're just an okay person, I think, if you get ideas you can't try to let – keep figuring out if they're going to hurt people or help people or whatever. You can't – as soon as you start thinking that way, you're going to start, you know, screwing yourself up.

KGG: You wind up not being able to do anything.

DL: Yeah, exactly. So you kind of have to just do it. And maybe you'll learn something, you know, but probably be okay.

KGG: How do you feel about the critical response to your films?

DL: Well, like which –

KGG: Well, I mean, I don't really think there was very much on *Eraserhead*.

DL: Uh-huh.

KGG: How did you feel about that fact? that critics didn't really notice it?

DL: Well, some critics did notice it. And I don't know these people, you know. They're just like everybody else. Some of them, I wouldn't care what they said. And some I would be real interested in their opinion. They're so powerful, critics are, and it seems like they're mostly – they serve the Hollywood movies and they don't really – there are not too many – you have to be kind of up the ladder before you even start getting criticism or reviews. And *Eraserhead* was never – it was a film that was easy to shoot down and no one – it didn't hurt them any at all. And – but some people saw something in it and did, you know, some – the French seem to be film people and they'll review anything. And they look at films – it seems like they love films and they treat someone who's made a film with some sort of care. I mean, they think about what the person was doing. And they write sensible, decent reviews. And – but here, I mean, it's like just mostly goofball stuff. You can't figure out what they're thinking, you know. And you never know whether – why they're writing that kind of thing, what's behind it all. You – so you can't really go by it, even a good one – it just, something doesn't smell right about it, you know. And I think it's – there's a couple of people that are really good and they really write, they're more like the French, you know. They write about film and, I mean, you can kind of tell who they are. But the rest of them are – I don't know.

KGG: I know what you mean. I find it very frustrating reading most critics.

DL: Yeah. And you can't – like, as someone was telling me the other day, that you can't go by them because they're not consistent, really. You know, it's hard to find – I think in San Francisco, this person was saying, there's some very consistent critics and you can actually find the one that thinks more like you do and determine whether you want to see a movie or not by reading his review. You say, well if Bill likes it, you know, it's got to be good. If it's a turkey, he's telling you. But – or if they – and then they might – I like, like Pauline Kael. She writes – she really gets into it and really writes a lot of stuff. And sometimes I don't agree with her, but –

KGG: The same with me.

DL: Yeah, but she really gets into it and her slant, whatever it is, she really explores it. And you feel – it makes you, excites you in a sort of cinema way. It's a good kind of thing. You can tell she really loves movies and stuff. And it's not just kind of like a popcorn review.

KGG: Why do you like black and white so much?

DL: Well, I've been forced to think about this because people ask me. And I've come up with two things. One, I think black and white makes things seem not so normal; because we're used to seeing in colour, it just removes you, even if it's just one step, from a normal feeling. And so it is – it makes it easier to go into another world, or to go back in time. And also it has – it – somehow it seems to me that it makes you see more clearly. Because it – like a frame to me in black and white is purer than a colour frame, unless you control every little bit of colour, which some people do. But even like if you weren't going to control the – a room – black and white would make it look to me better. And you'd be probably more apt to see the character and to hear the character in black and white – it'd be less distracting. And it, to me, it gives something of more importance. It has a feel – the film itself has a more solid – and it's like glue, it unifies a film. Colour, unless you really think about it all the way through – like when you go outside it's all blue and green, and you go inside and it's all some other way and the two don't relate to each other. But if it's all black and white, you can go inside and you can walk outside and it still feels unified.

KGG: Given all that – I would assume you'll have to do *Dune* in colour –

DL: Yeah. Yeah. *Dune* is – it's like – it could easily be done in black and white although people have blue eyes in *Dune* and it would be hard to get that across. But it's – I'm hoping that we can control the look of it so that it will be unified and – although there's different – there's three different planets involved, and so there's going to be some differences. But still, a film should have a feeling of a whole and have a unified feeling. And that's, a lot of times films don't have that.

KGG: I don't think I asked, but was *Dune* offered to you or did you decide on it and go after it?

DL: It was offered – offered, yeah.

KGG: Have you, considering all the projects there've been, have you – is there any carry-over from earlier – I mean, Dino De Laurentiis was planning one before with –

DL: Ridley Scott. Yeah.

KGG: Yeah. Is there any carry-over from that production, or are you going to start from scratch?

DL: Start from scratch.

KGG: Have you got designers yet?

DL: Tony Masters is the production designer. He did, among seventy other things, *2001*. And – a great guy. And he's already started doing lots of drawings and he and I are, you know, working pretty closely together. And that's really it. Freddie Francis is set to do – the director of photography. And – but he's not started working on the film at all. And, let's see, I think that Dino will probably have a long list of technical people that he'd like me to use. But he's told me that artistic people, I'm free to pick and choose.

KGG: What about cast? Has anything been set on that?

DL: Nothing's set on the cast yet at all.

KGG: Is there anyone you want to get for it?

DL: Well, there's several people I'd like to work with, but nothing has been set and I wouldn't want to say right now what it's –

KGG: Yeah. How long is it going to take?

DL: *Dune*? It's going to take a long time. I shudder to think how long it's going to take.

KGG: I take it since you've only just – it's a first draft script, is it?

DL: Yeah, but we've been working it for six months already.

KGG: I guess there's no – is there a production start date yet?

DL: We'd like to shoot next summer. But in order to do that, we really should start pre-production in January, and we're not. It's a huge amount of things have to be done in pre-production and – like everything that has to be done on a regular film and a lot more. So we need a lot of time and I think that with – we're still working on the script and it's going to be quite a little while more before we're through. So it's not probably going to be till fall. Next year. Before we start shooting. But we – I don't even know for sure where we're going to shoot. We might probably be in London.

KGG: And will it be sort of North Africa for –

DL: Deserts? Yeah. Well, see the thing is that I – you know, what we really need is – is not going to be found on this planet. I mean, it has to be kind of made and so I don't even think we'll go to the desert that much.

KGG: About *Elephant Man*, with the physical look of the world that you have there – things like the machines that you see in all these places, they seem sort of totally disconnected from any purpose – that's one of the things that makes it such a sort of claustrophobic, depressing sort of world to live in.

DL: Uh-huh.

KGG: It seems sort of purposeless. Were all these things actual replicas of –

DL: Machines?

KGG: – sort of things that had some function?

DL: Well, no. I don't know if we could take like – certain machines – I don't know what –

KGG: Well, there's one shot there that –

DL: In the street?

KGG: Well, it's two rows of men that seem to be pushing some sort of –

DL: The "elbow machine". Yeah, that's totally fabricated. Nothing like that ever existed. And this guy Tony designed it – he wasn't even the production designer, he just loves designing machines. And I wanted the guys to be working something – I wanted elbows. And so it was called the "elbow machine". And then I love smoke and steam and so –

KGG: You have that big steam engine out in the alley.

DL: – we had steam, yeah, that's right. Now that thing was supposedly a glue factory. But, I mean, like you say, you'd never see that. And then the thing that the guys were playing, the organ in one of the first scenes in the street, I made up that and the music – John Morris, who did the music, was looking at the film, you know, to get a sense of the music and all this, and he saw that and he said, "Boy, I haven't seen one of those in years." So, that was pretty good. But it did look fairly realistic, but it had a big bag of air and a fire burner underneath and it was a keyboard and a crank and so it was a pretty nifty rig.

KGG: The film doesn't look like any other Victorian film that anybody's done – it's very dreamlike. I think that's a large part of it, is all these weird glimpses of things that you can't tell what the hell it is, what they are or what they're doing –

DL: Right. Actually though it's based on a Victorian feeling. And--

KGG: Yeah. Well some of them are like engravings by Dore or something –

DL: Yeah, yeah.

KGG: – that same sort of dirt, the slum scenes and so on.

DL: Right. And I personally don't like Victorian times. And I like the Forties and the Fifties and early Sixties at best and then it just stops for me. I don't like it. And I don't mind the Twenties or Thirties so much – but Twenties electrical things I like. And Thirties, I'm sure there's a lot of things I would like, but my feeling of the Thirties is dry and kind of hot and I don't like that. Twenties is more dark and shiny black and like Forties is a dark sort of film noir kind of thing. And Fifties is just like my woodpeckers sort of and bobbysox and wild fins and plastics. And early Sixties is kind of really, kind of dreamy and the girl-next-door and sidewalks and stuff like that. And – but then it stops. And – but I – I'm not getting a film, you know, that I can go into those worlds, you see what I mean? I mean, it's really frustrating. *Dune* is not in that area at all. And here I am working on this and, although there's plenty of neat things that I like about doing it, I long to go into these other, back to those things.

KGG: You can't come up with a project yourself?

DL: Well, I came up with one for the early Sixties. And it didn't go. I – the film – the script needs a lot of work. It's a neat idea. The name of the movie was *Blue Velvet* and Richard Roth was going to be producer. But Warner Brothers didn't buy it and no one else bought it either. But it's a mystery in the early Sixties and a kind of a nice, a really – it would be a neat mood to it and – but, like I say, the script isn't right and it needs work. And it's right after Richard and I were working together on that that he acquired *Red Dragon* and that's how I got in on that. So – but even so I'm looking for stories or a script in the Forties, you know, detectives and that kind of thing, diner stuff.

KGG: So you've definitely decided to stick with film?

DL: Oh, yeah. Absolutely. Film is like what we were saying yesterday; it covers so many different things that you can't – you can't get that same feeling from any other art form. Even though I love painting and, in a way, I think now painting instead of dying out is – it will always be, because you – to create in – on – with that, on a piece of paper or on a canvas or something like that is – it'll always be something new and something that can't be done any other way, that experience. It's just like theatre, it'll always be. And film won't kill anything. But it – film – it's got so many more ingredients that if you can – if you can stand the pressure of working with all those different ingredients, if you can – if the good parts of it are worth all the bad parts, then it's great.

KGG: You talk about texture quite a bit –
DL: Yeah. Texture is –
KGG: I was wondering how dissecting the dead cat helped with *Eraserhead*?
DL: Well – well, did Jack tell you about the mouse?
KGG: He said you were the only person he ever knew who shaved a mouse.
DL: Well, I – I wanted to learn a few things, and so a veterinarian gave me a cat. And I just called him up and he said, "Okay, well I'll let you know if one comes in." And he called me fairly soon after that and said, "Come on down." And he said, here it is, and he put it in this box. It was like – it went in like a slinky. Just slinked in. And he said, "Just do me one favour," he says, "will this cat be recognizable in your movie?" And I said, "You would never recognize that cat." And so he said, okay fine. So I took it home and I had in my basement set up like a, you know, operating theatre. And I dissected the cat. But, first I put it in formaldehyde in a bottle with a kind of a narrow mouthed top. And so it got *rigor mortis* in the jar and I could not get this cat out of this jar. And I was pulling on this thing and it was just like a boat that you build in the basement; you cannot get it out of the door. And so finally it popped out and I – it was an experience. And it's like I examined all parts of it and it – I don't know. It's like, I don't know what good it did me, you know, really, but I – there was a scene in the movie where the cat was going to be in, where some kids had tied wire and, you know, did a cat in. And Henry trips on the wire. But it, it's just underneath the frame line in the tanks, where he walks through these oil tanks, is the – the cat was there. Well see, this tank area was very near where I lived, but you couldn't really see it from the road, and it was like going back in time, because it was built many years ago and it had a kind of a donut of dirt all around it. So if the oil tanks break, it captures the oil.... What was I – dissecting this cat?
KGG: You were talking about dissecting the cat, and the tanks –
DL: Oh yeah, the tanks – well anyway, the cat stayed there – see, the oil in the water – the shot where you saw the camera goes over this puddle of black water, the cat went into that, and so I came back a year or two later and I fished the cat out of that and so then it was covered in oil and sort of tar. And it stayed out in the dirt and preserved itself. And I came back even a couple of

years after that and there it still was. And so I've got a photograph of this cat and it looks like it's coming out of the ground. It's earth coloured and the earth, you know, everything has been rained on and dried and heated and all this. And it's pretty neat looking. And – but it really shows you how tar can preserve something. And then there's like membranes and hair and skin and there's so many different textures that on one side are sort of gross and – but on another way of looking at them, just isolated in an abstract way, are totally beautiful. It's the kind of thing where, if you don't name it, it's beautiful. As soon as you name it, they will see that and the rest of it will click in and they will be turned off. And one thing about *Eraserhead*, and one thing about things that I like is to me a lot of these things are really beautiful. And somehow I think other people maybe feel that in the work, I mean, and it's not ugly. It's sort of finding a beautiful thing – and beauty in something that was ugly. Or could be ugly. Like you don't smell smoke in – except with John Waters, you know, smell-O-rama.

KGG: Have you seen that?

DL: No, I haven't seen it.

KGG: I think it's a great film.

DL: Oh yeah?

KGG: I'm a big fan of John Waters.

DL: Oh, yeah, well great. And – I met John Waters. We went to Bob's.

KGG: He mentions you in his memoirs.

DL: Oh yeah? Oh great. And so – yeah, he – we went to Bob's together.

KGG: Have you seen any of his films?

DL: No, I haven't. I haven't seen them.

KGG: They're unlike any other –

DL: Yeah. He was real good to me, because when *Eraserhead* opened, his film *Desperate Living* was opening in New York at the same time and he told the audience – he made an appearance early on to promote his film – and he told them that his favourite film was *Eraserhead*. And he recommended that everyone see it. And that's just when *Eraserhead* was opening and so he really helped the film out. No, I'm sure I'd like, you know, I'd like his, you know, he's got a great sense of humour, I know. And –

KGG: Without it, his films would probably be intolerable.

DL: Right, right. Yeah, well I like that sense of humour.

KGG: I suppose I ought to ask why you have this passion for Bob's.

DL: For Bob's. Oh. Well, it's their chocolate shake. And – I don't know – when I first had – I used to go for treats in the afternoon, and I used to like this Dutch apple pie at Hamburger Hamlet. Then I got onto donuts and coffee at DuParr's. Then I was on to chocolate sundaes at Tiny Naylor's. And then I got – I had a Bob's shake. And I was really surprised at the taste and at the price – fifty-five cents for a shake. But it's not – I like chocolate shakes, but this isn't really like a shake, because they give you a spoon with it, rather than a straw. If they gave you a straw with a Bob's shake, it would be criminal, because your – either the shake would come up or your brains would go down. And they're thick. It's more like ice cream. And that they are – I don't know what they're made out of, but I don't think it's natural ingredients. And – but I always say there's an idea in every shake. And they come in a silver goblet. And they're made by a machine called a – the name of it is a Taylor machine, and it goes in liquid and it's frozen and comes out in these swirls like a Frostee Freeze or a Dairy Queen, but it's not like that. It, the taste is more like a fudgesicle than anything else. And – but the consistency and the texture varies. And I've had only about six perfect shakes in my whole life. Even though I eat like about three-hundred-sixty of them a year. And I've seen the price go from fifty-five cents now to ninety-five cents. And when they bump it up, they bump it up a nickel at a time. And so it's – the perfect shake is the – the silver goblet is frosted, you know, it's so cold. There may even be a little bit of frost on the shake itself, because it freezes up so cold. The consistency should be smooth and it should be dense like cold butter. And then you've got the perfect, perfect shake. And it should be chocolaty. Some of them are blonder than others, and you don't get the chocolate flavour. I've had some that are so dark brown, they're too chocolaty almost. But I think when they – the container, they don't shake it up enough or something, and a lot of the chocolate sits on the bottom and then never gets in the machine. So I think that, you know, that could account for why some are not dark.

KGG: Did you always have a passion for chocolate shakes or –
DL: Well, I –
KGG: – or did it develop at Bob's?
DL: Bob's is really – I always liked chocolate and chocolate shakes, but I like to go out in the afternoon for these treats. And I like Bob's, I like the feeling in Bob's. And I like diners. If I could find a real true diner that had a good feeling, I would like that. But I don't like dark places. I like light places with Formica and metal and nice shiny silver, you know, metal, mugs, glasses, a Coca-Cola, a good Coca-Cola machine. Another thing about Bob's is they have – you can get a vanilla coke, or a chocolate coke or things like this. And they've got a good soda fountain. And there's not too many, as you know, soda fountains are going away and true diners are going away. In San Francisco there's some good diners and, I think, more in the north are the true diners.

KGG: One thing I'm still not quite clear about from yesterday: what did you do in that year –

DL: Two years –

KGG: No, when you filmed for a year on *Eraserhead* –

DL: Oh.

KGG: – and there was a break –

DL: Oh, yeah.

KGG: What exactly did you do in that year?

DL: Well, not a lot. I don't remember too much about that year. I had a paper route, you know. I delivered the *Wall Street Journal*, and that was what I lived on. And I made forty-eight dollars and fifty cents a week. And I delivered two-hundred-ten papers. And the first night it took me about six hours – or six to eight hours – to do my route. And Jack had a route at the same time. And – but I got it down to four hours the next night and then I fairly quickly got it down around two-and-a-half. Then I more slowly worked it down and found short-cuts and studied a map, and finally I got this overview of the route. And I got it down to one hour. And I had a '59 Volkswagen and I would be almost flat out with that, and I'd fold as I drove. And pitched them out the windows. And I had some, about eleven places where I had to leave the car and run groups of papers in or place them in a certain place. But the most horrible thing in the world is to throw your first paper of the night, which was a long throw, and discover that the window was rolled up. And it – you'd see, you know, white light and there's these skid marks all over the road because you go totally out of control. And so like you don't do that, you learn to roll your window down, right. And – but – and I'd have about three or four throws that were real fun ones to do. Like one was – the lobby of this building had lights that would go on if you hit the door. And so it was a long throw again and I would throw the paper and whap the front door and all the lights in the lobby would go on. Then I had one throw where if you skimmed the paper along the sidewalk it would actually, you know, go right under the door. And then I had one throw that was this fish shanty on La Cienega – it has a big whale's mouth that you walk into the front door, and to throw it into the whale's mouth, you know, on a fast turn was a good throw. And you learn to lead, like if you're going forty you throw way before your house and watch it float and study how, you know, you learn about mathematics and all sorts of things on your route. And Jack Nance made two spectacular throws that he told me about. Once he said that going down Olympic Boulevard in rush hour is like shooting the rapids. But it took him so long to do his route that he was in rush hour before, in the morning before he finished. And so he had to give it up. Maybe he just was not cut out for the job. But he threw one paper and it actually went – there were two handles for the doors and it went in and, you know, stuck in the handles. And then he threw one paper and it went up on its end on the front porch of the house, just stood right up on its end. And those are – you'd never be able to do those again. But my paper route was my one, only really responsibility and like I said, I was – I have a power saw and kind of like a dream world to me is like being – in California, you can walk in and out of a house and not really feel the difference most of the year. And so going into my little back yard and having my saw all set up and everything, and feeling that sun on the back of your neck kind of warming, and to run wood through the saw is the greatest thing.

KGG: Is it true that you didn't make up your mind to hire Jack Nance to play Henry until he admired the home-made rack on top of your Volkswagen?

DL: That's right. That's right. He – we didn't have that great an interview. He – and I don't blame him – he had this attitude toward student filmmakers and he thought, oh brother, all he needed was some art, you know, art film or something to add to his resume. And I wasn't too – he – he's not the kind of guy that really shines in an interview, you know, because he's so low-key. And so I wasn't too taken with Jack. But we started walking out and we got outside where this little parking lot was and we were talking and sort of saying goodbye to each other, and he kind of said, "Boy, that's a nifty rack." And I thought he knew it was mine, but then it dawned on me that he didn't. I said, "Well, yeah, well, you know, it's mine." He said, "No kidding," you know and we started talking about this rack and he sort of lit up and that's – I saw this other side of him right away. And then we did a little bit of sort of testing, rehearsing sort of, and getting this – that's why he always says this Henry is a total blank. Any kind of like, when Jack had some sort of expression, it was wrong. And the more he could empty out and this – this – the closer it got. And so I just consider myself super fortunate to have had Jack. And it was, you know, there's not, like I said yesterday, there's no other person that could ever do it, in my mind. And I just was lucky. I – but I didn't see it right away. It didn't happen – you know, it's awful hard to make a decision for the lead in a film – even I never knew I was going to go that long, but I mean it's so important and you want to make sure and so I think that kind of gets in the way of making a – even if you knew the guy was right, it's like maybe, like you're buying a car, you'd want to see a few other ones before you decided. But I never saw anyone else. Most of the people on *Eraserhead* were the first people that came along, were the ones that did it. Like Jeanne Bates – are you going to talk to her?

KGG: I've got her number –

DL: Yeah. She's great. She would come in all dressed up and very stylish. And come into the X's house, you know, and she just didn't fit in, and it's like the first, up until the first night even, she never really became part of the film. But after the first night, I'd say she was with it a hundred percent. And, gee, everybody just got into it. And it was super. And they were all, like I said, the first ones. Even though we did, they read for the part and things like that. But I was real happy with the way they were and the way they worked with me and it seemed like they would be right.

KGG: Did you get much of a contribution to the detail in the film, or is that basically your own?

DL: What - like what?

KGG: I mean, all the little details like the tub of water, and the various decorations in Henry's room?

DL: Well, those are mostly my own in a way. I'm - Doreen Small, the production manager, had the job of - I sent her out to get any little knick-knacks and she went to swap-meets and things like that and spent - she got a whole boxload of these things for five dollars and she got a fan, an electric fan that was - I really liked. And I went to Salvation Army and Veterans places and - what do you call it? the place where you - Goodwill Industry, yeah. And Henry's whole wardrobe was gotten at Goodwill. And, you know, it was like we were going shopping and we got his shoes and his socks and his pants and his pen-holder and all his pens and got him all geared up, right, and got his hair out and his little tie tack and his tie and we got Bill's hat and had to sew Bill's thing onto his, you know, thing and we got some neat things for his belt. And it was great because it wasn't that I had pictures in my head of all those things, but when I find little things, then dressing a set I had a lot to choose from, but I could put in things and like in the X's centrepiece on their table, it's sort of a bowl with water in it and some sort of hair floating in the middle with a little duck on it.

KGG: I've never even noticed that.

DL: Yeah. I've still got the little duck and I've got the plates from the X's and I've got a couple of chickens and - let's see - I've got the fish from the X's wall. And Henry's bush I still have. And I've kept that - that's delicate. And - because it's in that mound of mud. And I've kept that for now, you know, eleven years.

KGG: I can't think of anything more right now.

DL: Well, you've got a lot of stuff, George.

KGG: Actually, I did wonder about - I take it this is something that was mocked up by somebody who did the poster for -

DL: That's the Japanese thing. I have somewhere the Japanese book - I hope Bernard or Herman didn't take that today. Is it over there on the floor? That's it. That thing there is pretty neat. They did a pretty good job. That's the way you read it, from the end, yeah.

KGG: What - it was given a real opening?

DL: Oh yeah. A regular thing in Japan. See, *Elephant Man* did so well in Japan that they paid quite a bit of money for *Eraserhead* and opened it regular, you know, in a regular way. And I don't think it was too successful. But, just like these Germans, they love *Eraserhead* but they know that it's not commercial. Do you know what I mean? And I think some places, some countries - like France and Japan primarily - they release it in a regular run and -

KGG: In France it's also -

DL: Oh, yeah. Yeah.

KGG: What kind of response has it had?

DL: I think it's done pretty doggone well in France. I don't know the figures because we're waiting to hear exactly what kind of business it's done.

KGG: Well, I think the French filmgoers are more accustomed to that -

DL: That sort of thing, yeah. Yeah. Yeah. I've got a - in fact, the French took some frames of the film and blew them up and they've done some real nice photos. And one of the things that I thought that I could - no American press or paper or magazine has ever done a picture of the baby. And I remember, you know, we were talking to you about maybe getting you a picture of the baby for the article, which would be good. And I've got some photos that maybe we could go over.

KGG: Well, I guess I'd better let you go again.

DL: Okay, well yeah. I - some more time, George, 'cause like this is a good week really. Because like Chris and Eric weren't in today -

David Lynch with a "Ricky." [Photo by the author]

December 15, 1981

KGG: First of all, did you photograph *The Alphabet* **and** *The Grandmother* **yourself?**

DL: Yes.

KGG: Okay. About *Gardenback,* **the script you were working on before** *Eraserhead* **-**

DL: Right.

KGG: Who was it you were doing that for? Was that at the AFI?

DL: Yeah, that was - the Centre has the same kind of thing - you submitted a script and previous work, and they of course knew about *The Grandmother* because they, you know, did it with their independent filmmakers program. But *Gardenback* was the script that I submitted to go to the Centre. But there, you know, like I've told you before, it was - it was a short film, it was supposed to be a short film - and some guy at Fox wanted to expand it into a feature. And he was going to have Caleb Deschanel shoot it - Caleb was also at the AFI and Caleb turned me onto this guy and Caleb was going to shoot it and - but it had to be expanded out. And when it got expanded out, it killed it, to me. And - but that was for AFI, *Gardenback* was. Yeah.

KGG: I was wondering, in *Eraserhead,* **did the grandmother ever figure larger in the thing, or was that -**

DL: That was it.

KGG: That was it?

DL: Yeah.

KGG: Where did it come from?

DL: Where did that little bit come from? George, I don't have the slightest idea. It wasn't something that I saw in real life. I almost made it up on the spot. It wasn't in the script. And I don't know how I got that idea.

KGG: Did you shoot it more or less in sequence, *Eraserhead*, or was it – did you sort of jump about?

DL: Well, actually, we shot pretty much in sequence. At least, all the stuff with the baby was shot in sequence. And, let's see – also, the grandmother, by the way, was the landlady of the building that we shot in for the – the kitchen was a location. And the landlady was – Jean Lange was the landlady, the grandmother, and she was very very nice and she didn't know what was going on, you know. I kind of felt bad about that. I mean, I sort of felt like I was taking advantage of her, although she was having a very good time, you know. But she did have a very fun time.

KGG: After you finished shooting, how long did it take to cut it all together and dub it?

DL: *Eraserhead*?

KGG: Yeah.

DL: Well, let's see. It's hard to say. The editing, in a way, was going on all the time. During that first year that we weren't shooting, I cut a lot of stuff together. And so it didn't take me a long time to edit it. But I had to edit it before Alan and I could start working on the sound. And so I edited, say, a rough cut, and then I stopped cutting the picture and Alan and I worked on sound effects. We worked for about two months every day on just sound effects, all day long. And then Alan had enough to start, you know – then he started cutting effects to scenes that I had, you know, finalized. And we kind of went from there. And it – the mix only took seven days. And – because, see, Alan had cut all the tracks – see, to me, there's no reason for a mix to take a real long time. Because, you know, Alan has sort of spoiled me; since he knows all the tracks since he cut them himself, and since he was doing the mixing, and we talked so much about every single thing, that it – it seems like it took us a long time at a week. But, I mean, there's just certain things that take time – I mean, there's transferring, you know, making protection copies and, you know, just cumbersome things like just moving film around, and then getting set up each night, because we did it at night at AFI. We couldn't do it in the daytime, and then I think we did weekends and nights. We had – so it took a week.

KGG: In the credits at the end, you've got that really long list of "thank yous" - were they all people that sort of helped out on the film during the years?

DL: Yeah. Some of them helped out with money, some of them helped out with equipment, some of them just sort of helped out at AFI with support and making sure that it, you know, it - really helped get it done, you know. And each person on there did something real important to keep the thing running.

KGG: I know, you know, you don't like to talk about effects or things very much - I was wondering what you used in the makeup for Laurel Near? I was talking to her on the phone this morning -

DL: Oh, you talked to her, huh?

KGG: Yeah.

DL: Oh, great.

KGG: And she mentioned this being something rather hot and hard on her face.

DL: Well, actually, let's see - see, she has very tender skin. And I think I used a bunch of different things on her. Let's see. I can't really remember what it was that burnt her skin though. But she had real tender skin and it really sort of irritated it. But, you know, it took a long time to make her up, even though I had certain things built that I used over again, you know. And - but, I mean, I would say I used a lot of different types of things.

KGG: When you got the distribution deal with Libra, did you sort of retain the rights over the film, or are they shared with the AFI and Libra?

DL: No, I have the copyright to the film and the AFI has a percentage of, you know, of the profits.

KGG: What was the overall budget, do you know?

DL: I don't ever say what that is, George.

KGG: Because I've heard figures, sort of twenty-thousand to sixty-thousand, you know, and, I mean, it sort of -

DL: Yeah, it's - neither one of those are true. But I've never really said. And I really don't really know.

KGG: Okay. I was also wondering: are you sort of drawn to doing bigger projects each time you take on something new? or is that just accidental?

DL: That's accidental. I like films that are, you know, I really do like smaller pictures. But, you know, the way things are going, they're getting bigger.

KGG: Are you worried about sort of maintaining your own personal vision on something that's getting as big as *Dune*?

DL: Well, yeah, see, it's a whole - like we talked, I think, about this a little bit. It's a whole 'nother thing. It's - it's a collaboration and - but the thing is that the collaborators all go through, you know, me as a sort of filter, right, so it's like it comes out coffee but it's filtered through a certain filter. And so I don't know – but, sure I mean I worry about it, you know, getting it – but I don't think it will be – it won't – it'll be the film that I really want to make, but it won't be like if I – it won't be as much that as if I did everything myself or more things myself, that I could do on a smaller picture. But at the same time you learn so much on these about, you know, lots of things on a big film that it's a great experience too. And then I can apply that to smaller films if I make them in the future.

KGG: I understand that you'd already shot quite a bit of *The Elephant Man* before Merrick's makeup was completed.

DL: Right.

KGG: Were there any fears that the makeup might not sort of come through?

DL: Well, absolutely. And the whole thing was that I was going to do the makeup on *The Elephant Man*. And what I did was a total flop. And it was about the lowest point in my life. And Chris Tucker saved, you know, the whole thing with his, you know, fantastic job. And the material that he works with and the technique that he, you know, works with and, you know, there's only about five people in the world that can, that can, you know, do what he does. And he works with this latex foam that is so light and so fluffy that it's like squeezing air if you have a piece of it in your hand. And it – what I learned was, you know, human skin, the muscles in the face and all this, you know, can't move anything much more rigid than that foam.

KGG: And your original one was a heavier –

DL: Yes. And I had a lot of – I had ideas for doing something sort of strange in a way. I was going to – I was making this sort of skin – and in theory it was a, you know, a nifty idea because I had tests made of this skin that sort of floated over something. It would move and just feel and look so beautiful, like skin. It was incredible. But it would not float and work over this other stuff because the other stuff was too rigid. And John Hurt was just, you know, was like working inside of a helmet, a diving mask. It was totally wrong. And it didn't work. But, you know, I still would like to go back in again sometime and try, you know, some things. But Chris Tucker, what he does is magical. And sure there were worries but once he got, you know, once we saw what he had done the worries just, you know, went out the window. And we knew we had, you know, the possibilities for a good film because all the ingredients were now there.

KGG: In *Elephant Man* I've always wondered about, you know, the mirror sequence. Why was it that you had that reflection so prominent in the window before they go through the thing where he's shown himself in the mirror?

DL: That's a good question, George. You know, it's like it's the idea – I think that John Hurt and I talked about, you know, the mirror thing. He was back in the circus again. And the scream was what the people wanted. And also it was

– it's a horrible – in a very very clear reflection you can play tricks on yourself too, with reflections in a window. But when it's right there in front of you and it's, you know, it's a little bit different.

KGG: Yeah.

DL: And I don't think that – you know, that he was that frightened of himself. It's – it was what he had to do for, in the scene. I mean, you know, in that – caught up in that night, that's what he had to do.

KGG: Yeah, I'd sort of thought that. It seemed like a moment that needs interpretation rather than just accepting it for what it was. You know, because it was sort of hard to believe that he had never seen himself before.

DL: Exactly right.

KGG: Getting on to *Dune*, I know it's sort of early and you again – but I was wondering, are you going to be using stop-motion for things like the sandworms?

DL: I have no idea. We're, you know, like the way I think that we're going to do it is using several different kinds of techniques. So there won't be like just one way that they're all done. And, you know, there again, you know, the sequences have got to be story-boarded and once they're story-boarded we'll see that in this, in this shot it's going to be something and in this shot it's going to have to be something else. And there's going to be several top quality people involved with the effects on this picture. And, you know, like I said, I think that probably two or three different techniques, or maybe even two or three different whole special effects houses will be involved with, you know, some things like the worms.

KGG: Yeah. I heard a rumour a while back which struck me as implausible, and it didn't come up before, but were you ever considered for *Halloween II*? Somebody told me that you were once in the running for that.

DL: Oh no, I wasn't. There is another director called Paul Lynch, and they ran an article in some paper, and they put David Lynch.

KGG: Oh yeah –

DL: And it wasn't me at all.

KGG: That makes more sense. Yeah, he did *Prom Night*.

DL: Yeah.

KGG: Yeah, that makes a lot more sense.

DL: Yeah. It wasn't me.

KGG: I also – the last couple of days I heard something which I think was probably one of the things you wouldn't want – wouldn't have wanted me to hear, but I thought I'd check anyway. It was to do with the fetus things in the film and the material used for them. I was told that you used actual umbilical cords for them.

DL: Uh-huh. I don't mind you saying that. Did Catherine tell you about that?

KGG: Yeah, she mentioned it and –

DL: Yeah, she went to the hospital. And she's the – she, you know, like – we got five or six or maybe even more real umbilical cords and, you know, like lots of, we had lots of little organic, you know, things around on the set all the time. But those were one of the things that we had in the refrigerator.

KGG: That again is a result of your concern with textures, is it?

DL: You bet. There's nothing like the real thing. And, you know, it's like that's why I say there's never been one, just one substance used or one kind of method used, it's always like, you know, bunches of stuff. And there's a lot of fiddling and, you know, getting it right before every shot, that – you know, that's another thing you can't really do on a bigger film because it – you don't have the time.

KGG: Yeah, yeah. Also, what did you mould Henry's rubber head out of?

DL: Well, that was pretty – you mean, how did we – what was the process?

KGG: Well, I mean, I imagine you took a cast of his head and so on.

DL: Yeah.

KGG: But what was it, you know, what was the substance you used for it?

DL: Well, I can tell you one thing: his hair was real. Yeah, it was real hair. And after you write "real hair", you've got to write "You better believe it." In quotation marks.

KGG: I think that's pretty well covered most of it – oh yeah, I wanted to check again: were any of the production photos and things you've got in colour?

DL: No. We got one roll of colour film on *Eraserhead*, but it, I mean, it was not for the stills. It was – they printed one roll of dailies on colour film. And it was – they developed it for black and white or vice versa or something, and the film came and it looked like someone had packed the film can with coal dust. And it was the weirdest thing. We never ran it through a projector, but the entire film was like made of coal. And there was dust, just kind of swarmed out of the can when we opened it up. But we found out that they had done something with colour stock with the black and white, you know, chemicals or something. And – but there was never any colour film used at all.

KGG: No – in, you know, the production stills –

DL: Not in the production stills or anything, yeah, ever.

KGG: The magazine's not going to be terribly happy to hear that.

DL: Well, see, the thing is like it's a black and white – it's a whole black and white thing. And black and white is coming back. So the magazine, you know, it's like colour to me doesn't sell anything, but, you know, any more. I mean, people are – actually the newer look or stranger look is black and white. People are used to colour.

KGG: Yeah, with my own still photography I prefer using black and white film to colour.

DL: Yeah, It's, you know –

KGG: I was also asked if there are any props still in existence that they could do that photo session with, like the rubber head or something?

DL: A photo session?

KGG: Yeah, they're still interested in doing that.

DL: What? I don't understand.

KGG: You know, send their photographer down so that they can get an atmospheric shot of you to illustrate the article.

DL: Oh, well, you mean – what would they like to do?

KGG: He mentioned specifically, you know –

DL: The head is no longer in existence. I'll tell you what we've got: there's a possibility that there's a chicken still around, but I'm not positive. But I do have an excellent photograph of chickens on tinfoil, a closeup. And it really looks good. But then, let's see, the fish, the mounted fish with no tail is, I've got that. And I've got the bush, Henry's bush, next to his bed. And I've got, let's see, I've got the bowl with the water and the pennies. I've got some dishes from the X's, you know, dinner. And I've got the little duck in the, from the centrepiece. But, let's see – I don't have a whole lot more than that. I, you know, in other words, I don't think – I think in the production stills they're going to get a lot more than they would get from sending a photographer or just to photograph those things.

KGG: Yeah, well, I mean the idea was to get the picture of you in that setting, you know, the sort of characteristic thing.

DL: Oh, yeah. Well, if we still had the set, that would be great. But so much has gone, you know, the whole mood, the whole world is, you know, totally gone for years now. That's the trouble.

KGG: Would you be willing to have their photographer come down anyway and do whatever he wants to do? I mean, they keep asking that, so –

DL: Well, I mean, you took a couple of pictures. I mean, if they want to come down, you know, it's like it won't be like on the set kind of thing because there's no set, there's nothing left. It might save them some money and time if the guy wanted to call me first and tell me what he plans, and see if it was –

KGG: Yeah, well I'll get them to do that, yeah. Okay. I also wondered if you could, if I could be sent complete cast and credits for *The Grandmother* and *Eraserhead*. Would that be possible, or –

DL: Yeah. I – I don't know. I'd have to get it off the film on *The Grandmother*. I think one has been written up for *Eraserhead*. And it possibly may have been done for *The Grandmother* too. I'll find out.

KGG: Okay. And the other thing is: I wonder if you could let me know, or get Steve to let me know, how it does on cable TV this New Years' Eve.

DL: Oh, yeah, yeah. For sure.

KGG: I'd like to know what kind of response it gets.

DL: Okay. I don't know how they judge that – do you know?

KGG: Well, that's on a pay channel, isn't it?

DL: Yeah, but see the thing is that, well people could phone in I guess, but no one has to pay specifically for *Eraserhead*. You see what I'm talking about?

KGG: I see.

DL: They buy it by the month. I don't know if there's any way for them to tell how many people actually watch it. Unless they get write-ins or call-ins or something like that. Or threats or something.

KGG: I think that just about covers it, what I've got so far anyway.

David Lynch's 1958 Packard Hawk in the Universal parking lot.
[Photo by the author]

February 11, 1982

KGG: I'm calling - mostly it's sort of minor points and little sort of connecting details that -

DL: Okay.

KGG: You know, I've got everything transcribed that I've got so far, so I thought I'd sort of fill in a bit where I can see holes.

DL: Right.

KGG: The first thing is a sort of obvious question that I never thought to ask before - is where did you get the name *Eraserhead*?

DL: From that one scene.

KGG: It came from the scene?

DL: Yeah, it came from that scene.

KGG: Okay. The other thing was, where did you get the name Spike for the baby?

DL: Jack named him Spike.

KGG: Oh, yeah?

DL: Jack Nance, yeah. He just called him - I think he called him a light bulb for a while, a little light bulb. And then he started calling him Spike. And the name just sort of stuck. He also named the - you know, in the corner, one of the corners, was a hat rack with a raincoat on it, a dark coat - it wasn't a raincoat, it was like a, just a dark coat – and he named – that was Uncle Edgar. And Jack kept his cigarettes in that, Uncle Edgar's pocket.

KGG: At what point was it that you were living on the set? I was told that there was a time when you were actually –

DL: Living there.

KGG: Yeah, living in Henry's room.

DL: Well, I was locking myself in at night. It was sort of illegal. But I – I found a way to camouflage the room to look like no one was in there. Because one door was padlocked and the other door was a cardboard – I mean, plywood. And I could bolt the plywood from within and so from the outside it looked like one board was, you know, bolted shut and the other one was padlocked. So obviously no one could be in there. And I lived there for quite a long time. And Alan lived there for a while as well and – but he lived down the way in the, in what we called the green room where people would make up and everything. But it was a little – little room and Alan would play his cello at night and we'd sit and talk in the food room and then I'd bolt myself in. Sometimes Alan would leave or sometimes, you know, he'd stay down in the green room.

KGG: Was there ever any trouble about that?

DL: No. I think they sort of knew, but no one ever – ever gave me any trouble. I was extremely nervous about it because I didn't have any money and I didn't have any place to live and so I – that's where I was all the time anyway, but I – you know, the only thing is that the garbage started piling up. And the parks department turned me in one time and they said that people must be living there because there's garbage piling up. Of course, we were eating there anyway. But so they asked about it, I think, one time, but I told them that, you know, of course we weren't down there. And we were working down there. And it's really true; I was working all the doggone time. I would just like go to sleep and then, you know, we were back at work again. And so I was very rarely out of those stables for a couple of years. And I had given my car to my ex-, my now ex-wife, and because I didn't have a car there so there's another way no one could tell I was there, you see. And all the cars would leave at a certain time, but I would be there. And Alan doesn't have a car. So we were – we were down there and it was very very strange there at night anyway. But a lot of times I'd be sleeping would be during the daytimes, you see. Because we worked at night.

KGG: You also mentioned that at one point you were living in a garage – was that towards the end when Alan was with you and you were working on the sound and so on?

DL: That's right. I rented a little guest house. It was in the back of a place and then it had a double garage. And the double garage we turned into a little studio, and Alan stayed there when we cut sound and - but then when I got remarried and everything, I sort of took over that garage and made it part of the house and then that's where I did all my shed building. And - but it was more like a garage always and the sheds were of like found wood as I told you. And - but it was a great little place, very private.

KGG: I sort of get the impression that most of the live action was done in the first year, when you were shooting continuously -

DL: In a way that's true. There was still a lot of live action done in the next couple of years, but it was piecemeal. And then we started zeroing in on one shot at a time almost. You know, just finishing, plugging the holes and all this.

KGG: Because I was wondering - Alan mentioned that for a couple of years he was off in Scotland and he sort of came back to do the final sound work in the last year.

DL: Right.

KGG: Who did the sound while he was away? if you were shooting live action at that time.

DL: Oh well, we really didn't shoot any sound scenes - I think, now let's see - one time I think we had a girl take sound and then one time I, on the Lady in, Lady in the Radiator, song; that was synced, you know, played to playback. And I - I got the soundman at the AFI to teach me how to hook that up and I ran that setup at night. But it - mostly we were shooting MOS and also Alan, since there was so little sound, location sound - but the thing is that - did he tell you about all the sound blankets we built?

KGG: Yeah.

DL: And so what sound there was was - there was - I mean, one or two lines were looped but the rest of the sound was just super super super clean. And we deadened the rooms down a whole lot. In fact when I would sleep there at the stables, inside I could hardly hear anything outside the room. It was - and when you spoke or something inside there, your voice was just swallowed up into the walls. It was very very dead.

KGG: The pencil factory scene - was that one of the last ones you did? Doreen Small mentioned that she'd left by the time you did that.

DL: Well, Doreen only worked the first year. And we did an awful lot of work in that first year. She did come back to shoot on the Planet. And then - but, you know, like a lot of people - well, not a lot of people - but people did sort of come in for a while and then go, but the main people stayed throughout the whole thing. But Doreen was there for most of everything, but then we - I mean, when we started going real piecemeal she was gone.

KGG: Was that her in the final shot when Henry reaches Heaven? She mentioned that she was in – you know, the woman that he meets in all that sort of glowing light and so on was actually her.

DL: No no no no no no no. That wasn't her at all. Now what is she telling you? By the way, where did you – how did you get in touch with Doreen?

KGG: I called her in New York.

DL: Oh, how's she doing?

KGG: She seems to be doing fine. She's at law school.

DL: Oh, that's right. Wow. Heavy duty.

KGG: Quite a change of pace.

DL: Yeah, you're not kidding. Well, I don't really like to, you know – I don't know if you should say this in the thing but the last shot is a shot of Henry with his eyes closed over the shoulder of the Lady in the Radiator, and that's Doreen there.

KGG: I think that's what she was talking about.

DL: Yeah.

KGG: You started building things long before you started shooting, with the sets and props and so on.

DL: Right.

KGG: So, I mean, how early did you build things like the Planet?

DL: Well, that was sort of an on-going thing. In fact, we took off for several months during the first year so that I could, well actually Jack and I were working on it, and it was real cold. And Jack and I would go out and work on various things. One thing we called the giant baby head. And we worked on that.

KGG: That was during the year-long break, was it? the baby head, or was that –

DL: Well no, that was during the first year, I think. Yeah. But then, you know, when things would get worked up to a certain point, and then we were shooting along the same time, but then when the thing was actually needed, I would like really concentrate on finishing it up and, you know, but a lot of things were started and they weren't finished until they were actually close to being needed.

KGG: What was the Planet made from? I had sort of conflicting reports from –

DL: What did they tell you? who told you?

KGG: Fred Elmes mentioned it, and I think Catherine Coulson. They couldn't remember exactly but they were sort of either plaster or fibreglass, sort of –

DL: Well, it was – it was both. And it was also made out of wax.

KGG: Wax?

DL: Yeah, there was some wax and some polyester resin and fibreglass, you know, and plaster.

KGG: How big was it?

DL: I don't want to say how big it was.

KGG: I heard at one point that Jack was more or less inside it, turning it for that -

DL: Oh yeah, it was pretty big. Let's put it that way. It was plenty big enough for, you know, people to get inside.

KGG: Did you build the little chickens yourself? I mean, they are artificial, I take it?

DL: Well now, George -

KGG: Oh, this is getting into -

DL: I don't know - what did they tell you?

KGG: Nobody actually mentioned them. I was, you know, this was just a thing that occurred to me.

DL: Everybody's being real good. Shoot. I don't know. I can't stand, you know, to say how things are done. You know that. And - son of a gun. It's just - but - well, I mean, it doesn't hurt it if I say, you know, I built them but - what else do you want to know?

KGG: Well, also you mentioned that you had real hair on Henry's rubber head. I wondered where you got it from.

DL: Oh, that was sort of a running joke. This guy - the line was, "That's real hair," and then you say, "You better believe it." And so I got that from a guy - I don't remember his name - well, there was a guy named Tim Baar and Tim Baar won an Academy Award for *The Time Machine* and he was a special effects guy, and I talked to Tim Baar, you know, about different things and he turned me on to this guy with real hair.

KGG: Okay. How late in the shoot did you do the Planet sequences, you know, the track on the Planet and the exploding Planet?

DL: Well, it was two - or about two years - well, I take that back. That might have been one of the last things at the end of the first year.

KGG: Before the long break.

DL: Before the long break. I'm pretty sure it was. But we had to shoot that twice.

KGG: Yeah, Fred Elmes mentioned that - you had a problem with the camera.

DL: Yeah. Well, a lot of times we shot things twice. And it wasn't always our fault. Like we, see, we had tons of lab problems, and camera problems.

KGG: Also Henry's decapitation and the final baby scene, I wondered were they done towards the end or -

DL: Let's see. Oh yeah, let's see. The final baby scene – you mean at the end of the film –

KGG: Yeah, with the giant head and –

DL: Yeah. Now that was done fairly early. But the – not fairly early. That was sort of done, parts of that were done later. But the Lady in the Radiator scene, all the stuff on the stage was done about two-and-a-half years after we started shooting. No, I take that back. We started shooting May 29th, 1972 – and, George, almost ten years ago. Can you believe that? And so May 29th we shot for one full year. It was almost May 29th again when we stopped. Then we were stopped for a full year and on May 29th two years later from the beginning, we started shooting again. And the first thing we shot was the Lady in the Radiator.

KGG: Which you had had the idea for during the long break.

DL: No. I had the idea for it before that. But we just – we had – we had stopped and we couldn't – it was, you know, a question of which things we were going to shoot first because we only had so much money to do one thing. And then we decided, well we'll shoot the Lady in the Radiator sequence and I told you I was at one point thinking of building Henry about, you know, six inches tall and animating the rest of the film. You know, just moving him around.

KGG: I did want to ask – I don't know if this is part of the forbidden stuff again – it was to do with sounds. I wondered what you used for the baby's voice?

DL: Oh, what did Alan tell you?

KGG: He didn't say anything. He thought that that was probably one of the things you didn't want to –

DL: Right.

KGG: Yeah.

DL: Right.

KGG: Okay. And I also wonder in the lightning during the storm which – as I mention in the essay I wrote – I can hear like a scream in it, and I wondered if that was actually there or is that my imagination?

DL: No. Yeah, you – you – you hear – you – it is like a scream, but you're not hearing a scream.

KGG: It isn't actually a scream?

DL: No.

KGG: Okay. Also, what happened to the baby and the giant head after the film was finished? Where did they go?

DL: Well, I have seen Spike from time to time and Spike is not in good shape these days. The giant baby head is in a dump somewhere.

KGG: You didn't sort of feel the urge to keep it as a souvenir?

DL: Well, I feel the urge to keep lots of things, George, but like I don't have any place to keep them. And I drag things all over the place and then I hardly ever get to see them, right? because they're stored away somewhere. I've got so many things from *Eraserhead*. I still have the bush, next to Henry's bed. I protect that, it's very delicate. And then I still have – hold on one second – I still have Mary's suitcase. I still have the plates from the dinner, and a lot of little knick-knacks from around. I have Henry's dresser and I have that sponge on the baby table. I've got a lot of the lamps from the film. And I have Henry's coat and his pens, but they're not in good shape.

KGG: It's getting kind of old by now, I guess.

DL: Yeah. And I've got a few more other things too. But I'm trying to keep as, you know, as much stuff as I can now.

KGG: I guess some of the stuff is a bit too big.

DL: Yeah, exactly.

KGG: Where did you learn to do makeup techniques? like casting – like Henry's head and Laurel Near for the appliances.

DL: Well, I don't know, George. No one ever really taught me. In art school, I would do, you know, I loved casting things and I – like I told you, my first film was, it was three heads of me, but my friend Jack Fisk cast them for me, took casts of me, for me so I could put them into this screen. And I think I cast his head a couple of times and I'll cast anyone's head that'll let me, you know. Because I really like it. But Jack went under three times I think before it got a good thing because we, I wanted him to have a Henry expression. And he was a trouper – Jack is the greatest not only as an actor but as a person that will go through, you know, practically living hell for you and for the film. And so he would, he really, you know – but I – people, you know, makeup guys really want you to hold a certain expression, right? Some are a lot easier than others. And a Henry expression is a subtle sort of thing and to kind of hold that for long enough for these things to set up is a real trick. And he did it, he did it fantastically.

KGG: Oh, I was wondering what you used for the blood or whatever it was in the chicken scene, that sort of thick oily –

DL: Well, that – I, George, I swear I don't really know because I hate makeup blood. And so I have bottles of like Technicolor blood, but it's always, even for black and white it looks too gray sort of. And it's too thick always. And real pig's blood would be the best thing to use but maybe put a little bit of darker colouring in it. But I would mix up things and like on Henry's nosebleed the stuff I mixed up I think was pretty toxic, and so he had to put it in his nose and it really burned the inside of his nose. And so –

KGG: Did the production move away from the AFI towards the end when you were – I mean, you were doing effects shooting at Fred Elmes' house and your house and so on –

DL: Right. It did. We kind of got kicked out of AFI. We were asked to leave – remember I told you we had about three more hours of shooting, no we had thirty hours of straight shooting we had to do in thirty hours because they were telling us we had to leave the attic. And after two or three years of being down there, they suddenly gave us this unrealistic, ridiculous deadline and were forcing us out. And they knew we were shooting, so we went for a thirty hour stretch with the only break, as I told you, was I had to go shoot my paper route. And we were, we were totally exhausted, but we got everything. And – but we weren't used to shooting like that. And in a way it kind of was like maybe good for us, but it wasn't really because we would work hard but we weren't used to being under the gun like that. And there's a lot of things that you, you might think of, you know, along the way if you have the time and do them, but we had to just race through that.

KGG: Yeah. Can you remember what things you were doing?

DL: Well, it was Henry inside the elevator.

KGG: So where did you cut and mix the film then? Was that when you were living in the garage there?

DL: Yeah. I was cutting the film and Alan, you know, we were making sound effects and Alan was cutting the sound, all in the garage. That was like in, toward the very end.

KGG: Where did you get the equipment for that?

DL: Well, I bought a Moviola, a real old-fashioned totally black one with a magnifying glass on it. And it was tremendously loud. And it would, it would really eat film if anything ever really went wrong. And I was kind of afraid to use it a lot, but it worked out real well. I mean, it did the job. And I sold it after the film. And then – but Alan – we bought quite a bit of equipment for Alan. And sold it after the film as well. And he had a pretty good console that we built and, you know, plenty of stuff to do the thing and then we'd rent like the odd thing that we couldn't afford, for maybe like a week or something. But he had a real good setup.

KGG: Considering you were doing it for so many years, where did you store all the film that you shot during those years?

DL: Well, for a while it was at AFI in the editing room. But then it was at my garage. And I just had shelves stacked with film. And it was not too well organized. But I knew in my head where things were. You know how it is. And – but it wasn't organized in the normal way, you know, because, Doreen had gone and we had shot – we didn't really take great notes. A lot of times things wouldn't get quite organized. And so I kind of like had to go by feel, you know, to find stuff but it was sort of uncanny how you get to know your shelves and you know, you feel where things are. And - but that's - all the film was there. And we shot quite a bit of film actually, but I forget - I think it was around ten-to-one ratio or something.

KGG: You didn't lose anything during the years?

DL: No. Not a frame. Not one frame.

KGG: Did you yourself invent the pencil machine?

DL: Yes I did, George.

KGG: I was wondering after what you mentioned about *The Elephant Man* - it sort of struck me that it was probably, you know, something that you had made up yourself. Was it based on a real thing or was it -

DL: No, I never saw a real pencil machine. But it was sort of like common sense, I figured, how they might go. And I had certain pieces of machinery and the rest I just sort of made up.

KGG: Can you recall which scene it was you completed to show to that producer that you were trying to get some money from?

DL: He saw quite a bit of the film but it was edited very loosely.

KGG: I thought you mentioned that you'd sort of put one whole scene together with the sound and so on.

DL: Well, okay, then it would be Henry's going to the X's, you know, for dinner.

KGG: That whole scene?

DL: Well, not the whole scene I don't think but, you know, but part of it. And that's when he said people don't talk like that.

KGG: After you first showed it - when you decided to re-cut it, was that after the screening at AFI or after the screening at Filmex?

DL: After the screening at Filmex.

KGG: Did you remix it as well?

DL: No. It didn't need remixing. The things I cut out, it needed just that twenty-frame pull up here and there. It - the stuff I took out was - were whole bits. It wasn't like an overall trim. I lifted out whole scenes. And I always felt they were, you know, they were too long, but I never had - I always wanted to fool myself that they could be there. And after that I knew that they couldn't.

KGG: I heard that Herbert Cardwell also came from Philadelphia.

DL: Yes he did.

KGG: And that he was connected with Alan there.

DL: Right.

KGG: Did you know him in Philadelphia?

DL: I met Herb in Philadelphia and – when I was over there with *The Grandmother* or *The Alphabet* or both, and he was shooting industrial films –

KGG: At the same company.

DL: Yeah. And when we came out – Alan and I and everybody came out to California, one day Alan and I were talking and Alan said, "You know, Herb really would like to get out of the industrial films thing." And I said, "Are you kidding me? You know, Herb would be great." Just technically Herb was just brilliant and – but he'd never had a chance to do anything except these industrial films.

KGG: So this was his first –

DL: Yeah, this was it. But Herb couldn't last more than, you know, nine months. And so Fred came in. And Fred is in a way, was not exactly like Herb, but they were very very similar. And it just, the segue from Herb to Fred was very very smooth and it really worked out well.

KGG: I was also told that at one point you took up meditation while you were doing it.

DL: Yeah.

KGG: And I was told that that had an effect on sort of lightening the mood of the film somewhat.

DL: Who told you that?

KGG: Doreen Small.

DL: Oh yeah?

KGG: She said it was much more sort of nightmarish in the original conception and attributed –

DL: Well, that could be. I think that might have been true.

KGG: I mean, did you take up meditation because of the pressures of the film?

DL: Well, I took it up because here I was supposedly very – doing what I wanted to do more than anything else, make films. And I had everything going, George. I had, you know, a little studio practically and we were working and everything and I just wasn't happy. And I was real innocent in metaphysical things and all this and I just – suddenly someone mentioned this, you know, meditation and whammo! that was it. And I knew it was for me.

KGG: Do you think that did have an influence on things like the Lady in the Radiator and so on?

DL: Well, I think, yeah, the whole Lady in the Radiator is, is, you know, is that, is that lighter line, yeah. This light coming in.

KGG: I was also told that you had people get their natal charts done.

DL: That I had them do that?

KGG: Yeah, to see if people were compatible.

DL: No, I didn't have them do it. But we have, we know this person who is really incredible at interpreting your astrological information. And this guy is unbelievable. And Alan and I were the main people that really kind of flipped out over these things. But most of the people did, did, you know, go to him and have readings done and we would sort of see more clearly how we all fit together.

KGG: I also did wonder – several people mentioned it – why at that time you wore three ties at the same time?

DL: I don't know, George. I wore a hat and three ties and I was – I still like to have my collar buttoned. And I think it's an insecurity thing.

KGG: It was also mentioned – you know, you were talking about the AFI and the problems with doing features there and so on. You mentioned Martin Brest's feature that he did there that was around the same time that you did –

DL: No, he did it quite a bit later. I think about four years later.

KGG: But I was told there was somebody – Stanford Kaye?

DL: Stan – now, it's not – Stanton Kaye.

KGG: Stanton?

DL: Stanton. Stanton Kaye. A filmmaker who was there the year before – the first year that it opened – was Stanton Kaye and Jeremy Kagan and Tom Rickman and Matthew Robbins and a whole bunch of people that have gone on and done a lot of things. Stanton Kaye was the one who was, out of all these people, picked to do the first feature film ever to be made at AFI. It was going to be quite an expensive picture, relatively speaking. And it turned out to be quite a fiasco which almost, almost shut AFI down. But everybody, everybody at AFI worked on it in some way. I went to Kanab, Utah, to build gold bricks.

KGG: To where?

DL: To Kanab, Utah. They told me, since they knew I could cast things, they needed gold bricks. And so they flew me up there for two days, but I was there for two weeks and I was working like twenty hours a day to do these ten thousand gold bricks. I was working in a basement with a guy named Happy.

KGG: And the film never got made, I take it.

DL: No. It never got finished.

KGG: Which is why they were very reluctant about –

DL: Features. It stopped features – the word feature at AFI was almost, you know, the death penalty. They just didn't want to hear about it.

KGG: I seem to remember reading a few years back that *Eraserhead* was shown at the Edinburgh film festival.

DL: Yes, I think it was.

KGG: And I wondered what other festivals it might have been to.

DL: Gee, George, it was shown at a lot of festivals, but I don't have a list of them all because a lot of the times Ben didn't want to send them to festivals because it costs a lot of money and then the territory in that area, you know, it wouldn't – the prestige would be great, but there wouldn't be any money out of it. We didn't have any money to send it and do it. So a lot of things were turned down, but I – they might be able to help you out at Libra concerning what festivals it's been in.

KGG: I wondered if it had won any prizes anywhere.

DL: I don't think it did. Oh yes, it did. It was – it won the Golden Antennae award and the Jury's, Jurors' Choice or something at Avoriaz.

KGG: Where's that?

DL: It's in France. It's a science fiction film festival every year at Avoriaz and I think Friedkin was on the board. Friedkin apparently really liked *Eraserhead*. A lot – Stanley Kubrick, you know, I told you it's one of his favourite pictures. A lot of directors, luckily enough for me, really, really go for it. And – but I mean I hear about it from time to time, but Friedkin was on the jury that year.

KGG: Let me see, something I can't remember noticing myself but somebody mentioned it, is that Henry – the picture on Henry's wall is of an atomic bomb.

DL: Yes, it is.

KGG: I'm amazed at the number of times I've seen it and people still point out things that I haven't noticed before. Oh, I never did ask where and when you were born. Somebody told me you were born on the same date as Federico Fellini.

DL: Well, I don't know about that for sure. I was born on January 20th, 1946, in Missoula, Montana.

KGG: And you lived at various places I take it?

DL: Yes.

KGG: Oh yes, another thing I didn't ask; is Frank Herbert at all connected with the *Dune* project?

DL: Frank Herbert connected with it?

KGG: Yeah.

DL: Well, in a way. You know, I talk to Frank from time to time and he's reading, you know, he read the outline for the script and I'll show him the script and so far he likes the way I'm, you know, the direction it's going. I – I don't – he's sort of a consultant and he wants to help and he's excited about the film. Right now he's in Hawaii.

KGG: How is progress going on the – have you got into pre-production yet?

DL: I'm still writing away like crazy, George. I don't know if you know that I'm writing by myself now. Yeah. Shortly after you left, we just sort of split up,

Chris and Eric and I. And it's – I don't know if you should even write that in your article, you know, because it just wasn't working out in my mind the way I wanted it to. And it's no fault of theirs, it's just the way it was. And so, since then they've gotten another job writing for Robert Redford, so they're, you know, they're really looking good. And I'm happy working on my own.

KGG: Are you getting into pre-production now?

DL: No, we won't till the script is approved. I'm going to write to the middle of March and then hopefully I'll be finished around then and then we'll get into pre-production.

KGG: So there's still no sort of set start date?

DL: No. We'll be lucky to shoot this year. There's so many things to build.

Cast and Crew

Everyone who worked on *Eraserhead* with David Lynch was very protective of his desire for secrecy and no one would talk to me without an assurance that I had Lynch's permission to ask them questions. And even then, there were areas they wouldn't go into – particularly anything to do with the film's special effects, and most particularly about the baby. But given those restrictions, everyone was eager to speak about their time on the film and how important the experience had been for them.

Jack Nance

Jack Nance, out of focus at American Zoetrope, December 1981.
[Photo by the author]

Jack Nance, a terrific character actor, was of course best known for playing Henry Spencer in *Eraserhead*. I met him at a Denny's on Sunset Boulevard. Although we both arrived on time, we didn't connect for more than half an hour, both of us wandering in and out of the restaurant; I was looking for Henry, but in real life Jack looked quite different (the hair, of course, was gone!). Eventually I approached the small guy who was hanging around the entrance and asked if he was, indeed, Jack Nance. We got a table, I set up my tape recorder, and we got started, initially on some background. He told me some very entertaining stories about the early days of his acting career. Unfortunately, I didn't get any of it down on tape because I had forgotten to flip the remote switch on the microphone! This error turned out to be a good ice-breaker as it gave us something to laugh about; from then on Jack talked and I listened. He turned out to be one of the wryest, most amusing people I'd ever met.

The day after that meeting, I was his guest at Zoetrope Studios, where he had a small part in Wim Wenders' *Hammett*, which was shooting at the time. It was quite a thrill for me to meet the director, whose work I admired (*The

American Friend, Alice in den Stadten, Im Lauf der Zeit, Die Angst des Tormanns beim Elfmeter), and to watch him shooting a scene with Fred Forrest and Peter Boyle on the Chinatown set on one of the sound stages.

Chinatown alley, Zoetrope Studios, December 1981. [Photo by the author]

December 9, 1981: Denny's on Sunset Boulevard

Jack Nance: Well, that hasn't been running. I didn't know if it was. Should I begin again?

Kenneth George Godwin: If you could just go back over a little of –

JN: How did I meet David Lynch?

KGG: Yeah. Sorry about that.

JN: How did I meet David Lynch? – I did that same thing one time. I was interviewing a gangster about some heavy business – car bombs and stuff like that. And this guy was talking to me on the QT, you know, and I got home with a completely blank cassette. I tried tapping his phone, I tried – you know, completely blank tapes. I wanted to cut my wrists. How did I meet David Lynch? I'd worked in San Francisco with a guy named David Lindeman, who was a terrific director – did I have all of this?

KGG: This was theatre work, was it?

JN: Yeah. Yeah.

KGG: Had you done any film before *Eraserhead*?

JN: Yeah, yeah, yeah. I'd done a couple of movies - one a movie with Jason Robards that was not a memorable movie, and one picture that was a good movie. It was a good movie. It was not a big commercial success, nobody ever heard of it probably, but it was called *Bushman*.

KGG: I haven't heard of it.

JN: David Schickele directed it. And it was a sort of a *cinema verite* kind of a semi-documentary thing about this Algerian - not Algerian. What was he? Nigerian. A Nigerian exchange student, a black guy, an Ebo tribesman. He came to go to school here in the United States during the Sixties and was caught up in all of the strife of the times, with student riots and all of that business. And was a black man living in a country where blacks had particular problems. And he didn't get - they weren't his problems. He was caught up in all of this at a time when his whole race was being slaughtered in Nigeria, in the civil war over there. And the movie was his story. It was really - it was a good movie. In fact it was the only worthwhile thing, I guess, besides *Eraserhead*, you know, that I've done before this. I've done a lot of American International hot rod movies and Chuck Norris karate movies and all of that kind of stuff. Now this - *Hammett* now is the first serious movie I've worked on in a long while.

KGG: That's Wim Wenders' project?

JN: Wim Wenders, yes. Yes. Francis Ford Coppola, the producer. And I'm really glad that's being done because it hasn't been easy. They've had a lot of problems and, you know - the good things never are; right. So I hope it's a big success because a lot of people have really had to hump to get it out. And it's good. It's really, really good. There's a lot of good stuff -

KGG: I like his work.

JN: Yeah, yeah. Wenders is great, and a lot of good people - Fred Forrest, and Peter Boyle, and Elisha Cook Jr, which is an incredible trip. He's great.

KGG: I didn't know he was still doing films.

JN: A great little guy, yeah. Yeah. So, yeah, I'd worked in San Francisco with David Lindeman. Lindeman came to the AFI, and introduced me to David Lynch when Lynch was looking for Henry. And we didn't really - we didn't really hit it off right away. I had done a couple of AFI projects before. We kind of kept our distance from one another at first. He wasn't sure and I wasn't sure.

KGG: What were you first told about it? how was it described to you?

JN: Well, I met this crazy guy with a beat up straw hat and three neckties, and he started telling me strange tales. And he gave me a copy of the script to read and it was a pretty sketchy script, but it was so bizarre, you know, that I was immediately, you know, I was curious about it at least. And, you know, I was reading all of these strange images and then I got to the final scene where there's the giant baby head. And I was struck by that because it was describing in some detail a sort of hallucination, I guess, that I had had at one time when I was very sick. And running a fever. I was taking codeine, and it was in a hotel room in Great Bend, Kansas, in a blizzard, dying, and I had a terrible nightmarish kind of delirium hallucination, that when I was reading that scene I thought, "My god, you know, this is exactly like that time in Great Bend." And then later, when he introduced me to Spike, the baby, I went, you know, "That's it."

KGG: Spike?

JN: Yes, the little child.

KGG: Who named him Spike?

JN: I think that's on the birth certificate. Well, in any case, I read this very bizarre script, and it was very sketchy. And he said, "Well, I'd like for you to see – to get an idea, I'd like for you to see *The Grandmother* – his first film. So we went into this screening room, he ran *The Grandmother* and it was like sitting for forty-five minutes in the electric chair. It was the most incredibly bizarre thing I had ever seen on the screen anywhere. It was genius, it was beautiful. And suddenly I wanted to do Henry in *Eraserhead* more than anything I had ever wanted to do in my life. I was obsessed with it. And things worked out, things worked out. He has a story to tell that we were discussing it, we were out on the parking lot, and we were talking about it and it was sort of up in the air about whether I would be Henry or not. And there was an old Volkswagen parked there that had this rack built on the top of it, a big wooden rack that was kind of an ingenious design, that you could probably load as much on the Volkswagen as you could on a truck, you know. This huge rack. And I had a Volkswagen myself and I thought what a neat thing, you know, to have a rack like that. So I said, "Boy, whoever built that thing must be on the ball, because that is a really neat –" So David said, "Well, thank you, Jack. I did that, you know, and you're hired." That's what he said convinced him, that when I complimented the rack –

KGG: How did you conceive of Henry? he's not exactly an ordinary character.

JN: Well, it was – I don't know. Henry was very easy. Henry was very easy. It was sort of – he sort of just – it was like putting on a comfortable suit, to put on that character, you know. The thing about it – the key to it, I guess, was that in spite of the fact that – you know, Henry's – the world in *Eraserhead*, you know, is strange and very bizarre, and Henry is a very bizarre character, the fact is he was just a regular guy, you know. A real ordinary joker. He – and that was sort of the key to the character really. He had, you know, certain traits that every ordinary workaday guy has, you know. He was a fairly responsible guy, held down a job, and got along in the world. He had his own ideas of what was cool, you know. He had a haircut that he probably thought was cool and, you know, he probably thought that the white socks with the suit was, you know, kind of flashy. And he had hip taste in music. And he was really just an ordinary, everyday guy. The story itself is ordinary, everyday, you know, common. Happens all the time. You know, it's basically your boy meets girl story that is, you know - it's a common thing. All of the, you know, the strange things that happen and, you know - they disturb him, all kinds of things happen. People are disturbed by all kinds of things. But basically he was just a regular good guy, I think. And, you know, seemed to be a likeable sort. And it was very easy to maintain that character. As you know, it was a very long term project. And there was - in one particular shot I get up off the bed and go to the door and, you know, open the door. And it was a year later before I came through the other side. The continuity held up, you know, because it was just one of those characters that you can just - you know, I would put on the suit and the tie and I was - there he was, there was Henry. And it didn't matter that months had elapsed or where I'd been or what I'd done - when I'd come back, there was, Henry was back and nothing had changed. It was one of those characters. It was just - I don't know if it was any kind of identification or whatever, but Lynch is really, he's really wonderful at drawing images and he, you know, he doesn't have a theatrical background, he has an art background. He can communicate with actors. Actors, you know, react to imagery. They see themselves in the big picture, you know, and so the best directors always give very visual kinds of images that you can work with and Lynch is just great at that.

KGG: He talked a lot about feeling and conveying feeling rather than a sort of intellectual kind of thing. But if you're going to work on something that long - almost five years - you must get into what you're doing and what it means and so on. What sort of discussions did you ever have about that?

JN: Well, yeah. We worked very meticulously, and shooting in black and white, it was going to be really good black and white, like *Eraserhead* is. It was, you know, it's a very slow, time-consuming process. And just as all of the lights had to be very meticulously placed - everything was like that. Every reaction and every look and everything that was happening inside Henry's head - which, much of it is going on inside his head. And so we had to get into that in great detail. I mean, it was - every little thing that was going on, you know, was very meticulously - I don't think it was analyzed. I don't know that we analyzed what was happening, but we were always aware of everything that was going on. It wasn't just now - I mean, it was more than just say the words and make the funny faces, you know, like a lot of stuff is. So we had these long strange conversations, skull sessions, and things would reveal themselves to us a lot as we were going along. We knew we were going in some direction. It's like, you know something's happening but you don't know what it is. And watching it, the audience is supposed to have, you know, a sense of that, and we did too a lot, you know. At certain points there's something going on here, you know, but you would have to figure out, you know, what was happening. Sometimes we didn't, but then sometimes - I remember one particular shot that was - it was, you know, a very simple, quick shot. I was supposed to say, "No kidding," or something and turn and walk away. And we worked on it take after take after take, a whole reel of film. And Herb Cardwell, the cameraman, had to change magazines, so he just opened up the magazine and started throwing the film out on the floor, you know, an hour's worth of work just piled up on the floor, and he said, "Well, at least we won't have to look at that shit in the screening room." You know, and it wasn't - it didn't work, it wouldn't work for some reason. For some reason. And so, you know, we had to sit down and think about it, you know, and figure out, you know, what's not - I mean, the scene worked, I mean, it played all right but there was something that wasn't there. And so we had to do a lot of that, you know. Unless we knew exactly what was going on in the guy's mind, it was no use cranking up the camera. I can't give you any kind of analysis of the film, you know. The main question I get, aside from questions about the baby, is: "What's it about?" You know, "What's it about?" And I can't tell you, you know. You can tell me what it's about, or what you figure it's about. You can't say what it's about. To say what it's about is to go back just to the simple story, you know. Just to Henry and Mary and the family and the baby and all that, you know. It's a guy, he's - you see him walled in, you know. The walls close in tighter and tighter and tighter - that's what it's about. But it's more than that, you know. The movie is more than just what it's about in that way. It's - what it's about to me is not what it's about to you or to the next guy. I guess in that way it's a lot like Lynch's paintings - you know, if you look at some of his paintings you'll say the same thing: "What's it about?" They trigger something in your brain, whatever that is that we react to. We see something. I sat in a room alone one time with a Rembrandt. And it was a fascinating experience. But my experience sitting with a Rembrandt is not, you know, what somebody else's would be, I don't think. You go up close and see the brushstrokes, you know - "Rembrandt did that!" So who can say what it's about?

KGG: Did you have any trouble getting the feeling between characters? There's a sort of odd pacing in all the scenes involving dialogue. The dialogue doesn't seem naturally paced, it's not the way people sit and talk.

JN: No, no.

KGG: Is that something that just sort of emerged or was it planned?

JN: A good example of that: we had - when - before the film was finished, we went broke a half a dozen times, you know, and we brought in a guy who was a big movie producer, to show him what we had done because we were putting the touch on people for money, you know. And we ran a bunch of film for him and the guy blew his stack. He was enraged, he was offended, you know. He went storming out of the screening room. And he was yelling, saying, "People don't talk like that!" He said, "Look, I know people and people don't act like that! You people are crazy. People don't talk that way, people don't act like that. What do you think you're doing?" He was – anyway, people don't talk like that, you know, they don't talk like that. There's – the mother says, "What do you do?" and Henry says, "I'm on vacation." It's got nothing to do with what was asked. But then that's, I think, part of the dream image, you know, in dreams people say strange things to you. And it's sort of what happens, you know, it's not – there wasn't any difficulty with it as far as, you know, relationships among actors or whatever. I mean, it didn't cause any kind of problems with what you're saying has nothing to do with what I'm saying, because that's what we're doing. You know what I mean?

KGG: Did you find working that long on it, with its very distinctive own world, that it had any effect on you outside the film?

JN: Well, yeah. Yeah. Sure, I mean, I wouldn't ever have to want to make a movie like that again. But I wouldn't take anything for having done it, you know. At the time, you know, I was going around Hollywood and agents' offices and casting offices, doing hot rod movies and all of that kind of stuff. And I had come from several years of doing a lot of really good work in San Francisco, that was really where I made my bones as an actor, you know, when I was a young, real hot shot actor, you know, when I got a chance to do a lot of really flashy stuff. And, you know, I had quite a bit under my belt before I came to Hollywood. And I came here with a show that was a big hit, you know, but memories are short here in this town and, you know, I was going through this grind – pictures and resumes and all of this – and there was nothing really stimulating, you know. Some TV shows or whatever. It wasn't the kind of real meaty kind of stuff that I'd been used to at all, and playing the game and all of that. And, like, I got involved in *Eraserhead* a hundred percent, you know. And at the time it was good because it got me out of that – I was getting very discouraged with the rat race and the Hollywood game and all. And it was good for me to get involved in something that I was really enthusiastic about. I didn't realize of course that it would turn into the next several years of my life, you know. And that cost me, I guess, a lot because, you know, when it was finally done I had been out of circulation for a long time, you know.

KGG: You didn't take on anything else during *Eraserhead*?

JN: Well, no because we – not in movies. I, you know, picked up radio spots and stuff like that, which I'd done a lot of. With a haircut like that I was pretty limited as far as that goes.

KGG: You maintained that look all the time, did you?

JN: Well, you know, that's my hair and that's all it would do. Besides, you know, it took – mean, we worked weeks at a time without a day off, morning, noon, and night. When you're broke, you've got to do it the hard way, you know, and when you're doing it all yourself it's – I mean, I got an appreciation for the movies in a way that, you know, it was – I realized, you know, what a monumental task making a film really is. I used to think, here they've got all these dozens of people, hundreds of people working on these movies, you know, and here's one guy to move this wire and here's another guy to do this and another guy to do that. But really, I mean, there's a lot of work involved in making a picture, and everybody works really hard on movies, you know. I've never been on a movie where anybody sat around, you know. It's hard work and I got a real appreciation for that. But, you know, like I say, it was –

KGG: Was it easier or harder, considering all the time you had on *Eraserhead*, working so slowly and carefully, than it is on a big feature where you've got the time pressure – it has to be produced right away?

JN: Well, it's really, really tough to walk onto a set on a picture that's been shooting for four weeks, and jump in and do a bit and then you're done and the movie goes on. Because you're not, you know, you're not involved in everything that's going on. All of this stuff is happening all around and you don't know what all is happening. And everybody has a vocabulary, a dialogue that, you know, you're not familiar with. And it's really tough to do something like that. On *Eraserhead*, you know, I was involved in everything, even the editing – I was running machines and matching up my own voice with my own lips, you know, and all of this stuff. And I like – I really like, you know, having the experience of, you know, behind the camera and all that, but I wouldn't want to do that stuff because everything is heavy in movies. You know, everything weighs tons – it'll be little bitty boxes like this that weigh five-hundred pounds a piece and they, you know, you have to carry them up. There's a lot of, you know, schlepping. It's hard work. I wouldn't – I don't envy those guys their job, but it was neat to do it, you know. And in that sense, yeah, it makes it a lot easier to, when you know everything that's going on. When I first started acting, I went to the Dallas theatre centre and the first thing that they did was, you know, give me this baptism of fire in the technical theatre, in hanging lights and building sets and props. And my first job really was stage managing a show, you know what I mean? I think, you know, you've got to have at least some knowledge of the workings of that, you know. It helps a lot when you're in front of the camera to know what's going on behind the camera. And *Eraserhead* in that sense was like getting a university degree in that. So that's – it put me in good stead really, you know, because I feel a lot more comfortable now going onto a set, knowing exactly what's happening ahead of time. I think it's good for any actor to put in some time behind the scenes, you know, sure, sure.

KGG: After it was finished, when you saw the final film, what was your reaction? were you still too close to it to experience it as a film?

JN: Well, there was really no sense of it – of sitting back and saying, "Ah, it's finished." You know, it wasn't finished all at once. It was like one frame at a time. And when we first screened it, it was a very, very long film – when we first screened it for an audience. So we knew it still wasn't finished, you know. And Lynch went back and was cutting again. And I guess it was when it premiered at Filmex, it was locked in. And that was the first time that I saw it in toto. And, you know, all of these bits and pieces that I'd seen ten thousand times all of a sudden ran from beginning to end, all together – and hell, I was ecstatic, I loved it. Yeah, yeah. And to finally get an audience reaction like we got was a big kick.

KGG: What kind of reaction did it get?

JN: It was – at the end of the screening there was complete dead silence. And I knew that it worked. And I said to Lynch, "You see, I told you it would turn them into zombies." People were stunned, and there was this long, shocked silence. And then, you know, a huge burst of applause. It was beautiful. I'd been waiting five years for the applause, you know. It was great. It was great. And then I haven't really sat down and watched it since, I've been in and out of screenings, but I haven't – I, not in *Eraserhead* so much, although there are certain bits, but I have problems watching myself. There's always something I want to do different. But you can't do it. There are a couple of things I've done that are just maddening, maddening, like that. And a few little bits in *Eraserhead*. But for the most part I like *Eraserhead* a lot. It's so clean, you know, everything is just right on the beam. Because that's how we worked, you know. So it's good. We weren't under any pressure, you know, and we didn't have to – we'd get the shot and break for lunch, and if it played it was okay; we didn't work like that.

KGG: Was there any response after it went into distribution, I mean as far as your career is concerned? Did anybody see it and offer you more work?

JN: Well, you know, it's put me in very good stead, you know. It's sort of – right now, it's sort of my main claim to fame, you know. I'm some sort of midnight movie cult hero or whatever. Although I'm totally out of touch with whatever the cult is. I've made personal appearances at the theatres and, god, the fans, groupies, and the punk rockers, you know, I mean, guys like Devo are fans, you know. But that sort of has passed me by. I don't understand it. Maybe it's, I'm not of today's generation or whatever. And when we were doing it, you know, it's like I always felt there's a market out there, there's an audience – not "market", I don't like "market" – but there's an audience out there somewhere and, you know, at the time there was no midnight movie circuit, you know. And the midnight movie craze or whatever it is sort of came along as *Eraserhead* came along. So maybe we were somewhat ahead of the times or something, because things, I mean the audience sort of grew up after the fact. And – I don't know. I'm just sort of – sort of out of touch with whatever the phenomenon is. It's – I mean, I love having people line up in the middle of the night in the rain to get their tickets, you know, but I don't – it's not my scene. I guess I'm – I don't know. What am I? Straight? Something of the sort, you know. I don't know that I would be an *Eraserhead* fan. I don't know that I would be lining up in the middle of the night. And people go to see *Eraserhead* again and again and again. People in the audience are saying the lines with the movie. It's phenomenal. My girlfriend, Laurel, is my biggest fan – she's been to see *Eraserhead* nineteen times, you know. I don't know that I would be a fan like that. I can't think of anything – well, *Giant* maybe I saw several times, but that's because – yeah, it's really phenomenal. I'm really tickled to heck by it. I'm always shocked whenever I sneak into theatres, you know. Who are these people? who are these people? I don't know. But I'm glad they're there. I like them. They're neat. As far as the movie people go, the Hollywood people, it's done me – it's done a lot of good for me because there's an incredible amount of mystique that's built out of that. I go into these offices, you know, and I get, "Oh, yeah, you're the guy in *Eraserhead*. Yeah, I haven't seen that movie but I hear it –" You know. And I sort of – "Tell me what's it about?" And, you know, I'm kind of burnt out with that, you know. I mean, if – it ran for four and a half years here in town and it's – people haven't gotten out to see it, you know – only I can dig that, you know, so you guys aren't going to go out at midnight, a lot of people. But it's like maybe what they don't know won't hurt them, you know. If they haven't seen it, there's some sort of mystique about it because of the talk that goes around about it. And so, that's sort of done me – opened some doors for me, yeah.

KGG: You've done films between *Eraserhead* and *Hammett*?

JN: A couple, a couple. Well, I don't want to mention them. Yeah, there's one in particular that I'd rather forget and another one – I don't even know the name of it. They had several different titles for it. But after *Eraserhead* I got involved with this phenomenal group, the Doo-Dah Gang. We were – I became a 1925 gangster gunsel, I was Tony Robozo. I was a lieutenant to Big Jim Valenti, a bigtime, rich and famous, powerful gangster figure. And we shot up Los Angeles and were on TV. We were famous, an incredible phenomenon. *Time* and *Newsweek*, the front page of the *National Observer*. And it was another one of those things it's kind of hard to describe exactly what we were up to. People – it was the same question with the Doo-Dah Gang: "What's it about?" But we – I went to Las Vegas and I played the Flamingo, which was the greatest. I mean, never did I ever dream that I would play Las Vegas, you know what I mean?

KGG: What did you do there?

JN: Well, that's – what would I do, you know? I'm not Wayne Newton, you know what I mean? What am I going to do in Las Vegas? But we were an incredible smash hit in Las Vegas with the Doo-Dah Gang, 1925 gangsters. People loved it. And we were up there with the – that was the big, glamorous showbiz world, all the glitter, you know, the cars and the parties and the – all of the Hollywood big-shots, you know. It was incredible. It was – it conformed much more closely to the image I'd always had of what it would be like to come to Hollywood, than *Eraserhead*. Yeah, playing Las Vegas, I thought, well this is a lot more like it. Yeah. So that was what occupied me most after *Eraserhead*, but then again that sort of took me out of, you know, out of the horse race, as far as that goes. So I guess, you know, there's always some price to pay, but again I wouldn't take anything for that, it was fabulous, Las Vegas. I hated to leave Las Vegas, man, I could live like that. Yeah, that was fantastic. So, after that – that was for – that was another pretty long-term project. I spent three years doing that, yeah. But – I don't know – I've done stage plays that have run for a year or more, you know what I mean? Eight or ten months in a play, that's a nice run. I don't mind really. *Hammett* has been in the works for a long time.

KGG: What kind of character are you playing in that?

JN: Well, I'm right back to 1925. It's very much Tony Robozo. I mean, the suit fit, you know, the bow tie and cap and all of that. Not at all the same character. But I play a character named Gary Salt, who is trying to pull off a caper and is just in way over his head. He's bitten off a lot more than he can chew, you know, and doesn't make it at all. Gets it in the end. The caper is kind of – rather convoluted, complex series of events that, you know – and Salt gets lost, he's lost, you know, along the way. But it's – I like Salt a lot. He's, again he's a regular guy who's just – he shouldn't be where he is, is all, you know. He gets himself in trouble. And it's a good shoot. It's a good movie. I hope it goes.

KGG: Have you got anything else coming up after *Hammett*?

JN: Well, a couple of things that have been left hanging for the time being. Where am I right now? I'm doing – I'm really in better shape now than I have been in a long time, you know. I've been – I've got some really good prospects coming up. The whole business is a crap shoot, you know, so you never know. But, you know, I've put in a lot of years, had some good years and had a lot of bad years, you know, in a long period of time after *Eraserhead* – during *Eraserhead* really, you know. So some of the kinds of hard times, I guess, every actor goes through, that are common at least, you know. Divorces and booze problems and a lot of, you know, some bad times, some bad times. And now things are going really, really good. I'm really happier and more enthusiastic about a lot of things that are going on now. Not that there aren't, you know –

there haven't been a lot of disappointments, you know. Some things have been cancelled and some things have been postponed and some things are sort of in limbo right now. And it's sort of just – I'm playing a sort of waiting game right at the moment. But I've gotten together with a lady who's my agent now who I really like a lot, Maggie Preston, and I've been all over town, some good things, I've met some good people, and some good things coming up. So I can't tick off a half a dozen projects, you know, but there are good things coming. And I'm looking forward to a pretty good year this year, I hope. Last year was probably the worst, I guess, for everybody – a series of strikes, and threatened strikes. Things are tough all over, but, you know, I'm in good shape. I think I'll be busy this year, I hope. I'd like to have a few good years, you know, and then go back to New York and completely retrain, is what I'd like to do, because I'm getting old, man, fast. I'm thirty-eight years old, but, you know, that's old for a boxer, but it's like I'm not the same hot shot kid that I was when I started out, you know. I trained hard and worked hard, but, you know, I don't have the same voice or the same face or the same body – or the same brain, you know, and I think I'm coming to the time when I'd just like to retool, you know. I'd like to go back to school. I think there ought to be – I don't know if there is such a thing, but I'd like to find some kind of program for me, whatever it is, after putting in a lot of years. I mean, it's easy if you're starting out and you're young, you know, you can jump into a lot of parades, and you can get – you know, I really believe in training hard and there's lots of opportunities for young men, young actors and whatever. But as you get older there aren't too many things that are geared for – you know, you don't stop growing up, you know what I mean? You're not grown up when you're twenty-one, you know, you keep growing and changing and whatnot. So, yeah, I'd like to put in some more time in Hollywood and then I'd like to go back to New York and get back on the stage. And I'd like to – I'm very hot to direct – stage, never a movie. I wouldn't want to get involved in directing a movie, but I'd like to direct some stage. And I'd like to get married again because I'm in love. So I'm hoping for a few good years, the next couple or three years, you know, till I'm able to make it easy on myself. But now I couldn't afford a ticket to Pomona, right. But I like a movie – you know what I like about *Eraserhead*, or movies in general, being in movies, is that the show can go on and I don't even have to be there. You know what I mean? It's like, if I'm not there, they can start without me. That's great. I think that's neat. I mean, it beats hell out of doing eight a week, you know what I mean? Hell, *Eraserhead* plays in sixty-five cities in France, and a hundred cities across the country on the same night. If that was a stage play, I couldn't keep up a schedule like that, you know. I mean, that would be a rough grind. So that's kind of – that's what I like about the movies, yeah. David Lynch. David Lynch. The only man I've ever known that shaved a mouse. Yeah, yeah, yeah. Quite a character, quite a character. He's made one of the greatest movies I've ever seen in my entire life – *The Elephant Man*. And he really did himself proud, I thought. It's a beautiful film. I was very moved by that, you know, like I haven't been by a movie – I don't take movies seriously really. I think *Elephant Man* – it's beautiful.

KGG: Would you work with him again, if something came up?

JN: I hope so. I hope so, sure. Sure. Yeah, yeah. I would like to work together again. He's terrific to work with.

KGG: Is he very open to contributions from the other people working with him?

JN: Oh sure. Working with Lynch – to me, you know, enthusiasm is a very important element. And Lynch has such enthusiasm for whatever he's doing that it's incredibly infectious. And you find everybody gets caught up in it really – and you find ideas popping all over the place all the time. And we would just knock ourselves out, you know, we would hit on something and start laughing, you know. We were just – it was great, you know. I'd say, "Well, David, this is going to have them bolting for the fire exits. There ought to be a jail sentence for what this will do to them." You know what I mean? We just relished it really. He's great. He's terrific to work with, because of his enthusiasm for whatever he's doing, you know. If it's building one of his sheds or whatever. So yeah, something'll come along, something will come along. I really – well, I don't know – I like working, you know. I work hard. I like a happy set. I usually get along with people and, you know, stay as good natured as I can and have a pleasant time of it. I mean, working can be a pleasant thing and I'm really happy with the Zoetrope people, *Hammett*, and, you know, people have been really great to me on that movie. And I'm working with a lot of people that I've known for a really long time. Fred Roos and then Ron Colby and a lot of those people I've known for a long time. And it's been a pleasant experience. I like a happy set, you know. There's been a lot of problems, you know, that had to be worked out, but there hasn't been the kind of strife or bloodshed or anything like that, you know. I've been on pictures where that's been the case and it's miserable, it's miserable. So I've been, you know, happy with *Hammett*. What can I tell you? I haven't really been in touch lately with anybody else on *Eraserhead*. I don't know – I haven't seen Charlotte for a while, but she was recently married, I think, and they're doing well. I guess she's sort of settled down. Judith Roberts, the beautiful girl across the hall, is back in New York doing well, I think, the last I heard. The little lady in the radiator, Laurel Near, is doing well with, I think it's the Seattle ballet – I think it's Seattle – she's with a very good ballet company now. Fred Elmes I haven't seen in a while – he was one of our cinematographers. I never worry about Fred. He works a lot and he does okay.

KGG: Was there any disruption when they switched cinematographers?

JN: No. Herb Cardwell – David brought Herb out from Philadelphia, I think. I'm not sure if they'd worked together before. And Herb did some remarkable work, you know, designing lights and whatnot – he brought Fred in pretty early in the game, so when Herb had to leave, you know, for other things, Fred had already been doing much of the stuff. And then Fred is really good, he's a talented guy. You know, a lot of his special effects stuff was really – you know, a lot of difficult stuff. Herb Cardwell died a couple of years ago, which was sad. He was a young guy and, you know, a new baby and all of that. That was sad – I guess all the people involved, you know, spending that much time, working that closely – we're all pretty good friends, pretty close – I don't think, you know, we see each other all that much, but – Alan Splet, of course, has been doing well. Johnny Carson has made him a household word. So – it's doing good. *Eraserhead* is doing good. Wim Wenders had been in France doing a picture and just came back recently, and evidently it's really big over there, and it's doing good over there. The Japanese have gone crazy over it, you know. So I'm very pleased, very pleased with *Eraserhead*, yeah. What else can I tell you? I should be able to tell you something, anecdotes – I have three good anecdotes. You've seen *Eraserhead* several times.

KGG: Nine.

JN: Nine times? Well, see, you're a better man than I am.

KGG: Actually, the last time I saw it was after I wrote that essay – and I regretted writing the essay.

JN: Why?

KGG: It destroyed the film for me. All the feeling was gone. I was sitting there with all this – it was about a year between screenings and I wrote the thing in between. It took on and off six months to write the essay, so the whole feeling had been totally intellectualized and lost for me.

JN: Well. Yeah. I guess you can do that, you can do that.

KGG: I'll have to let it rest for a few years then try again.

JN: Yeah, yeah. Well, you know, I don't believe in doing that. That happens. You can cerebralize something to death, you know. I was doing a scene thing for a guy not long ago. It was a class project of his that he asked me to do. And we sat and read through the scene and we sat and talked, and did an enormous amount of scene analysis, and got into all of the psychology involved, and all of the motivation involved. But never got it on its feet, you know. Doing it was disastrous. Acting is a physical art or whatever, you know, you've got to get on your feet. You've got to think, you know, and know what's happening up here, but you can't – there's more to it than that, you know. So have I given you some stuff? I have to –

KGG: You're shooting again today?
JN: No, I'm shooting next week.

Fred Elmes

Fred Elmes, Los Angeles, December 1981. [Photo by the author]

December 10, 1981

Fred Elmes, who has gone on to a major career as a cinematographer, took over shooting *Eraserhead* after the original cameraman, Herb Cardwell, left the production during the first year.

Kenneth George Godwin: How did you get to meet David?

Fred Elmes: How did I meet David? I met David at the American Film Institute. I was there as a fellow, as a new fellow, as a cinematographer, and I really didn't have any films to shoot. There was a problem because there were older cameramen there who were doing all the films, that I didn't have anything, and one of the instructors there --Tony Vellani – who has always, you know, thought very highly of David, put me in touch with David. What had happened was that the cinematographer, Herb Cardwell, who started *Eraserhead* – so Herb Cardwell had started the film and was unable to do any more and David needed someone to, you know, to replace him and I stepped in. And, you know, we talked about this commitment of, you know, a month or two of shooting which of course turned into, you know, several years of shooting. But that's how it all came about. It came about through the American Film Institute because it was a film being done there at the time.

KGG: Did you do any work with Herbert Cardwell?

FE: Yeah, we had a sort of transition period of, you know, several weeks of shooting where I helped out, and then Herb left.

KGG: Was it difficult to continue something that had been going –

FE: Well, it wasn't so difficult, because David has a real clear view of what he wanted. You know, he had no trouble saying, you know, what it should look like. And I had done enough work before that I knew how to get a certain look in, you know, with a black and white film. So it was a matter of carrying on the style that David had established pretty much.

KGG: Is black and white more difficult than colour?

FE: Yeah, I think it is. Yeah, it relies more on lighting. I think in colour you have the advantage of the art direction. You know, the art direction fills in a lot because you have all this colour palette to play with, but in black and white the light is so important and – you know, not that it wasn't art directed because it certainly was as well. But we did tests, you know. We photographed gray walls, painted different shades of gray, to see how, you know, how dark is what gray, or how dark is what kind of makeup or, you know, hairstyle – or this or that. We would shoot, you know, a piece of film and test it, see what we liked and then, you know, kind of go from there.

KGG: There was a lot of experimentation?

FE: It was a lot of feeling our way, yeah, because David had not made this, you know, exactly this kind of film before. You know, we were both in sync as to what it should look like, but, you know, how to do it was a little bit new, you know, especially when it got into some of the effects. And we had a great time. We had made contacts with various key effects people at different studios, and David would come to me and say, "Well now, today, you know, we're going to try to do this and we want it to look like this." You know, "How do we get that?" And I'd say, "Well, gee, you know – I think we could get it by doing such and such." And we'd try it and it would either work or not work. You know, then we'd go to somebody at the studio and say, "Well, you know, here we are making this film for no money, you know, at the American Film Institute, can you help us?" And they would. You know, they would give us little secrets and little tricks on how to do this and how to do that and how to save money doing it. And, you know, we would try these things and that's how the film was made. It was a little trial and error, you know, every step of the way. We knew what we wanted and we stayed with it. It wouldn't have taken four years if we hadn't, you know, stayed with it.

KGG: Were the effects sequences the last you did on it?

FE: Most of the effects were last, yeah, the mechanical and the optical effects.

KGG: How long did it take to do things like the stop-motion, the little worm?

FE: Oh. Well, again, that's the sort of thing that took – I think it probably took a day to shoot it, but it took, you know, another day to build it, you know, and another day to do the test on it. And, I mean, it – everything took longer. I think if we were a major studio, you know, you would build it in the morning, shoot a test in the afternoon, and photograph it the next day. With us everything took a bit longer because, you know, we didn't have the money to just go out and do it. I mean, we had to work – we would rent special cameras to do pin-registered effects and things like that. And, you know, we had to rent it over the weekend because you could get two days for the price of one, you know, and that was the only way these things were feasible. We would build lots of things, you know, for weeks and then, you know, shoot it in two or three days because that's the period of time we could afford to rent the camera for.

KGG: What kind of set ups were there for – like the thing where you're tracking along the surface of the planet?

FE: We did effects in every imaginable situation. Some of the miniatures, most of the miniatures, I guess, were done actually in my living room. I had – David and I had, were given an animation stand for a little while by, you know, someone who helped us, helped the production. And I had this – it was a horizontal job, it was twelve feet long and I had it set up in my living room. And we just – what we would do is, with like that surface of the planet, we would just build the effect, bring it into the living room, you know, mount a Mitchell camera – I think in that case it was sideways, it was actually shot sideways, you know, trucking along this thing. And then I think that shot actually took us about two hours to do because it was stop-framed. It was actually stop-framed. That's another thing. We did tests. We did tests to do it another way – you know, we tried it in real time and we tried it in slow motion, and it didn't work, you know, it just wasn't what we were looking for, so we ended up doing it stop-frame, which fortunately we could do on this animation stand because it was rigged to time out things. But, you know, we didn't know till we tried. And it all worked that way. You know, we just took it as we went along very much. But a lot of those miniatures were done in my living room. Some of them were done at David's house. Some of them were done at the American Film Institute.

KGG: Did you shoot the scene on the stage with the decapitation?

FE: Yeah, yeah.

KGG: Was that a difficult set up? or was it fairly simple?

FE: Well, no, it was actually – it was difficult because we didn't have – we didn't quite have all the right tools. David had built this – that's actually one of the earlier sets made, was this round stage platform. And it was built, you know, in an area at the AFI, and it just sat there for months and months and months until we could finally get around to shooting that scene. But we knew where everything was. We knew where all the black curtains were, you know, and we'd sort of made plans about how we would hang lights. But the problem was there was nothing up there to hang lights on - it was an exterior. So we had to build, you know, a scaffold. We took a big extension ladder, you know, that we borrowed from the AFI and, you know, suspended it in the area over the stage and started hanging lights on it - knowing that the only time we could shoot it would be at night. You know, after sunset and before sunrise was the only time, you know, that we could actually do it.

KGG: This was outside?

FE: This was outside. So we had a situation, which we actually had several other times on the film, where the only place we could build something was out of doors, you know, therefore it had to be shot at night, you know, on that night schedule. And we had to call it quits, you know, at dawn. That was it. In fact, some of the times, you know, we had to stop - I mean, there was too much light, you know, from the sky to make the shot that we'd rehearsed. And it ended up that the first - the first shot in the film is the long trucking shot in, you know, on this planet, and it's a massive set up. I mean, for our means at the time, it was like a thirty foot dolly on an Elemack with a crane arm and a Mitchell camera going, you know, high speed and a model that had to move and coordinate and the light - and this big black curtain, you know, twenty - it was like twenty feet high, sixty feet wide with stars in it. This was the sort of thing that we couldn't - we needed a tremendous area to shoot it. We only had the weekend to do it because the only area available was in the gardeners' set up down at the stables at the AFI, and they wouldn't allow us in there during the day. You know, there was no way we could interrupt their schedule, so, you know, Friday at four when they left, we moved in and we hung the curtain and we put the dolly track up and, you know, started lighting it. And it took us the whole weekend to do, so that Monday morning at like three, we actually shot it, because it took all the time before that just to get it in place to do. And that happened, you know, time and time again. The only time we had to do it was over a weekend, and we had to work very quickly and then, you know, grab the shot, then clean up real fast so we disappeared by the time they came in at seven in the morning.

KGG: So a lot of the effects are purely physical then?

FE: Most of the effects in the film are, yeah, are all done in the camera. I mean, they're all real effects that were done at the time of principal photography. We thought about doing it, yeah, we thought about doing opticals and we decided that for the most part it was too expensive. I mean, it was really out of our ballpark money-wise, and also the quality that we got, you know, we found that we got when we did, you know, it real was better for us. I mean it was better to have those stars there, you know, at the time of the photography. You know, it was better to go out of our way to try to make a mechanical effect work rather than do it an optical later. Because the opticals – we lost control of the – you just never have as much control when you have to send it into the lab and work with them. I mean, not that they can't do a good job. It's just that it's one more thing that's taken out of your hands, whereas if you can take a little longer, you know, where you're shooting it, it's usually better. We found that, you know, what we lacked in monetary resource, we had in time. Because we could just take longer for the most part. We could take the time to build something right, you know, and we could shoot a test, and if it didn't look right we'd go back to the drawing board and build it again. You know, and that worked in our favour because we, you know, we just did things the right way. So I think that in the end it really worked for us.

KGG: It took so many years to make – were you involved in other things while that was going on?

FE: Yeah, yeah, I was. I had several other films that I shot, you know, during the time. For one, I was a fellow at the American Film Institute and I had, you know, several projects to do there. And I had some other commercial films. I was offered a film by John Cassavetes, so I shot a film called *Killing of a Chinese Bookie* during *Eraserhead*, during a little hiatus that we had, you know, I shot that. And Catherine Coulson, who was the camera assistant, came with me on the Cassavetes film. But I had to support myself in the meanwhile, you know. Unfortunately David could – I really admire David though. He had enough money to pay us, you know, for a long time, and he really wouldn't – he said he couldn't shoot without paying people. It just made him feel real bad. You know, we had a real comfortable situation at the AFI because we had a facility and the space to do it, and we had enough equipment from them and we had enough money in the budget to provide food. He provided meals and he provided, you know, kind of a stipend salary for everyone, which he felt was the only way to do it. And when the AFI finally could no longer finance the film, we stopped. I mean, we really, literally shut down for a year because the AFI couldn't do it and David had no other source of money to fund the film. And when we started to shoot again, it was with the help of the AFI, it was with the help of some cameras and things, but not with the money. And David, you know, felt real badly that he had to ask us to work for nothing. And, you know, we agreed because we wanted to see it done, you know. Obviously no one was in it for the money. You know, we'd worked for a couple of years already for relatively nothing – the last year or two, you know, would be easy.

KGG: Did you have any trouble starting up again after that long break?

FE: No, we didn't. We didn't because we talked about it a lot. It was like David and I were always in contact the whole time. You know, we didn't know quite how it was going to be possible, you know – if we could get the right camera, you know, if we could get all the lights we needed, if we could get the space, you see, if AFI needed us to move. You know, I mean there were lots of "ifs", but, you know, we talked about it all the time, so it was just kind of assumed that it would be finished. One way or the other the film was going to get finished. So, you know, one day we just started shooting again, and were able to do it. With all the same people. I mean, you know, everyone – all the regulars, you know, were available basically.

KGG: How did it look in rushes? because so much of the effect comes with the sound. So how could you tell when things were right before the sound was added?

FE: Yeah, I know what you're saying.

KGG: Did you ever see rushes and have to scrap it all and go back and do it again?

FE: Yeah, occasionally. Occasionally we did. David has a very specific feel for what he wants and he pretty much knew if something was working or not working. Sometimes it was hard to tell when we were shooting it, but always on film we could tell whether, you know, whether an effect or a scene or a mood was right. So occasionally, you know, we did shoot things and then see them the next day and then shoot it again that night a little bit different. Just because the mood wasn't right or because, you know, either for the acting or for the technical effect part. He really had a pretty clear view of what was necessary. I think that's a real tribute to, you know, to know what you want going into it so clearly that you can make those decisions, you know, as you go.

KGG: You sort of get that feeling just watching the films – no matter how weird they get, they're still clearly done. Even *The Grandmother*, which is more bizarre –

FE: Yes, it is. It is. I never forget when I – when David and I first met, we met one afternoon and there were, gee, I think there were like five people working on the film at that point – six people. And I went, you know, David came up and sort of – very typical warm handshake, you know – "Hi. How are you?" – and we chatted for a couple of minutes, then he took me in to see dailies. And they had selected a couple of reels of film that had already been shot to give me a feel of what was happening and to see if, you know, to see if I wanted to be involved as well as, you know, if they wanted to be involved with me. And they started with the real tame stuff – and, you know, it was Henry in his room, where Henry lives, and walking outside and so on. And then we got to the baby, which they saved for the end and, god, I didn't know what to make of it. I just didn't know what I was getting involved in. It was real strange. Because I was sitting in the darkened theatre with these six people who I didn't know, you know, I mean it was an intimidating situation – and then see some of these real powerful images on the screen, you know, without sound makes no difference, you know. It's just bizarre, but it's captivating at the same time. I mean something in it appealed to a sense of – I don't know – a sense of wonder in me, is what got me hooked. I really was hooked, you know, right from the beginning, you know, before I went down to the set, you know, before I helped shoot anything. You know, just talking to David, and meeting the people involved, and seeing what he'd done so far was enough to, you know, kind of get me going. And that was it, you know, I was in. And it worked. I mean, you know, three or four years.

KGG: What sort of work had you done before that? before you went to the AFI?

FE: I went to – I've always enjoyed photography, and I started taking pictures in high school – still pictures. I went to the Rochester Institute of Technology and – I went to RIT and studied mainly still photography and then got interested in films. RIT is a school in Rochester, New York. I'm from New Jersey actually. So Rochester wasn't too big a move. Then I went to NYU, to graduate film school, and studied there, and that was – that's what confirmed that I really wanted to go into films and that I wanted to shoot films. And I had a teacher there who was a cinematographer. I worked as a – I mean through a stroke of luck I became his teaching assistant on my first day of classes. He said, "You went to Rochester. You know about Kodak. You will be my teaching assistant." He was a big Czechoslovakian cameraman, Beda Batka – he's a wonderful man. And I learned so much from him. You know, I learned firsthand about, you know, shooting feature films because the guy had shot thirty feature films in Czechoslovakia. And even though he hadn't made any in this country yet, you know, he was going to and he was talented. So I got a good start at NYU and, you know, was a student there, shot things on the side, you know – mostly documentary things, a little bit of dramatic things, a little bit as a camera assistant occasionally. And stayed in New York for a couple of years afterward. And then decided that California was the place I should probably go. And having never been here, you know, drove out one summer to look around, you know, and thought the AFI would be a good excuse to come to California to be a student again and not – chuck the responsibilities and live in a safe environment. So that's how I got into AFI. I mean, I just applied and they liked me and it seemed like a good idea at the time. And it was. It was a great introduction to California. It was a real good way to come here and, you know, kind of learn the ropes of the film business. Because I had, you know, at AFI, I had to work to support myself. You know, I mean I did everything from, you know, xeroxing at the American Film Institute to being a projectionist to, you know, shooting films. And, you know, in fact last year they called me back to shoot a promo for them – Charlton Heston saying, you know, "We're moving to a new campus. We need your dollars." You know, "Send us money." Which was a kick. It was fun. It was fun to go back. It was fun to be there. That's kind of how I got there.

KGG: Do you have any preference between black and white and colour? David is extremely strong about black and white.

FE: Yeah, David is. I learned a lot from David. Because I had done black and white films as student films, and always kind of looked down on it because I think we shot in black and white because we couldn't afford colour mostly. That's the way I looked at it. And I think with David I learned to really appreciate all the possibilities, you know, of black and white. Now, I've gone on and have shot some other things in black and white that I'm real happy with, that have been dramatic films, sort of dramatic films. So, I don't know. I think that you really have to go by what the story calls for. And black and white, you know, was right for *Eraserhead*. I don't know that black and white's right for everything. I think that what's – I don't know, I think you really have to decide, you know, by the story. That's the most important thing.

KGG: Do you have any interest in doing anything other than being a cinematographer? to direct or –

FE: I – no, actually directing doesn't appeal to me quite that much. I really get a kick out of shooting films. I really get a kick out of creating images and creating moods and telling a story, you know, visually, telling a story through, you know, using the tools, the things that I've learned. I think that producing appeals to me because I've done a little bit of that. I've produced some short films and I've produced some short plays, and I would consider that, you know, a creative thing, and that I would like to go into or at least have as something that I do sometimes, more than directing. Rather producing, I think.

KGG: Did you have any problems on *Eraserhead* with the quality? I mean, did you ever find that something that had worked well had gone bad in the lab?

FE: Well, you mean things out of our control?

KGG: Scratches, or problems with the developing.

FE: We had – I think we had all – we sort of suffered all the typical problems that any production goes through. The added burden of black and white caused us some trouble in that when we were shooting the principal part of it, fortunately it was at a time when – I think it was Peter Bogdanovich was shooting a black and white film in Los Angeles, so the lab – CFI was the lab – was processing black and white every day, and they had pretty tight controls on things. After, you know, that black and white film was shut down, there was less need to do, you know, to do black and white work in town because everything really was in colour, so we started to have little problems. They switched over to developing black and white twice a week which means that the machines weren't always run and they weren't always, you know, in great shape. So we suffered, you know, little problems because of that. It was really a matter of staying in contact with them, and communicating, and saying, "Look, you know, I don't care if you only develop it twice a week. It better be good on those days." You know, it's a matter of letting them know that you know what you're doing. That, you know, that they're not going to, you know, to pull anything on you. Because I think they try, they try to do that. They try to get by with as little as possible. And unless you call them on it, and establish that from the beginning, you know, you're off to a bad start. So we did. We stayed close with them, you know, and we developed good relationships with a couple people, you know, who became our key liaisons at the lab. And for the most part, you know, we did pretty well, I think. We suffered, you know, problems with cameras – that big shot, that opening shot where we dolly in on the planet, you know, that we set up over the weekend, the first time we shot it and viewed the dailies, you know, the next afternoon, we found out that the camera was bad, and that we had a very strange flickering, due to something wrong with the high speed camera. And we had to re-shoot it. So it meant, you know, after having torn it all down, it meant taking it all out and putting it back up again on the next weekend, you know. And going to the camera house and saying, "Look, there's something wrong with the camera. We need it again, you know, we need a good one." You know, regardless of the money we spent already, trying to do this. So we had problems with that. You know, all those little problems we suffered, I'm afraid. And at the time they were really earth-shattering because we didn't always have the money to re-shoot something, you know, and we hadn't had the years of experience to know exactly what it was that went wrong. So it was sort of a trial and error to find out what was the problem, and then to solve it before we re-shot. So it was a little more trying then than I think it would be now. We never expected it – well, we thought it was a real long shot is what it amounted to, and we worked on it because we wanted the film to get done, we wanted it to be done right, and we knew – you know, we respected David and knew that he was going to do it right. I mean, if it was going to be done at all, it was going to be done the right way. And, you know, I for one really appreciated that. But I never thought that it would find a wide audience. Well, I guess it hasn't found a wide audience. But it certainly has become something of a classic at least. It was shown – it was a funny thing. We showed it at the AFI, the premiere performance at the American Film Institute, which was mostly cast and crew and friends and, boy, the theatre was so quiet after the screening, it was a little bit spooky, you know, and no one knew quite what to say, you know. It was really completely different. I mean, no one had seen it first of all, except for the couple of close people, nobody had seen the whole movie together. And it was, you know, sort of different than I think anyone had imagined it to be. It was really a shock. And it is - it does take your breath away at the end, you know, and it's hard to know how to respond to it. Which I think depressed David a bit, because he was kind of expecting, you know, some responses. He didn't get much right at the beginning and then it was accepted at Filmex, which was really the first break. I mean, that was the thing that made, that, you know, made it possible for the film to start to have an audience, because through Filmex a distributor saw it and liked it. And Filmex is a good calling card when it comes to promoting the film. So -

KGG: Did you ever, while you were making it, think what it was about?

FE: Yeah, I wondered. I wondered what it was about. It wasn't until pretty near the end of shooting that David came out and told us what some of the imagery was and told us, you know, specifically where things came from. Which made it of course all that much more personal for us because, you know, we sort of knew these little secrets involved in the film. But it was - see, there was no shooting script per se in the traditional filmic sense. David had it all - I mean, he had it all in his head and he could tell you what happened in any scene, he knew what dialogue was, and he knew - I mean, he could draw you a picture of any scene. You know, that was all very very clear to him and he had no trouble communicating it, but what didn't happen too often was, you know, to have it laid out in front of us. You know, we kind of took it a step at a time, and let the whole - let the process, you know, be part of the evolution of the actual film. It was a real growing process. I think it was, you know, it was for me and I think it was for David too, to go through that, you know, kind of artistic unfolding of an idea over a period of time like that. Because it's something that David, you know, lived with, you know, for that many years. I mean, I went home and I did other jobs. And I, you know, supported myself, you know, shooting films but David, you know, kind of lived, ate, and drank this film and kind of, you know, supported himself by delivering the *Wall Street Journal*, you know, sometimes, or doing this or that.

KGG: Did you ever wonder what the things did mean? or could you work over that period of time and just accept the physical elements that you were shooting?

FE: I wondered. I wondered what it meant and I would talk to David about it and he would give me little clues as to what it meant, or how this related to that. And he gave me just enough to go – he gave me enough to keep me involved, and to keep me hooked with it. You know, it was fascinating work and I felt confident that David was a talented person, that this would all, you know, not be for nought and, you know, the film would disappear after we'd shot it. I really felt confident that it would be completed in one way or the other. And it – you know, and David just had an ability to keep us involved, just kept us, you know, just kept us going on.

KGG: How do you feel about the film now, all these years later?

FE: Well, I like the film. I like the film a lot. I really think that it's a brilliant work and the imagery that he's created, not just in a visual sense but in a, you know, sort of an encompassing mood, is a really unique quality, and I don't see that in a lot of films. And I think that David's outlook on life and society is, you know, is also buried in there somewhere and I like that. I mean, I like the way he thinks about that, so it appeals to me. But I'm kind of prejudiced, so you shouldn't be asking me.

KGG: Do you think you'll work together again some time?

FE: I think we will. I think we will. It's hard to say when. You know, it was much easier for me to get the job on *Eraserhead* than it would be for me to get a job with him now. Just because of the other forces involved in the films that he's making, both financial and, you know, all the way down the line. There's many other people involved so the decision isn't always explicitly in his hands. But he's expressed an interest in working with me and, you know, we're talking about films now, talking about *Dune* now. So I hope that it'll be possible. I know somewhere down the line it will be. I would like it to be on this one.

KGG: The project interests you?

FE: Yeah. Yeah, *Dune* interests me a lot. I like science fiction and it's a story that's always fascinated me – and being real intrigued by trying to create a different world like that and, you know, think about how you would approach that visually and how you would, you know, create a world where the sky was black and the horizon was yellow and how, you know, they have different kinds of lights and they have different kinds of situations on this desert planet. So it's fascinating. It's always fascinated me. And I hope it's possible. It remains to be seen.

KGG: It could wind up taking longer to make than *Eraserhead*. Had you ever worked with any of the other people in *Eraserhead* at all before doing the film?

FE: No. No, I never met anyone on the cast or crew before – it was a real, completely new experience.

KGG: Have you done anything with any of them since?

FE: Most of them, yes. Actually, I've worked with almost everybody, you know, on various projects again. It's been – they've really been friendships that have lasted, you know, all the way down the line. The woman who was the camera assistant on *Eraserhead*, Catherine Coulson, is someone who I work with, you know, fairly often now as an assistant. And since we've, you know, both gotten into the union we've been able to work, you know, work together again on union films. So it really is on-going, it's a real treat, you know, to have that. Because it doesn't always happen. I mean, that's one of the things that was special about *Eraserhead*, is that it was a special group of people who were all interested in seeing the film made. You know, it wasn't a job for anyone. You know, it was a real labour of love and we all wanted to be there. Which is real different than most films today, unfortunately. And I mean that's not always possible, that, you know, the man who builds the set or pulls the cable can love to see the film made, but still there has to be some happy medium for me at least. I would feel better about that.

KGG: It's certainly made my interviewing a lot easier – everybody seems happy to talk about it.

FE: Yeah, yeah.

KGG: Are you working on anything right now?

FE: Right now, I work – I've been working as a camera operator on *Star Trek II - Star Trek: The Motion Picture*.

KGG: I didn't know they were actually filming that –

FE: Yeah, it started a couple of weeks ago and it was fun. It's sort of on-going and I don't do it every day.

KGG: Who's doing it?

FE: It's being done by Paramount Studios, and it's being done, you know, by the same people who made the TV show.

KGG: Who's directing?

FE: I don't remember his name. It's a fellow who has been a writer for years and wrote *The Seven-Percent Solution*.

KGG: Nicholas Meyer.

FE: Nicholas Meyer. A wonderful fellow. I just fell in love with him when I met him. He's just wonderful, wonderful sense of humour. A great guy to be with, to be around. It makes it real easy. And it was a real treat to be, you know, on the bridge of the *Enterprise*, you know, and see all those familiar faces from the TV show, you know. It was like a real deja vu to see – everybody's back. It's great.

KGG: Are you interested in getting into more effects type photography, or do you prefer the soundstage?

FE: Well, I'll tell you. I really like effects a lot, and I find it intriguing. But what I find best about it is that you can make magic, you can make something happen – you can make almost anything happen, you know, in movies. You can, you know, pull strings and do this and do that. And it's not so important to me to know how to do it, it's just important to know that it can be done, and if you can use this or that or the other special effect to make something more convincing, you know, to make a character more convincing, or to make a story point then, you know, I think anything's fair, you should just go for it and use it. I really hate to see effects used for the sake of effects. You know, that bothers me a lot and I'd, you know, sort of rather steer clear of that. So I have, you know, since spent some time with special effects and kind of gotten good with certain things and know, you know, what's involved in photographing them and how the opticals work and how the laboratory treats it and feel pretty comfortable with, you know, knowledge on one level at least. I have a grasp of what's possible. But as far as, you know, as far as learning it further and, you know, working for an effects house or working sort of – specializing, I'd rather not. I'd really rather, you know, be someone who photographs the film in the best way possible, you know, what's right for the story and, you know, use my creative talent as sort of a way to interpret the story, but not get hung up on, you know, an effect or, you know, a particular way of doing something. And I think that's important, I think that's really important. I think that's a quality that David has too. I think that he – I mean, *Eraserhead* required certain things, it required certain kinds of moods being created to, you know, to convey a thought, and we found a way to do it that was best for that film. But, I mean, *Elephant Man* was a film that he treated differently. I mean, it's really, you know, rather straightforward and traditional in its approach, and it isn't tricky, except there's a couple of dreams in it. But it's not – I don't think it calls on the photography the same way *Eraserhead* did. So I think that David sort of has the ability to differentiate, you know, and use what's necessary for the story. And I think *Dune* will be the same way. I mean, from the little we've talked about the story and how he feels about approaching it, you know, I think that he'll really – he'll bring, you know, his stamp to it, it'll definitely be a Lynch film by design. I mean, even bigger than by direction, but by entire design it will be David's film. But it will still be the story that Frank Herbert wrote, you know, it's still *Dune*. And I think that's a really unique quality. It's so easy to get hung up on one way of doing things, to sort of find a formula that works for you and stamp them out. You know, find something that's popular and do a whole bunch of them and make your mark that way without any regard for what it is you're doing, you know, what it is you're photographing or what is your – what story, you know, what the guy in the story is doing. You know, I think that it's real important to differentiate. It's a real rare quality to be able to differentiate between this story and that story, and this one requires an approach that's different than that one. And then be able to, you know, to do them differently. But I would hope that I could bring that to, you know, films in the future. I mean, I think certainly working with John Cassavetes was real different than working with David Lynch. I mean, David is someone who's very controlled and very concise and has, you know, minutely specific ideas about the way something should look or something should be, you know, down to the "t". And with John Cassavetes, it's a little bit the opposite. I mean, it's a little bit the exact reverse, though the ends are the same. I mean, you know, John makes films that he – he makes the films that he's good at making. I mean, he makes films that are moving – and certainly, you know, they move me a lot – but he does it in such a different way than David. It's amazing. I know – it's funny, in *Eraserhead*, I had one of the first days that I was there on the set and, you know, on the job, and the crew had been, you know, working on this set for a couple, you know, a month or two before me, and kind of knew – there were sort of ground rules. I mean, everybody knew where everything was and what everything was and how David worked. And I was the new kid and I didn't know how David worked or what – kind of what to do or what not to do. So I kind of went into it the way I normally would when I photograph things, which is to sort of in a very quiet way take charge of what needs to be done. And to do it, you know, do it myself. And in the case of *Eraserhead*, you know, really do it myself because there was nobody else to say, you know, to tell to do it. So I remember on the – we were doing some closeup or something, the baby I guess it was, and I went and, you know, David had looked through the camera and lined it up and this was, you know, it was all ready to go, and we'd adjusted the lights and I went over to the table and I moved this little prop over so that it was not hidden so much by something else. And Catherine, who was the assistant, turned to me and said, "Fred, we don't move things on that table." And I said, "Well, look, you know, it's just that it was blocked and I wanted to see it more clearly." And she said, "Well, David has never moved anything on the table." "Oh, well I'd better go and put it back then." Heaven forbid David should see I was meddling. It certainly wasn't my intention. But it was real funny being thrust into that world, and kind of sink or swim. And we did – it was one of those situations where David was on a night schedule because of – well, partly because a lot of it had to be shot at night and partly because he enjoyed working at night better. But I would, you know, be up at AFI all day, you know, working or doing things around the classes or working on other films, and then at five-thirty we'd watch dailies from the night before and then go down and start shooting, and shoot until three or four in the morning, you know. Sometimes later. And then I'd get up, you know, at eight or nine and go to AFI or go to whatever other job I had. And everyone did this. I mean, everyone had at least one other job, you know, during the majority of the time we were shooting. And we just, you know, we just maintained, I mean, we just – just became a way of life. I used to live out in Topanga at the time and I got – sort of put the car on automatic pilot going back, you know, because there was no way I could manouevre the hill by myself. It was a great time. I really – I look back on it real fondly. It was a lot of work, you know, we really did work hard. I mean, I look back at diaries that I kept, you know, over the years and I really – I don't know when I slept sometimes. I mean, I used to work on something during the day and work on *Eraserhead* all night, then, you know, meet my friends and go horseback riding at seven on Saturday morning, you know, and I don't know quite how I did that. But it was a real good time, you know, and it was real fulfilling in a certain sense to be working, to be that immersed in a film project, because I came to California to get involved in films and I had looked at the AFI as sort of the answer to kind of fulfill the dreams instantly. And it wasn't working out at first. I mean, there was nothing for me to do there. It wasn't quite what I had hoped it would be. And then *Eraserhead* came along and kind of filled in a gap where I could – you know, I mean, I was shooting a film and I – I didn't know kind of what film it was for a long time, and I didn't know if anyone would ever see it. And I didn't know – there were a lot of unknowns, but I was involved. I mean, I was really involved in it and I, you know, I had responsibilities and I learned a lot about the laboratory and I learned about new equipment and, you know, we explored new things together, which was real fulfilling. You know, and then I – in an artistic sense, I was creating something. Which for me is real important, you know, to have happen. It's important to be, you know, working on something. And because of the sustained nature of the project, it was, I mean, it was something that David and I could just talk about for years. You know, we used to live, you know, a block from each other, so we would, you know, go over and have coffee wherever in the afternoon, and even in the time when we weren't shooting, we were planning. I mean, you know, we would have so many napkins and place mats that have, you know, block diagrams and little storyboards written on them as to how, how we were going to do effects and what we would have to build in order to do the effect, you know, and where we were going to get all this equipment from for free, you know, and how long it was going to take. I mean, we really had that planned out and gone over so many times.

KGG: I guess you've never worked on anything quite that way, besides *Eraserhead*.

FE: Not – no, nothing like that. Well, partly obviously because of the length of time involved in the production. Partly because of the nature of the project. It was, you know, it called for so many special things that – and every one had to be thought out somewhat. You know, every setup required a certain – a certain new thing. Every effect or every scene required, you know, pre-thinking it. And partly because David's so meticulous. I mean, David really, you know, requires that. He sort of – you really have to know what you're going to do in a situation because he does. I mean, he's sort of done the homework ahead of time and he knows what he wants and looks to me, as the cinematographer, to, you know, to be able to provide, you know, a certain, you know, feeling. Which is real challenging. I mean, it was great. It was real wonderful to be involved – and to be involved with someone who was so – I don't know, so undemanding. I mean, in a personal sense, you know. I mean, the work was demanding and we certainly, you know, worked long and hard, but there was no ego involved. And all these things that are the trappings that I find in a lot of, you know, commercial Hollywood productions were completely missing from, you know, from that whole film. I mean, it was real nice to be in that situation.

KGG: Can you think of any more anecdotes about the shooting?

FE: No. I can't think of anything right now. Let's see. We had some – actually, there were so many funny things. All these things are funny in retrospect because at the time they were – they were horrible. I mean, they were horrendous problems. Some of the production problems where we had – something we were shooting outdoors – oh, I know. We were shooting the stage, the Lady in the Radiator and the stage. We had – we had the oddest schedule because I would – I would be working all day, Catherine would be working all day, and David would be sleeping all day. And then we'd kind of converge at five-thirty or six o'clock on the set and start, you know, to shoot as soon as it was dark, so I'd be lighting then we'd start to shoot. But the problem was that the woman had to wear makeup. I mean, it was quite a makeup job, quite an event. And it took a couple of hours to get her set. So we'd, you know, we'd really rush to get into it, and get lit, and start shooting it as soon as it got dark. But then David was on this schedule where he had to deliver the *Wall Street Journal* and it was a night job. I mean, it was a job that – I don't know what time other people did it, but I know that – it seems to me David would leave around twelve-thirty or so, you know, in the morning, for a couple of hours. You know, and then we'd – sort of like, it was time to take a break, you know, we ate and, you know, kind of held the fort or changed lighting for a new setup, while David went out, picked up the papers, folded them and threw the whole paper route, and then came back around three-thirty and we would get a few more shots in before dawn. And this went on for a few days; I don't know quite how we did it when I look back on it. I know occasionally the *Wall Street Journal* didn't get delivered. Once in a while there were some complaints. But the movie got done.

KGG: Who did things – do you know who did things like Henry's rubber head and so on?

FE: Oh, these were all – David built everything. David built everything, you know, right from the beginning. And he had – I still don't know quite how he learned about all these things. I mean, some of it came out of the former films and some of it came out of his kind of inquisitiveness and, you know, want to tinker and learn about building things, because that always intrigued him. But David built it all and it was all – most of the props were built before we actually started shooting, the baby and the – you know, I mean, all the properties and things, you know, were built early on. I don't know if David wants – did David talk to you about building the baby?

KGG: No. He doesn't want to talk about it.

FE: That's something that we really shouldn't talk about at all. But, you know, David built everything and, in fact, the sets as well because the whole film was done on sets. There's I think one practical location that's in the film for, you know, a minute. And the rest of it's –

KGG: The oil refinery thing?

FE: The oil refinery was, yeah, was a section of town not far from the AFI where, you know, that he found that we – he changed around a little bit, but basically it was – there are those couple of exterior locations, most of which don't exist now any more. Unfortunately, the refinery, that little – it was like a holding area, is what it was – there was a pump there and some tanks and stuff, and it was defunct for years, and then it was finally, they took it down and put a new building up. And a couple of the scenes downtown that we, you know, we searched and, you know, found these areas that looked like nowhere in the world. You know, these industrial zones are pretty much gone now unfortunately.

KGG: Was the outside of the X's house, was – I mean, that was a set?

FE: No, that was a set. Yeah, we built that. That was another one of those things that we built starting at five o'clock on Friday – we started hauling in dirt. It was the craziest we'd ever tried, but we, I mean, hauled in dirt, you know, planted plants, built a sidewalk, built the facade of the house – I mean, the front, you know, the window, all pieces of sets, you know, tacked them up down at the stables where we were working. You know, and that was kind of all Friday night. Then all Saturday night we lit it and then Sunday morning we shot it and took it down again before the gardeners came in at seven o'clock in the morning. I can't believe we did that. I still don't believe we did that. Time and time again, we did these crazy things.

KGG: It certainly paid off anyway.

FE: Yeah, I think – I think it was worth it. I think it was worth it. I mean, we certainly developed strong friendship binds, you know, ties.

KGG: I guess you'd have to, working in a situation like that.

FE: And we're all, you know, we're all still close now, which is good. And, you know, we have a movie. I mean, a movie came out of all that. It was really a surprise when David told us, though, that, you know, that he had a distributor. The distributor, after seeing it at Filmex was really interested in showing the film and he was going to sign a contract with him. I mean, it was such a sort of dream come true, because none of us had ever imagined that, you know, that there would be an audience out there for it. I mean, not looking at it selfishly at all, just for David it was such, it was so nice to see him happy that it was all for some good, that people were, you know, actually going to see the film.

KGG: Were you surprised when it did get an audience?

FE: Oh, yeah, yeah. Absolutely amazed, completely amazed. It was just, you know, we used to, you know, buy New York papers and find reviews for it, I mean, you know, we would go out and search for reviews and things, and see how people liked it and what the responses were. And we'd get reports from, you know, the distributor: well, it just opened in Cleveland, you know, it just opened here and it just opened there. It was just great. I mean, it was really wonderful to hear this for a film that, you know, as much as we wanted to see it done, we never felt would muster any wide audience. It was great. And we certainly never – I never imagined that there'd be any financial return. I mean, I certainly wasn't in it for the money that I was being paid at the time. It was really maintenance money and most of it was free anyway. And then the last thing that David did when, you know, we started shooting again was, because he couldn't pay us, he, you know, had offered us a percentage of the profit of the film – if and when it should ever make money. And, you know, for so many years it was just words on a piece of paper that, you know, we did and we accepted because we knew David felt strongly that he wanted to repay us, he wanted us to be reimbursed somewhat for our effort. But, you know, we were all certain that it was not possible for the film to make any substantial amount of money. So it is a surprise and a welcome one, a welcome surprise that, you know, there's some money coming back in for it, to be profit participants in it. It's nice.

KGG: We were talking about effects – when the planet explodes, how was that handled? did you shoot that?

FE: We, yeah – that's actually a real good one. We – this is another one of those effects that we didn't know quite how we were going to do it. And, I know David – I mean, David knew, felt confident it could be done. And when he built that model of the planet, he had built the nose section without any structure behind it, so that it could pop out. Because he had planned – I mean, it was planned right from the beginning that, you know, that was going to happen and we were going to move through and in, into the blackness. And, you know, he had painted a white rim around it so that it would read right once it was broken away and it was all scored and, you know, we had to be very careful not to bump it 'cause it would fall apart. But when it came time to shoot it, we still really hadn't come up with a plan of how to pop it open because, you know, we couldn't use – I mean, explosives were kind of out of the question 'cause there was smoke and fire involved and that was not the effect at all. It just had to be this breaking up explosion. And we knew what it wanted to look like but not how to get it. So we – Jack Nance, who was the actor in the film, was somebody who, being around the whole time, helped build sets and helped, you know, helped with whatever needed to be done, you know, when he wasn't in the scene. So, he and David came up with a plan to build a catapult. And they were going to take these lead weights and put them on a catapult, underneath the planet model, and on cue we were going to release it and these lead weights were going to spring out and explode. I mean, that was going to be the device to explode it. I said, "David, look –" you know, "I'm sitting there with the camera ten feet in front of this – do you want me to just stand there?" David said, "No. Well maybe we'd better build you something." So we built this enormously elaborate shield where, you know, it was four by eight foot plywood boards with holes cut in them with plexiglass on them, because it was a special – it was the only three camera shot in the film. We had three cameras because we knew it could be done once, and we were going to get this shot no matter what happened. So, you know, we set up the cameras and they were high speed and they were running at different speeds so we could, you know, choose which one we wanted. And we had this special – you know, we had it lit in this special way so that we'd see all the pieces fly out and then they'd be all backlit and stuff. And the problem was that the catapult rig hadn't really panned out. We talked about it a lot and we tried a little test shot and it just – I mean, the lead weights went about two feet and that was it, you know. And no one knew quite why they only went two feet, but the fact was it wasn't going to happen. So, this was one of those situations where we'd shot, you know, a whole bunch of other stuff during the night and it was like five-thirty in the morning and the sun was coming up. And we had, you know, we had to get this thing to break apart, right, so we could shoot it because the gardeners were coming in a couple of hours and all this had to disappear. We had to be gone. So I – I don't actually remember what happened. I only know that David, in a frenzy after finding the catapult wouldn't work, you know, sort of threw the thing halfway across the driveway and picked up the weights and did it himself basically. So that shot is done, you know, with David under the planet, throwing the weights up through the nose and out at the camera.

KGG: How come you don't– I don't recall, I mean –

FE: Oh no, you didn't see it. You didn't see any weights. I mean, it was – that was one of the miracles of it, the trajectory was such that you weren't going to see those. All you were going to see was pieces. I mean, it was one of those things that worked out and, fortunately it did, because it would have been very very difficult to shoot that again.

KGG: It was made out of clay, was it?

FE: Plaster. Well, no it was actually, it was actually fibreglass. It was fibreglass. It was – I'm pretty sure it was fibreglass. But David is wonderful with all those materials, with rubbers and fibreglass and plastic and plaster. You know, he has a wonderful technique for working with them. There were so many stories like that where, you know, we had to get – where we started building canopies over things to keep the daylight out so that we could get one more last shot in before, you know, it was too light to shoot. You know, and I still look at shots in the film and I think, "My god, that shot looks a little different," and then I remember that actually there was – there was skylight, you know, everything was very subtly filled from the top by the skylight, you know, because it was like the last shot of the morning before we had to wrap it up. I don't think anyone else would notice, but all of a sudden this comes back to me.

KGG: In the opening of the film, when the Man in the Planet starts pulling levers there, how was the shot done with the thing which sort of comes out of Henry's mouth? I mean, it's obviously a composite, but –

FE: Yeah, that's a super. That's – I know – it's a little hard for me. I'm not sure exactly what David wants to reveal. I feel a little –

KGG: The shot is so well lined up –

FE: Yeah, it was – you know, that shot, plus a lot of shots, were done, were planned out so well in advance – I mean, it's like, that's one of the few opticals in the film, and we knew, you know, we knew exactly what we needed. And, I know in that one we shot a couple of tests because we couldn't get Henry to float right. It was the hardest thing to get him to, you know, to sort of float in space. And we knew – we knew where he was going to go in the shot, we knew what the move was, and how long and everything about it. We just didn't know how. And we shot it a couple different ways. And then ended up – ended up doing it in such a way that he was – he was not actually sideways when we shot him. He was sitting upright and the camera was sideways, and he was bobbing up and down and actually he was sitting on the dolly; we had locked the camera off and he sat on the dolly and we just dollied him back and forth, you know, against a black background. See, it's him that's moving and on the, you know –

KGG: That's a real background there, is it, like the stars behind him?

FE: No, that was – the stars were photographed with the planet. So it was – it was him against black. But so many things like that and the fetus, you know, coming out of his mouth and so on were lined up so carefully ahead of time – we would take, you know, we learned how to shoot one scene and take a clip of the scene and put it in the viewfinder of the camera and line up the camera, you know, like they did in the old days, to be sure it matched. Because, I mean, that was the way that we had to do it. And it just, you know, it wasn't easy and it didn't always happen the first time. But we eventually got there, you know. I mean, we used tricks – they're not new tricks in the industry, but they were new to us at the time. You know, ways to like I said make people float or ways to – some things, it was easier if you turned the camera sideways or upside down even – we shot things upside down. We shot things oftentimes with the camera running forward and then printed backwards to make an effect happen, because that was the only way – I mean, it was – some things that defy gravity, you know, require special handling. You know, we had to figure out a way to do it and we, you know, being babes in the woods, you know, had to feel it out as we went along. I mean, we would call some old guy at the effects houses and they would sort of give us a clue and then we'd run back and, you know, try this out and it would work a little better and then we'd sort of make refinements and we'd shoot it again, and it would work, you know. But, I mean, it was all – it was all tricks that we learned as we went. I mean, no one gave us a book and said, you know, "Here's how you make the fetus float." Because, I mean, obviously there's lots of different ways to do it, but for what we needed, you know, this way seemed to work and, you know, and we got it. But it was –

KGG: So, you sort of rediscovered a lot of old techniques.

FE: Yeah, we did. We really did that. I mean, much as I – I did lots of research. I read books on how to do this and how to do that. But, you know, we still had to invent as we went along. We had to put this technique together with that technique, and gave it a try, you know.

Catherine Coulson

Camera Assistant Catherine Coulson (centre) behind camera.

December 12, 1981

Catherine Coulson, married to Jack Nance at the time of *Eraserhead*'s production, became involved in the shoot as camera assistant and assistant director.

Catherine Coulson: Well, anyway, they decided to make another one [*Star Trek*] and this time they got a very good script and they found a wonderful young director named Nicholas Meyer, who –

Kenneth George Godwin: He wrote *The Seven-Percent Solution*.

CC: Right. And he did a film called *Time After Time* – did you see that?

KGG: Yeah.

CC: I really enjoyed that. He showed it to us the other night.

KGG: I was a bit disappointed actually.

CC: Oh, really? I had never heard anything – for some reason it escaped me. So that was his first film and I thought it was a good first film.

KGG: Oh yeah.

CC: So he's directing this one and it's being made "in spite of" the studio. It's such an amazing thing to make a big studio movie, specially after doing things like *Eraserhead*, you know, which were so kind of personal and rewarding and you got to do everything. And now this big union situation in which you're so compartmentalized and there's so much political bullshit, you know. And it's like you really are making it in spite of them. It's still kind of fun to be spending all this time on a spaceship.

KGG: Fred Elmes mentioned that, you know, he was –

CC: Yeah, he came in on second camera a couple of days, yeah.

KGG: He said it was great being on the bridge.

CC: Yeah, right. I got to hire Fred because my job as camera assistant is to get the second crew when we have two cameras. So really since *Eraserhead*, which is when I met Fred about ten years ago, we kind of trade back and forth jobs, you know. I assist him and he hires me, and then I get to hire him to come in as a camera operator and – it's a real nice little – we keep it as much family as we can, in spite of the bureaucracy of it all. – How did you become interested in *Eraserhead* to begin with? Did you just happen to see the film, or –

KGG: Well, I'd heard a few things about it, you know, just – I mean, I'd never seen a real review of it, just sort of a critical mention from time to time. It turned up in Winnipeg for a four day run – I guess it was around late winter, early spring last year, so I went along to see it. And I saw it twice that weekend. And it started a midnight run a few months later and I used to go quite regularly to that. But the first time I saw it, it just blew me away and, you know, I sort of became slightly obsessed with it, which is why I wrote this thing last winter –

CC: I see, and you wrote that and sent it to the same magazine?

KGG: Yeah.

CC: Say the name of the magazine.

KGG: *Cinefantastique*.

CC: Oh, I know that name. David said something that made it sound like some sort of French –

KGG: Well, I mean, it's supposed to be pronounced in French.

CC: Right, right. But David – so –

KGG: The editor of the magazine apparently likes *Eraserhead*, and had been considering trying to do something on it. In fact, I think he said he'd tried once before and it had fallen through.

CC: Yeah, it is hard to get David to talk, I think, because he's a little reluctant to answer questions about things he wants to kind of not talk about and so forth.

KGG: So anyway, the magazine sent this essay down to him to see if he was interested and he was impressed, so he agreed to do it.

CC: If – only if you did it.

KGG: But only if I would do it.

CC: Oh, that's just fabulous.

KGG: Which is great for me because the magazine would never have agreed to me coming down here.

CC: Oh yeah, that's great. So you do kind of freelance journalism?

KGG: This is my very first assignment.

CC: Oh, really? Oh, good for you. What did you do before you did this?

KGG: Not very much. I've sort of done odd jobs, I went to university for three years, got fed up with that. I don't like to work very much.

CC: But you like film?

KGG: Oh, yeah. I've been a sort of fanatic about film for years. I mean, I spent a year doing reviews for the university student newspaper.

CC: I see. You might enjoy then – I haven't read this particular article but – in here, in this *L.A. Weekly* – Michael Ventura. Kind of – people – it's a little bit the underground magazine, only it's not so underground anymore because it has this big circulation. But they do rather intelligent reviews of films oftentimes.

KGG: Kind of hard to find.

CC: Yeah, it is. I've always been intrigued by the idea of doing that too. I think from the point of view of being a filmmaker, when I first began working on *Eraserhead*, I had really not worked on a film at all except as an actress – I hadn't been on a crew. And so suddenly I got this whole new perspective on how films are made. Then I began going to films and seeing them totally differently. It almost destroyed my kind of childlike approach to watching films for a while, and then I'd start going, "Is that a dolly or a zoom?" you know, and noticing every cut and all that stuff. And then I gradually lost that sort of super self-conscious awareness and became – went back to being a film-goer. But even now when a film's not real good I start noticing all those other things. When it really sucks me in, I don't notice them. Oddly enough I'm real kind of squeamish and don't like – really don't like suspense or horror or anything like that and a lot of people who know of my association with David and *Eraserhead* are always surprised if I've taken them to see it. You know, "Well, how could you stand it?" and I never think of it as a horror film or I never think of it as anything uncomfortable because it was so organically made and it didn't – David didn't come out of any perversity. He came out of just the real story that he wanted to tell. And as a result of that I – that became my reality, that – Henry's room, and the baby, and all the things that we made and built together, became my world and didn't seem at all out of the ordinary. And in fact, when I saw the film, you know, I had no qualms at all because of course I had been there and now once in a while if I take someone to see it and they have a hard time dealing with it, it always still surprises me, that it in any way is, you know, something that would provoke one's stomach to turn. This always shocks me. It doesn't seem very shocking to me. But then we lived – we really lived that world –

KGG: Were you one of – the whole five years?

CC: Yeah, really. Steadfastly. Jack and I were married to each other, Jack Nance. And he met David – we were doing an acting workshop at the AFI and Jack had been recommended to David and I had been recommended to David by a man who was conducting this workshop, who had directed a theatre group that Jack and I were both in as actors. And so Jack met David first and said there's – there was a part in the film which is not in the film of the nurse. She was this crusty woman. And Jack said, "You should meet my wife, she'd be perfect for this part." But he came home and said, "Wow, Catherine," he said, "this guy is really amazing. He's built all these sets already and he's really quite, quite brilliant and I'm really excited about playing the part. I really want to get the part. I really want to do it." And Jack is not the kind of person who gets very enthusiastic unless something really catches his imagination. So he really wanted to do it and he said, "Why don't you come and meet this guy. He's kind of an oddball. He wears three ties and he's – always wears this hat, but he seems real, you know, real. He's real sweet and very innocent. He has all these sets built down in the stables at the AFI." So I went and met David and I – I was auditioning basically for the part of the nurse and I wore my hair back very severely, and a prim little dress. And I met David and I always say I met David as a young woman and by the time I finished *Eraserhead* I had aged quite a bit, because we worked such long hard hours. And we worked all at night. And I also had daytime work, so it was really a moonlighting life. But I auditioned for him and I read – I read the part of the nurse, and he said, yeah, and you know he thought that I'd be real good for it. And then he was rehearsing Jack and Charlotte, who played Mary, in the scene, the scene when Henry comes home after the long walk where his shoe gets wet and he lies on the – lays on the bed and Mary's had a rough time with the baby and he asks if there's any mail – and that was the first scene that I saw. I had not read the script yet – oh yes, I had, I'd read the script. It was very short. Seemed like it would be a very short film. It was supposed to take a few weeks to shoot. I think the original shooting schedule, which I still have, is, you know, it's like six weeks or something. So, we started – he asked me if I'd time the scene, that's right. And I – so – but – it was a combination, I was an actress auditioning, I was also Jack's wife. So by that time he had decided he definitely wanted Jack, so I – I remember holding the stopwatch and we were working in Henry's room, which David and his brother were building at the time. And David had just found this fabulous carpet. So, it was all rolled up and I was standing over on this carpet doing the timing of the scene because he wanted to be sure that the film would be the right length.

Which now is so amusing to me. So we timed that scene and he – so he really rehearsed the major scenes. And then I was going to play this part which was scheduled for, I think, the third week or whatever. Then about a week before we began shooting he asked me if I would like to, since I was going to be there – I think what was happening was I was kind of going to rehearsals with Jack and he was saying, "Well, since you're going to be here, you know, because of Jack, why don't you see – you know, would you like to maybe hold the boom or push the dolly or something." Because we really didn't – he really didn't have a crew. And so I said, yeah. I had always thought when I had done acting in films that the crew had much more fun. And it seemed like – seemed like the crew had a lot more to do and that would be interesting. So I just started off first of all doing Jack's hair, because David had this idea of how he wanted the hair done and I – since Jack was my husband, he would let me touch him – and I got this, you know, kind of maniacal pleasure of back-combing his hair. I really – the one credit I really wanted in the film was "Hair – Mr. Nance's Hair by –" because I – I always felt that was quite an achievement. It was David's design, of course, but I executed it. And poor Jack, I mean, every few weeks – the first time he went to a barber, and then became too expensive, so I learned how to trim around the ears and do the back and the back-combing of course. I got so that I could really get the shape down. And then it became, "Well, why don't we take some production stills?" So the cameraman taught me how to take stills, which then I got really into and enjoyed doing. I took a lot of production stills during the years that we shot the film. And then I held the boom, I think, at first and I pushed the dolly a few times. It'd be just various jobs. And I started learning about the lighting, which I really enjoy a lot – and I started learning what inkies and babies and 2Ks were, and learning how to hang them and stuff. And then pretty soon it became apparent that we would all have to be eating, not just getting takeout food. So I – and first of all we were shooting at night because it was the only time it was quiet in the stables. I began making dinner for the crew and I really enjoyed that. It was – sort of took care of my nurturing self, you know. And then my art self was also getting satisfied by getting to do these other jobs. I really didn't know anything about cameras at all, but after the first few weeks the guy who had been the camera assistant had to go back to school or back to work or something – I can't remember. And so, I remember Herb Cardwell, the cameraman, said, "Why –" ... it was a scene with Henry in the hallway, walking down the hall toward his room. And he said, "This is the follow-focus knob and as he walks toward us, you have to hit the number on the knob, you know, on the lens how many feet away from the camera he is." So he taught me how to tape off the hallway and then he said, "As he comes forward of course you turn this faster." And that was my really first instance of doing that, what later I found out was a highly technical job. But I just kind of took it on because it needed to be done. And it was fun, and I was learning something. And now, you know, I'm one of the sort of well-known women camera technicians in Hollywood. I'm in the camera union, and I'm doing *Star Trek* and all. And it seems – every once in a while I think I would never have done this, this way or done this job if it hadn't been introduced to me in kind of an off-hand way and out of necessity because it – there was – I had no mystique about it. I just knew it had to be done, and I learned how to load magazines and gradually, you know, the crew was so small that we just all did everything. So now I, every once in a while when I'm on the bridge of the *Enterprise* pulling focus and being in charge of several cameras, I think back on that time when he said, you know, "You pull this knob faster the closer he gets to the camera." So that really basically started off a whole new career for me. And of course we became like a family. We really got involved, so that really what happened was that I got the opportunity to know David better and better and we became really good friends and besides making the same sandwich for him every day – I think in those days it was egg salad; he always sort of eats one thing for a period of time – or grilled cheese. And since Jack was playing Henry and almost in every scene, basically Jack's and my home life became *Eraserhead* and oftentimes after we were through shooting David would come over and we would all eat pancakes at our house, and then David and Peggy, his wife, and Jack and I became real good friends. And when we had to stop shooting because we had more sets to build and the money was running low, we spent a lot of time that first fall with David and Peggy while Jack and David built the giant baby head in David's back yard. And Peggy – that's when Peggy and I became real good friends, and we still are real good friends right now. Actually she might be somebody you might be interested in interviewing – she's a wonderful, wonderful woman who is very fond of David and is very happily married to someone else and doing real well, but she can tell a lot of stories, I mean, Jenny – she and Jenny used to come down to the stables and Jenny would ask David if she could go, you know, play with the baby. So we really did become a family. And we worked odd hours and everybody sort of did a little bit of everything and gradually we practically were living there. I mean, I remember spending one New Years' Eve at the stables. We were all drinking champagne which – David really didn't drink – and we had a lot of fun and Jack kind of gave Jenny, who was about four, a couple of sips of champagne so she would go to sleep. We all listened to music and had a real nice time in our little home away from home. I started helping David in the afternoons build things. And I – I remember he taught me how to hammer. He had very precise ways of doing things and – painting sets and so forth. I – the first thing I had to learn was how to wash brushes. I learned lots of techniques and skills and things from David that I really have used and probably will use the rest of my life. So as a result of that we, you know, we really became very close and I did lots of sort of – started doing more and more errands. And it was always very clear that it was David's vision and David was the boss, but he had a way of including us all in a very warm way, because David is so beguiling and so real that you just sort of did things out of a love of doing it. I don't think I've ever worked harder in my life, those four years. During the time when we stopped for a year, I learned some, a little bit of editing skills, enough so that when we cut it, David and Alan cut together some pieces and I started learning how to file trims and all that sort of thing. But then I – I went out and worked. I worked at the AFI in the grant program and also washing windows and waitressing. We would – I worked in a restaurant and David would come down in the afternoon and do some odd jobs for the people who owned the restaurant in exchange for a grilled cheese sandwich and fries. And he was always doing odd jobs. We found him lots of things to do to support himself, and after he and Peg separated, then, you know, he really had to do some work, and that's when he got the paper route. And the paper route really was a good bonding thing, because we all helped out folding papers and stuff. And Jack would go on the route sometimes, or I'd go on the route. And then David would want to go home for Thanksgiving or whatever, then couple of times I took the route. And he tape recorded it for me, you know, "And now the orange house on the left, and then you turn right here," and I used to throw the *Wall Street Journal* when he wasn't there. It was a pretty funny job. When we were shooting the Lady in the Radiator, which was after we had broken for the year and then came back, he – we'd have to stop every night at a certain time and he would go off and do the route. And I'd usually take a nap, because then I was working during the day. A lot of my friends were – acted in the film. Really, because Jack and I had all these actor friends from all of our days at the theatre and so forth, so Laurel Near, who played the Lady in the Radiator, was the sister of my very good friend Timmy Near and Holly Near, and she came to stay with Jack and me. At some point David moved in with Jack and me and we lived there for about six months, and we – I think we were – we probably were each others', all of each others' best friends. D. Phipps-Wilson, who played the landlady, another woman who's not in the final version, was also another real good friend and Neil Moran, who plays the boss in the pencil factory and Hal Landen was an old boyfriend of mine – he plays the man who operates the pencil machine. And then my nephew Thomas is the little boy who finds the head. And Tom Coulson was, you know, a young teenager and was just thrilled to be working on this, and David – I remember when Tom came to get interviewed, David – Tom has seven brothers and sisters, and everybody was there at the stables when Tom went up for his interview and they were all standing down outside, you know, sort of like a cheering section. And my brother and sister-in-law were there, and Jack and I, and David came back down the stairs and said, "Well, Tom has the part." And everybody cheered. And then Tom stayed with us for a while during the summer and helped David build a lot of sets. He was like David's young assistant. Then we would shoot a few scenes. I remember one time down – going downtown to shoot this scene on a Saturday afternoon, the scene in which the boy finds the head in the Eraserhead dream sequence, we had to stop at the market to buy some jellied consomme which we were going to somehow use underneath the head. It had a kind of glistening texture – David's very into textures as you must know by now. I remember running in and buying the jellied consommé and thinking, "Other people don't spend their Saturday afternoons doing this." It had become such our world that it seemed impossible that there was anything else beyond that. We were out there with this huge camera, this BNCR that we had borrowed from Mark Armstead (?), and a lot of people were very nice to David and to the film, a lot of people really cared about David and really contributed a lot and one of those people was this camera company. And we had this thing where, if we ever got stopped by the police or whatever for not having a permit, we would say, "Well, we're just a student film," which it was. But it somehow never really felt like a student film. It was a real artist's film, a film being made by quite a wonderful human being who I think is quite a genius, and had a very clear strong vision, and enough of an ego that he would let people, you know, help him but always made it very clear that it was his film. But somehow was a lot of reward working with David because you knew he wasn't ripping you off. You know, he was really loving and generous and – we, I remember work – making twenty-five dollars a week; he didn't want me to work for free, didn't want anybody to work for free. And I had worked on other AFI films where it was just assumed that the actors and technicians worked for free. But David took his initial money from AFI and paid everybody salaries. And I remember when we ran out of money, or we got real low on money, we cut everybody's salary in half and I was making twelve-fifty a week. Which of course I always put back into the food which we then, you know, would – by the time we were really in the thick of it, I was – we were making breakfast, lunch, and dinner. We had a little hotplate and a frying pan and we just made every meal. We really practically lived together. So he was – that was a real special time. I really knew it at the time and I didn't even – but I didn't know it really until afterwards when I started working on other films and Fred came and joined our crew and – I was already by that time the camera assistant, so I was – he was sort of assigned me. You know, I was already there and we did a lot of the lighting together then. And David would come in and do a lot of the lighting. After a while, it became apparent that there wasn't really a separate crew and director; it was really everybody doing everything. And Jack really helped out a lot too, in the few scenes that he wasn't in, he worked on. And oftentimes he would just go down to another room down the hall and sit and read or wait to be on as Henry. And Alan would be down the hall playing his cello - Alan played a cello then.

KGG: I take it David sort of designed all the sets and so on.

CC: He didn't sort of: he did. Everything to the last detail was David's. Occasionally he would accept suggestions as to how to do things. There was this one scene we did that's - I don't think it's in the final film - when the baby's sick, Henry went to get the vaporizer out of the drawer. And it was in a drawer that was full of vanilla pudding and peas. And so the problem was how to make a drawerful of vanilla pudding. And Doreen and I - Doreen was another woman who worked on the film - Doreen and I went out, I remember we went out to the grocery store and we tried to figure out what kind of vanilla pudding would mix up the fastest. So we hand-beat instant vanilla pudding and filled this drawer with it, and then these green peas right on top of it. So when Henry reached in he had to reach into the vanilla pudding and pull out the vaporizer which was then covered with peas and vanilla pudding. Now the vaporizer - I had this wonderful aunt, Aunt Margit, who has one of the credits in the "gratefully acknowledged", Margit Laszlo. This is my favourite auntie, who lived in Beverly Hills in a big huge seventeen room house and had years and years' worth of stuff, and Margit was a bathing suit designer and a very flamboyant woman, and loved David and really supplied a lot of props. Whenever we needed something that we didn't have, we'd go to Aunt Margit, and she would give us a vaporizer or some old worn sheets which then - I remember one of the jobs I had first was dyeing the sheets for Henry's bed so that they weren't white-white - this was black and white and you don't want to have white-white - dipping them in tea and coffee to make them the right colour. Aunt Margit supplied the old blanket on Henry's bed, which got - one of the problems was continuity because over a period of years, not only did Jack age, but the blanket had more and more holes, so - one of the hardest things was keeping Jack's haircut all those years. When he wasn't shooting for a long time he would let it go, but then, you know, it was, poor Jack had to have another haircut, right, before starting to shoot. My family didn't know Jack any other way really, except with that goofy hair, which he would try and kind of comb down but it really never looked very good. And we have a lot of sort of family pictures at Christmastime with Jack with this goofy haircut. I think that was one of the most fun times in our marriage too, which was just, you know, being able to work together like that. We had quite a lot of fun. I never played the nurse. What happened was, during that year off, I became very involved with the fund-raising and oftentimes I would – any waitress tips from the restaurant where I pitched in at lunchtime, you know, we would kind of pool our money to some extent. And I never felt that it was right any other way. I mean, it really did seem like our film even though it was David's film. There was a sense of collaboration. So a lot of the – a lot of my work in these days really kind of went back into the film both with energy and financially. Which is why David gave us all such a nice percentage of the film – something we did not even write down until after the film started making money. He said, "Gee, I think we'd better get this in writing." Which is pretty impressive for a filmmaker to do that. And now it's really nice to get a healthy cheque every quarter from the distribution of it. All those years of working for twelve-fifty a week and then, you know, gradually giving twelve-fifty or more a week back into it. The reward artistically and emotionally was great, but to be able to also get some money back from it is a real rarity, I think, in this particular business. I think David's unique ability to handle people is something that has made him successful because he's very real, but he also has the ability to jump into the other person's place really and be compassionate and loving. He gave me his Bolex the first birthday that I knew him, that he had made *The Grandmother* with, because he said, you know, now that I was getting interested in camera and he was very appreciative of all the pancakes and grilled cheese sandwiches that I had made him, so he gave me this Bolex which I still have and use, and I really appreciate a lot. One of the things that we used to talk about was wouldn't it be fun if this film were really successful and there'd be pictures outside a theatre. We used to joke about people wearing their hair like Henry Spencer.

KGG: Which has happened.

CC: Yeah, I understand people do that. It's so amazing. It really does happen. When it first was on at Filmex – I remember the very first screening of the long version; nobody knew what to think. It was at the AFI and they came out with this kind of quiet – David was real depressed. Because people really didn't respond in the way that – they didn't know what to say. And as it gradually became more successful and more people picked up on what it really was, it's always been kind of a surprise in a way. Because it wasn't a film that was made to make a lot of money or to make anybody famous. One reason why, I think, it's successful. Because it was made because it was somebody's vision, that they wanted to create and share with other people. And that remained steadfastly the reason for the film being made. And as a result of that I think it's been very well received because it didn't – he didn't compromise.

KGG: Yeah, it's an extremely pure sort of film.

CC: And all those, all those negotiations with them, with the AFI, that we did and just, you know, talking with the bigwigs and so forth, I used to - by that time I was working up there full time in the grant program; I was also still doing some acting in some plays here and there and so forth - so, oh, I used to hear stories about David from the AFI people who didn't really realize how close we were, kind of wondering what was going on down there at the stables. But something in them, I think - they harassed him to a certain degree but for the most part I think they kind of stayed away because I think they - somebody must have known somewhere along the line that there was something good going to come out of this. Even when they decided not to give any more money. I think they might kick themselves all over the place for giving up such a big percentage of the film now, but it would never have been finished if they hadn't. I remember when we used to go to dailies. David is very very very secretive and he didn't want anybody judging it before it was done, he didn't want anybody to know anything about it ever, except for these two projectionists who were quite wonderful guys, so David still has some contact with. And they used to just - I remember when we first showed dailies of the baby, with the baby, and we were looking at it and they were - nobody could believe it, you know, it was like - so little rumours would leak out here and there, I think, that just kept the AFI being indirectly supportive and pretty much staying out of David's hair, although when David started living at the stables they used to come and, you know, kind of harass him, that - he never admitted that he lived there. And they never admitted that he lived there. But I think everybody kind of knew. And David used to go to sleep in Henry's room and in case there was an unexpected AFI inspection, we would put up sentry stands with black drapes all around him, big black cloths, and flags and stuff so that if anybody happened to peek into the set they wouldn't see that David was asleep in the bed. It was pretty amazing. They just - I think they pretty much knew though and just let him alone. When it went on so long it became a little bit of a joke, you know, that we were still shooting *Eraserhead*. And Jack's and my friends couldn't believe we - my parents couldn't believe I was still working on this film. They were worried that I was giving a little too much to it. But I'm really glad I did it. I certainly learned a lot. And I certainly made some wonderful friends and we're still, you know, friends to this day, although I don't get to see David as often since he is working so much and I am working so much, we don't really get to see each other very much. But I always feel like we're going to be friends. I actually see more of Fred because we work together. I've just been chattering away here. Do you -

KGG: That's fine.

CC: - want to ask me things? or - because I -

KGG: Well, the only thing I can think of is if you have any sort of little stories about sort of interesting things that you can remember that happened during the filming, little anecdotes.

CC: I do. I'm not sure that I can talk about them. I'm not sure – can you turn that off for just a second?

KGG: Sure.

CC: One of my favourite stories, I think, is making that vanilla pudding, but since it's not really in the final film it's not as good a story. Oh, I was going to say why I didn't play the nurse. By the time we got down to shooting that scene, one of the hardest things I had to do, I think, was to say that, because I think David would have filmed it anyway, was that I didn't – it really wasn't a critical scene to the making of the film. By the time I – by the time we got to do that scene, which was like three years later, I really had such an investment in getting the film finished and in trying to find money and so forth and so on, that I remember saying, you know, I didn't think it was probably that necessary a scene. And David –

KGG: This was the scene where Mary is picked up at the hospital by her parents?

CC: Unh-hm. Right, and she – the nurse gives them the baby and the nurse is very disgusted with the whole thing. So we kind of gave up that scene. Now I did act in another scene now, which is not in the film also. It's just down the hall from Henry – there's some women who are in a room with a very strange man that has this black box. And we were, my friend Phipps-Wilson and I did this scene where we were lying on this bed – now, somehow it didn't seem at all sexual, but we were bound by these kind of battery cables. And the guy had this black box and he was just kind of walking toward us with these prongs or something and I remember wearing this slip and some pearls. It wasn't sexy really, it was sort of David's sexy which is always kind of pristine in a way. And what happened was, Henry hears these strange noises and he walks down the hall and he opens the door a crack, and this is his vision of what he sees. And the women kind of look at him and then he shuts the door real fast. And that was it. That was in the first version. I wish that sometime David would show those particular scenes.

KGG: Yeah, he said that he had some sort of favourite scenes that he had to take out –

CC: Oh yeah. Oh yeah. It was too long. But the digging for dimes scene was another scene where Henry's looking out the window and he sees all these people digging. And then we used all of David's friends and their kids and everybody. We – I think probably the biggest challenges were finding things that needed to be found at the last minute. A lot of little – like making that vanilla pudding. Hairballs. There was this particular tar pit where there's this oil rig that was right in the middle of L.A. and we used to go down there and get this kind of sticky, oily hair stuff – it wasn't really hair – to put under the radiator. And what happened was, I used – to me this stuff was real oddball and then after a while it became very normal. And I remember one time when David was editing the film a friend of mine was working next door in another editing room, a woman named Michal Goldman, and she got a call one night from David and Alan saying, "Do you have a radiator in your room?" And she said, "Yeah." And they said they needed the sound of a radiator. And she said, "Well, I don't know if it's that kind of radiator." And he said, "No, no. We don't need the sound of the radiator hissing. We need the sound of somebody jumping off a radiator." I mean, there's a scene in which Henry's peering out of the window and he jumps back down again. I remember learning to make them – we tried – we used to – David used to invent ways of doing things which now when I think about it really involved a lot of special effects that, working at the studios, I see are very complicated and very expensive. But I remember doing the rain outside the window of Henry's apartment by building this little tube and this little drip thing and punching holes in the tube and – David would paint everything himself and make everything look very real, or very real from David's point of view. I had to research one time – David, in this one scene where the baby just kind of explodes and this sort of mush stuff comes out – one of my favourite things to do was to find out how to do things, and I used to call around and ask questions, you know, "What kind of substance?" I remember calling the Universal special effects department and saying, "Do you have any suggestions as to how to fill a room full of mush?" And, you know, in my perspective that was a rather normal question to ask. It was always interesting to hear people's response. Usually the suggestions that they made were not applicable to the film, but we – one of the things that we did during the film was do other little projects occasionally. David always kept other things going, he always did drawings. I remember when he came up with the idea for the Lady in the Radiator, which was really after the film was in the process –

KGG: Yeah, he mentioned that.

CC: He came up with this idea of this line "In Heaven everything is fine." And he did this little drawing of this little woman and that really is what the Lady in the Radiator sprang from. All those squares on the stage of the Lady in the Radiator, David painted all those one by one, you know. He made a little stencil, then he painted them all. I mean, he didn't do anything in the normal way really. A lot of times we gave up our furniture, like our – the living room furniture – I can't remember if this is in the final film, the scene in the apartment, in the lobby of the apartment, Henry's apartment, those chairs were our, Jack's and my living room chairs. When we would give something up it would be gone for months because of course we would have to take it so slowly. It really - it wasn't that David really - it wasn't that it went on so long because of any kind of inefficiency, just went on so long because the job was being done basically by a couple of people. So the room that the pencil factory is in is the same basic attic room in the stables that was the same room that was the apartment lobby, which was the same room that was some other scene. It was like David kept striking the set and then building a new one - oh, the office of the pencil factory. All those rooms were the same space with different sets built in them. And now I work on union films and I see these, you know, art departments with ten people on it doing the same thing, not quite as well sometimes. He really pretty much did everything himself. He had - David has tremendous energy. He still does. I mean, he just can go and go and go for something that interests him. I remember one time we had these, I found these canvas jump - not jumpsuits, but overalls, at Standard Brands and they were a dollar-ninety-nine, and we were all wearing them for painting the set and stuff and David wrote *Eraserhead* on them like you'd write "Al's Garage", you know. We all wore those little things. We didn't have too many clubby little things, but that was one of them that I always enjoyed. Going to the grocery store was a big event because it was not only going to the grocery store to buy food for the crew, but really to buy things for the film. I mean, what would look good? what kind of texture would look good for the head? Jellied consomme was David's idea and turned out to be the best.

KGG: What was the head made from?
CC: Oh, that was another one of my jobs; helping clean out the mold. David made the head. Jack sat for - oh, that's another thing we did - god, it's bringing back a lot of memories. Jack's face being covered with plaster of Paris with straws coming out of his mouth.

KGG: He actually took a cast?
CC: Yeah. Is that okay for me to tell you, I wonder?

KGG: As far as I know, the main thing he didn't want people to tell me about was the baby.
CC: Okay.

KGG: He hasn't specifically mentioned anything else.
CC: Well, the head was made from a mold from Jack's actual head. And that was very strange for me because I remember kind of working on the plaster and filing it down. I was filing down the face of my husband. Jack was a very strange person and quite wonderful. I'm sure you know from having talked to him, a very funny man, we just couldn't stay married to each other. But I really do - I'm just crazy about him. But, yeah, there were lots of little odd - there

were always odd jobs to be done, like, you know, filing – well, doing the giant baby head in David's back yard. Has anybody talked about that?

KGG: No.

CC: Sanding the giant baby head was such a big deal. It was huge and, you know, the neighbours called it "that big egg." David lived in this little house right in the centre of the city and on either side of the house were these big, it was these like three-storey apartment buildings, so people would look down into David's back yard where there was this giant thing which he had also made out of a mold. And they were – Jack and David worked on this for a long time. I think that really cemented literally their friendship. And David and Jack would be sanding the giant baby head, and little Jenny, who was like four or five, learned how to mix cement and she, you know, she would stir the cement and then give it to David and they would put it on real fast and then, when it'd come time – we were always waiting for the head to dry. That was the big thing. We sat around David's house and drank coffee and ate sandwiches and watched TV and waited for the head to dry for months it seemed like. We were always waiting for something to dry. And when David did *Elephant Man* and I talked to him and he was in England, he was waiting for the Elephant Man cast to dry at his house in England. I couldn't believe he was still waiting for things to dry. So it – I remember they found they were – the cement they first used, or this plaster that they first used, was gravelly and they would be sanding it, and they would sand down all their fingerprints, so Jack and David were like, they were like, you know, criminals. They had no fingerprints left on their fingers. And the neighbours – I remember the neighbours said to me, you know, "What is that big egg there?" It was – so we would call it the big egg and then one day the big egg disappeared. And we had – oh, Jack's brothers came out from Texas to help. We always were getting, when we had a big scene to do like the planet scene, which we worked on at night, all one night – I remember one night we shot it, we had Jack – was not actually in that scene obviously because it was just dollying in on the planet's surface – was inside the planet rotating it, when we were dollying in on it. And we got the shot right before the sun came up. We always got, seemed to get our best stuff right before dawn. I remember Alan would be listening to the sound and say, "Wait, I hear birds." You know, we'd have to stop when we started to hear the birds.

KGG: How big was the planet?

CC: Is the planet in it?

KGG: Yeah.

CC: He made that too. I can't remember what he made it out of. You would have to ask him.

KGG: How big was it?

CC: Oh, it was pretty big. I don't know. Maybe ten feet in diameter. It was huge. Now it's so interesting because I'm working on *Star Trek* and the special effects people are photographing planet surfaces. And I'm thinking, you know, we photographed that planet surface, it looks quite good. And David just thought that all up. And Fred thought about how to light it. But we did it – he had made a big black star field. Big – kind of big black with pinpoints and lights behind them and – I mean, that's the stuff that now, that George Lucas and Industrial Light and Magic do on a much more sophisticated level, but in a way the same kind of results. When we did the opening scene, which we didn't do until the very end after several years, with Jack Fisk as the Man in the Planet, that was the day Sissy Spacek, who's married to Jack, came and helped out; she was the script supervisor. Oh, that's the other job that I did, Doreen and I traded off – we were the script supervisor as well. And Sissy came and we taught her how to be the script supervisor for the day, so that we could do that scene. She was great. She really enjoyed doing that. She said the next time she acted in a film, she'd have a lot more appreciation for that particular job. We – I really think that probably the most unusual tasks in my life were on that film, the finding of things sometimes. I remember collecting dust balls that would be under the bed. There's another whole scene that's not in the film now: Mary roller skating through the – she leaves, when she leaves him, she pulls the suitcase out from under the bed – there's this whole scene that, where she used to go into the bathroom and get her stuff and then she – she just roller skated through the room. I mean, you didn't know she was on roller skates, it was like she just flew through the room. And we had this fan blowing so that it would blow her hair in a real unusual way. And things like that took a lot of time because David had never done them before. He had a vision of how to do them, and there'd be a lot of figuring out how to do it, and I think that's why it was so richly rewarding. Because we had the opportunity to work things through and then see them happen. And to actually see them on film and to have it be good was so wonderfully rewarding. I'm very happy I had that experience. I will always remember that as my first feature film and little did I know it was a feature film when I started. And I do regret now, I think, not having acted in it. I think that would be fun to say I acted in *Eraserhead*. And now when I say what I did on it, nobody really believes me because it was so many different things that in a way it's almost too much, you know. It's like too many excuses; you kind of don't believe any of them. And I think when we were doing the credits we were trying to decide what we would call each of us, you know, what we did. So I remember I said, well I liked, you know, camera assistant and assistant to the director, and I guess that kind of covers going out and buying the pudding and – but I really do regret that I didn't say

"Mr. Nance's hair". But David did design it, you see, that's the thing. He really designed everything and then we just kind of all helped to execute it. And it's not a situation in which I feel at all ripped off, which is unusual. I'm really glad that David gets to make other films. I hope that it doesn't get too far removed from what he wants, you know.

KGG: That's what I was sort of wondering; each one is getting bigger. I mean, *Dune* now is going to be enormous--

CC: I still think it'll have David's particular imprint.

KGG: But it must get more difficult to maintain that individual thing, working on a big corporate thing like that.

CC: Absolutely. Yeah. I think so. It's probably very hard. I wish I could come up with some more interesting anecdotes. Most of them concern the baby, I'm afraid. But - you know, can you think of anything else you would like to ask me?

KGG: Do you know Doreen Small's number?

CC: She's in New York.

KGG: Yeah. I can call her from Canada when I get home.

CC: Yeah, yeah. I can give you that.

KGG: And Charlotte Stewart?

CC: Charlotte is listed in the San Francisco phone book.

KGG: And do you know Judith Roberts -

CC: No, but you could get that from the Screen Actors' Guild.

KGG: Oh, yeah. Do you know what Laurel Near is doing now?

CC: Yeah. She lives in Santa Monica and she's a - she was in a wonderful dance group called the Wallflower Order for a long time and she's been teaching dance and she's really still interested in acting. I have her number too. And when you see Laurel, give her my love. I wonder if David - well, I guess you'd probably get the same information from John Lynch. His brother - David and his brother and Alan really worked on the very original sets. His brother helped build them, but I don't know where he lives now. I think he's in Washington. He probably wouldn't have that much more to offer.

Alan Splet

Sound artist Alan Splet jamming with David Lynch.

December 17, 1981 (by phone)

Beginning with David Lynch's early short *The Grandmother*, Alan Splet became a long-time collaborator with the director on the complex and imaginative sound design of all the features up to *Blue Velvet*.

Kenneth George Godwin: First of all, I'd like to know how you first met David Lynch?

Alan Splet: We met at Calvin Productions back in Philadelphia in 1970, and David had come to Calvin with *The Grandmother*, which he had done on a grant from the AFI. And he came to Calvin to put sound on the film – it was a thirty-five minute film but he had – it was just totally silent. And initially he was going to work with a friend of mine who was actually running the department there, and through some quirk in fate he wound up with me. And we got along real well and the film turned out really well. AFI was really pleased and David and I formed a lasting friendship.

KGG: When you were doing the sound for *The Grandmother*, how did you arrive at what you arrived at? It's very distinctive.

AS: How did we arrive at that?

KGG: How did you build it up?

AS: Wait a minute now. You're talking about something we did eleven years ago.

KGG: Yeah. I realize -

AS: How did we build it up?

KGG: Yeah. What did you start with because - although a lot of the sounds are natural, there's sort of distortion and - altered quite a bit?

AS: Well we - and maybe I'm not answering the question right - but we started with - most of the things, most of the sounds are from normal everyday things that we found around the company. David and I would talk about the sound, and David usually had ideas about what he wanted to do but they were very abstract. And then we'd talk about actually getting it down to concrete terms, and then we'd start scouring the company for things to make sounds with - you know, like crushing a plastic box, or in one case we used a pencil sharpener, and in another case we used a staple gun. We didn't have a lot of stuff available. We didn't even have a lot of equipment available there, not like we do now, because it was industrial film producers so they weren't - it wasn't like they had a lot of equipment around. So we often had to make do with what was there. One time we wanted to - there's *The Grandmother*'s whistle in the film, and we wanted that little reverb to it, and we didn't have a reverb device - I mean, that was just beyond our means. And so we got the sound basically by rerecording the whistle through a piece of aluminum heat ducting which we just happened to find in the shop. We re-recorded it, you know, maybe fifteen times through this piece of ducting to get the sort of little bit of echo on it that we wanted. So I mean that was the way we sort of worked. Everything was improvised from the materials we had on hand.

KGG: So they were all natural sounds you started with - you didn't create anything electronically?

AS: No, no. We've never done that on any of David's films. I've never done it on any films I've worked on, I've never used a synthesizer. You know, they're all basically original sounds - some of the sounds of course are just from sound effects records, like there's the sound of a babbling brook in, this is **The Grandmother**. And there's some other sounds that we - you know, thunder and things like that - that are just from a library. But a lot of the other, more unusual sounds, we made, you know, just from things laying about.

KGG: How did you get on to *Eraserhead*?

AS: How did I get on to it?

KGG: Yeah, were you with David right from the start?

AS: Well, after **The Grandmother** was finished, David took the film down to Washington, D.C., where - which was the headquarters of the American Film Institute - still is actually. And he played the film, he ran the film for George

Stevens Jr, who was then the director of the Institute, and Tony Vellani, who is now the assistant dean – in fact, I think he's the dean actually, at the Centre for Advanced Film Studies down in L.A. And they just flipped out over this film, they loved it. So anyway, he took it down to Washington and played it for George and Tony, and they just – they loved it. And, you know, they were talking about it and they started to talk about the sound. And then they wanted to know how the sound came about. They thought the soundtrack was really good, and they were really impressed with the mix also. So then David started to tell them about me. Well, they were real excited because they were just opening up this Centre in Los Angeles, you know – where it used to be at the Doheny mansion – and they were looking for someone to run the sound department. And so, they were real interested in me having the job. Well, I resisted for a long time, but eventually one thing led to another and I wound up with the job at the AFI and David was a fellow at the AFI. So there we were. Both of us came out to Los Angeles together actually. And of course *Eraserhead* was conceived at the AFI and most of the early, most of the major shooting was done at the AFI. So, and I was there working, so I just naturally fell into, you know, working with David again on the film. And eventually I quit the AFI, but I still continued with David on the film.

KGG: Did you just work on the sound or did you do other things on the film as well?

AS: Oh, yeah, I – we did everything – I mean, everybody helped out doing everything. I mean, there was nights where we'd work all night on production and I'd help, you know, do the lighting and carrying things around and, you know, help – just help-—yeah, lots of different things. Help build sets. Yeah, we all helped out wherever we could. I mean, everybody, even, you know, Jack Nance helped David with the giant baby head and did all sorts of things. Any time we ever had a shoot, you know, even often when there were shoots where there was no sound I would come down and do other things, you know, like push the dolly or, you know, if it was a complicated scene where there was, you know, maybe somebody had to run a rheostat for a light or something like that, I'd do that, you know. And everybody helped out, you know. Jack would help out when he wasn't acting. And Jack's wife at the time, Catherine, would help out. Everybody just plunged in and did whatever they could. It was a great sort of group effort, you know, and the lines were – there were no really sharp lines in who did what. I mean, when we – of course, when we recorded sound I recorded the sound. But even one night – I remember one night where we had – we were so short of – we needed so many functions, we were so short of people that everybody moved functions. I remember our cameraman at the time, Herb Cardwell, was running sound. I was doing something else. David was running the camera. It was like everybody shifted to another function because we had so few people to do whatever we needed to do. I don't remember what it was at the time, but –

KGG: Were you sort of building the sound for *Eraserhead* while you were shooting? or did a lot of the sound come after it had been finished?

AS: Well, a lot of the sound came afterwards. But I remember David and I, we built the sound for one scene completely very early on. I think it was because David needed to raise some more money, and we wanted to get a real finish that, you know, that had full sound and picture. So, the scene where Henry first enters his apartment early on in the film, through to the scene where he goes over to the, let's see – no, I think we stopped at the end where he's looking at the photograph. We went that far. We built that scene completely. We got all the sounds and we even did a mix on that section. And that was very early on, because I remember we were still shooting down at the stables at the AFI. But then we didn't do any more after that. I don't recall really working much more on the sound until the film was pretty much complete. I was actually – I'd been in Scotland for a couple of years, while David was struggling to finish up, the last year and a half or so, where he would just shoot like once every couple of months. And then I came back to help David finish up all the post-production. And that's when we really got into it. We spent a whole year from summer of – what was it? 1975, I think – to the summer of '76 – or the spring of '76 – we spent really going through and, you know, making sound effects and laying tracks, and the mix of course. We had a real, a real push at that time too because we thought we could possibly get it into the Cannes film festival. And I remember at some very late date, David and I finally agreed to go do it, and it meant really working, you know, like almost around the clock. So for about a month and a half I was working, you know – I was sleeping in the same room that I was editing. So I would work all, you know, 'til like three in the morning, then I'd crash right away, get up the next morning, eat breakfast, go right back in and cut again. And we actually got most of the film done very quickly to screen for them. They never accepted it, but – I think it was a little too *avant-garde* for them.

KGG: Can you remember any sort of details of sounds that you used? I mean, like for the baby's voice?

AS: Well, see there I would have to talk to David first. I don't know what he wants to divulge about the baby. So I'd rather not say anything relative to the baby. Because I know David's usually very secretive about it. And I'd prefer not to say in that particular case.

KGG: Okay. In the thunderstorm sequence – the thunder sounds very mechanical. Can you recall what was used for that?

AS: I think we started with regular thunder, just library thunder, but we processed it I'm sure. But, you know, it's hard for me to remember what we did really. I can recall one interesting thing that – the opening sound where there's a sort of presence and it kind of widens out as you move in on the planet, the egg planet. And we were kind of wondering, you know, David and I were talking about it and really wasn't sure what to do and I just took this one presence that we had in the library, called "early morning presence", and while we were sitting there I was sort of fiddling around with it and I just stuck it through this one-third octave graphic equalizer that I had and I started to push the – each little equalizer, each little third octave, I started to open it up, push it open. And the sound started to open out and we said, "My god, that's it." So it was like it – you know, you don't know how something like that happens. You know, was it conscious? Or did it just – was it a lucky accident or what? But it was the right sound. And there it was, you know.

KGG: So a lot of it was sort of trial and error?

AS: A lot of stuff is trial and error. You know, it – very rarely do we hit things the first time out. Generally what happens when David and I work is, we'll talk about the sounds, whatever they happen to be, and then usually I'll try to get more concrete. David usually thinks in very abstract terms, so he says something like, "Well, gee, it would be nice to have a low sound here. Let's find –" But then we have to start, you know – what low sound? what kind of sound? And I have to start probing a little bit just to get it a little more concretized. Then when I think I've got an idea of what it is, I'll try to think in terms of what I've got and how – you know, something I can use to make it. And I'll try something on David. David'll say, "Ah no, no, no," you know. "Let's – it should be such and such, such and such." Then I think back and I think, oh maybe, you know, maybe I'll do such and such, and such and such. And then I'll approach it again and try something different. Or maybe even try a different sound, you know. Sometimes I find sounds that, on my own, that I know David's going to like. Like, there's a low sound in *The Elephant Man* – and I got that sound, I discovered that sound about a year before and just sort of kept it away on ice, you know, sort of on the back burner. And then when David and I finally got together to work on *The Elephant Man*, one of the first things I did was, I said, "David, I've got this low note for you that I think you're going to love," you know. And so I played him some of this stuff and he flipped out over it, you know. I knew he would, you know. And so some of this stuff found its way into *The Elephant Man*. So, I mean, occasionally I find sounds that I know he'll like, I sort of file them away in my head and then when we work together again on something I'll, you know, pull them out and play them for him, you know, then get his reactions.

KGG: Had you done this kind of sound work before you met David?

AS: No, no. The first time I ever did anything like that was with David on *The Grandmother*. Before that I'd worked on industrial films, you know, just kind of nuts and bolts films. So it was like, meeting David was like, you know, expanding my world of film by about a million percent.

KGG: What are you working on now?

AS: I'm working on a film directed by Carroll Ballard called *Never Cry Wolf*. It's based on a novel by Farley Mowat. - The old gang. We still all know each other too. It's funny - that period of time was so intense that really we formed lasting friendships from it, you know. It's like, you know, we still all know each other. Catherine was up here recently and stayed with us for a couple of days. I see Jack every so often when I'm down in L.A. And of course Fred - every - when Fred comes up to San Francisco we all get together. So, it's like, that period, that *Eraserhead* period sort of spawned all these friendships, you know. I've just got to say one more thing: it was a really unusual way to make a film. It's too bad that most films can't be made this way. It really was a real group experience, where everybody really shared. I mean, it was like a family for a while. I mean, everybody shared everybody's problems and, I mean, we shot the film, but there was all sorts of other dramas going on too that we all shared in. And it was a really, kind of an exciting time. And it's sad that other films aren't made that way, you know. Most films are such a mechanical process; they come, they work on it, and they leave, you know. That's kind of too bad. It was a very rare moment in filmmaking. It was certainly good to be part of it.

Doreen Small

Production Manager Doreen Small working on set.

December 22, 1981 (by phone)

Doreen Small was *Eraserhead*'s production manager.

Kenneth George Godwin: I'm writing an article on David Lynch and *Eraserhead*.

Doreen Small: Oh, really. Hello.

KGG: And I wondered if I could talk to you about your connection with the film?

DS: Sure. What is the article for?

KGG: It's for a magazine called *Cinefantastique*.

DS: Does it have David's permission?

KGG: Yeah. I was down a week ago in L.A. talking to him and Jack Nance and others.

DS: Oh. Okay. We're all protective of David.

KGG: Yeah. Well, I'm not supposed to ask about the baby and so on. But apart from that everything was okay. So, are you free to talk now?

DS: Sure. This is fine.

KGG: Okay. So I guess I'll start at the beginning: where and how did you meet David?

DS: Okay. I had come to Los Angeles and I had worked in the art business in New York first, at an art gallery here. And one of my neighbours was an assistant art director on a black exploitation film called *Cool Breeze*. And he said, "You're artistic, why don't you be my assistant?" And the art director was Jack Fisk and Jack Fisk and I became very friendly and after we finished *Cool Breeze*, he said that what I had been doing for *Cool Breeze*, which was getting props and organizing that kind of thing, that his friend who he went to art school with in Philadelphia was over at the American Film Institute and needed somebody to help out. So he introduced me to David. And it started out that I just was getting props and helping him with – they were – all the sets were built in the stables, he and his brother were building the sets, so I helped him with that and building a lot of incidental small props. And then he said, "Well, I don't have a production manager and I don't have a script girl, so why don't you see if you can talk to anybody around the American Film Institute and see if you can learn how to be those kind of things." And so I learned how to be a production manager and I learned how to be a script supervisor. And it was sort of on-the-job training. We, all of us did pretty much everything. It was – from the very beginning. And all of us believed in – it was extraordinary. When I first met David, he used to wear three ties at the same time. I don't know if anybody's ever told you that. But it was the kind of thing where we just trusted that what he was doing was really worth helping. So we only would shoot at night and all the rest of us would deal with the world during the day, like get equipment, which was my job – equipment and film – and get the actors and get the costumes and get the permits and just work out all the logistics of things. And then we would shoot at night, so we were all awake for twenty-four hours a day. Anyway, that's how we met.

KGG: Had much work been done on the film when you became connected with it?

DS: No. No shooting. When I became – it was – they were still building Henry's room, which I lived at for – David and I went and we got all of the – we decorated it. We got all that black stuff, the tar – there was a kind of oil well over on Robertson Avenue. And we got the picture of the bomb. We went into – all of the things, I was around – the only part I wasn't around for was the carpentry of Henry's room. That was the only thing that I had missed. And the first building of the baby. But – and I guess, of course, the writing of the script. But, no, nothing had been done before this, so I was there from the very very very beginning.

KGG: What were your first impressions of the project when you – I mean it's rather a strange film, so –

DS: Well, to us it was just a simple love story. And it was about what it meant to be trapped. And we – we had a – David went through enormous numbers of changes during the filming. He found – he went from somebody who smoked lots of cigarettes and drank lots of coffee and woke up in an extremely foul mood – we used to rotate who would wake David up – to – then he started meditating. And I think that cleared up a whole, was an outlet, a certain kind of outlet for a lot of the bleaker visions he had. So the script changed actually from – it was much more of a nightmare and less of a dream, much more of a nightmare when we began. But, see, David from the beginning told us that he had been bamboozling the American Film Institute. They had, unfortunately had – Stanford Kaye had tried to do a feature, which he called *In Pursuit of Treasure*, otherwise it was *In Pursuit of Pleasure*, and he just went on and on forever and nothing ever got done. And so they were very chary about giving money to directing fellows to do features. David knew this was going to be a feature and it was, written it was twenty pages. That was the script, was twenty pages. And he said, you know, they said to him, "Oh, twenty page, twenty minutes." It was very difficult for me to get film out of them after a while. He said, "Well, maybe – maybe more like forty minutes, but I'll shoot it in black and white if you let me shoot in thirty-five." And they agreed to that. And then what we all had to do, all the crew, me and the cameraman and someone else, what we had to do – David screened *Sunset Boulevard*, that was the only movie we all saw together before we started working together, and then – no, we didn't think it was strange, we didn't think it was a strange movie. We thought – we just believed so thoroughly in David that when he told us god was his co-pilot we believed him. He's – I don't know how much you've talked to him, but he's extremely charming.

KGG: Yeah, I had several interviews with him.

DS: Yeah, he's a – he was, I don't know, he was married to his first wife, Peggy, then and his daughter Jennifer was very small. He just – he was very secure in his painting and in his first film – we all saw **The Grandmother**, we all saw his first film, we also saw *The Alphabet*, that little film that he made. We admired his paintings. We – nobody second-guessed him. Alan especially had been working with him for a very long time in Philadelphia. And the first cinematographer, who is now dead –

KGG: Herbert Cardwell.

DS: Yeah, Herb also was from Philadelphia, had worked with Alan in Philadelphia. And so Fred only came along – Elmes – only came along later on. Catherine – Catherine – do you know Catherine?

KGG: Yeah, she was the one who gave me your number.

DS: Right. Catherine was married to Jack and, anyway – so – but all of us, all of us were just so, so thoroughly convinced that it was, what he was doing was worth doing.

KGG: How did you manage to survive through such a long shooting?

DS: With great difficulty. My mother – my mother was extremely generous to the production and to me. She gave money to David to keep him going and to buy the treats that we all felt David needed. And she supported me, for all intents and purposes. I didn't make any – yeah, I guess she supported me for every intents and purposes. She felt it was – I had not gone to film school, and I was still fairly young then and – I don't know, I was happy and she had the money. And so she said, why not? And –

KGG: Were you with the film right through to the end?

DS: No. I'm actually in the last shot. The person in the blond wig in the last shot is me. And I am in a whole bunch of other shots, but you can't see me; I'm under the table working the chickens and I'm working the baby most of the time. But when the baby gets crazy, and the baby gets very hyperactive, it's Alan working the baby because he plays the cello and he has a certain kind of touch. But, no, after about three years – after about three years, the film went into a very very very long hiatus when David was building the giant baby head, and I had a very pressing personal crisis – not crisis, sort of – well, I suppose it was a crisis. I had to go to Santa Barbara to live with somebody for a while, and David – it was difficult to commute from Santa Barbara, and so there are a few scenes that I wasn't involved in; the scenes at the pencil factory, which David built – I had ordered the pencils a long time before that, but we – David and I – I had helped David – David built – I had helped David build the Eraserhead, the cast of Jack's head. And – but the filming of that scene, I wasn't there for. And I wasn't there for the filming of the scene of the Lady in the Radiator, and – the one with the pudgy cheeks. And, let's see – that's about it, that's about it. And, oh yeah, and the giant baby head scene. So I wasn't there for that. But that was about two months' worth of work. I mean, it was like five days' worth of shooting and about a lot of building, a lot of building. So – but I think I was there for pretty much everything. A lot of stories, I've got three years' worth of stories.

KGG: Can you remember any sort of particular incidents that, anecdotes about –

DS: Oh, lots of things. Charlotte Stewart is my room- – was my roommate then, the one who plays Mary X. And from the – there was a scene that's not in the film, where – well, you still see part of it; the scene where, where there are the fetuses, when she's in bed and something, you know, her eyelashes are clicking and stuff like that, something's wrong. Well, David and I built a body cast of Charlotte and we had a – he has all these techniques for doing these kind of things – and so anyway we had to get her undressed and cast her body and his wife was around and Charlotte undressed, you know, we were casting her – but he made a planter later of it – but what we had was, we had a torso, very very thin torso, and we cut out a hole in Henry's bed and Charlotte would sort of settle in underneath it and we put this very thin shell of her body on top so there was a space between her actual body and the shell. And it – originally Henry broke through that when he first found the fetuses. And, well, the umbilical cords are actual, are real umbilical cords, and for that particular – did Catherine tell you that what happened was one of them coming into Jack's house slipper?

KGG: No.

DS: Well, I was under the bed to keep tension on the umbilicals – the "billy cord" as Jack would call them – and I was there trying to keep tension on them. And Jack pulled and we sort of missed and one of them landed in his shoe and he got so grossed out that we had to stop filming for a couple of days. Poor Jack. I mean, he put – Jack put up with – Jack put up with more, more things – he got his hair done like that every day. He had to have it spray painted by the end. There are a lot of personal things, I mean, the time David – the things that David and I did. But there – I mean, if you have, if there's any scene that interests you, if you want some kind of glimpse behind a certain scene –

KGG: Well, the ones I'm interested in are the ones he doesn't want anybody to talk about, I think.

DS: About the baby?

KGG: Yeah, basically. Yeah.

DS: Well, the baby has its own mystery. He – the baby – the baby just has its own mystery.

KGG: Yeah.

DS: But it's a – I don't – the other scenes, I mean, everything that's there – the reason we shot, one of the reasons it looks so good, I think, is because we used a lot of real organic kinds of products. Instant cream of wheat and mashed potatoes and grape jelly. There are a lot of nice stories about screening dailies and things like that, but those are mostly I think just nice for us because we really cared, all of us cared a lot about one another. But – I don't know. I don't know what you'd be interested in hearing.

KGG: Have you worked with any of the other people involved since?

DS: I worked with Catherine a few times, and Fred a few times. But I started doing different kinds of things. I mean, I started – I'm not in the film business right now, but I started – I'm going to law school. But, well, I worked for Albert Brooks for a long time and I worked at a lot, but it's – so I sort of left, I left low-budget filmmaking. It was – there was a lot of wear and tear. There was a lot of wear and tear. We all had to do so much that it takes a lot out of you, no matter how much we cared about one another, it just takes so much out of you that – and I've never found any other, any other – I haven't found any other project I've believed in as much as I believed in David. I saw David when he was here to screen *Elephant Man*, but I don't – I don't really have an on-going relationship. David's now married to Jack's sister, Mary, and she's – well, I just don't have an on-going – I get letters from them, but it's -- I have no insight into David's personal life or present life or – he's there, I'm here.

KGG: Was there, when you were filming, was it basically David had a clear idea of everything that was to be done and sort of told everybody how to do it, or was there any –

DS: David was in thoroughgoing control. David was in thoroughgoing control. He – we had a couple of actors, like the – Mary X's – the X's – old-time Hollywood actors. Jeanne Bates had, was under contract to Harry Cohen at Columbia and David did not doubt for a moment that he could tell her what to do. And he'd tell me, "Keep them calm. It's going to be six or seven hours before I get to them." The lighting – he would wait, he would take forever to get a lighting setup. First of all because everything – he wanted everything to look a certain way. He knew exactly how he wanted it to look. The dailies would come back from CFI and they'd say, "Are you shooting this with one candle in a tunnel?" You know. And David would send them that back saying, "Not dark enough. This is not dark enough. I want this darker." And he would keep actors waiting; he didn't like to keep them waiting, but he'd come out and schmooze with them and do what he had to do. But it was extraordinary. From the beginning, they also – they trusted him. And he had a very, a very clear idea. Not only visually, because he would think just from his background that visually he would be very sure of himself. But he was very sure of his directorial skills. And we were told what to do up to a certain point. I mean, David I think – David and I had a very strong personal relationship for a while and so he and I were more – he trusted me to do a whole bunch of things. I mean, the fact, I mean, a lot of the way things look are things that I brought around. He could have said no at any time and that would have been fine. There was that amount of control, but I think he realized that he had certain people who he could trust to do certain kinds of things. And – but no, this is David's show. This is really David's. We were all hand-maidens to genius. That really – it was David's vision, it was from – and

I think we were, the crew was part of David's vision. If he trusted us, he trusted us because he, David Lynch, trusted us – no, very much his, it was all his. He's not an egomaniac in – ostensibly. But he's – he's a director.

KGG: When you finally got to see the finished film, was it anything like what you thought you were doing at the time you were making it?

DS: Oh sure. Sure, we saw dailies every day. We had – we saw at the screening room at the American Film Institute, it was wonderful, very lush, very posh. And it was a big part of our day and we would see them. Sure. We knew what was happening. The first cut, the first finished cut with a mix which was sort of, was very long. It was unremitting. Just didn't give you a break. And there's the roaring in the sound effects and it gets a little loud and it gets a little difficult. A lot of scenes that David had put a lot of time into, he felt close to and couldn't cut, but then he did. He cut it and remixed it. And still, what I feel about *Eraserhead* is that it's a, it's a wonderful film and David's a wonderful director, why don't we give this boy some money and let him go and make a regular movie, almost. You know, it's – I think the fact, the stricture of – we started with ten thousand dollars, you know. He made ten thousand dollars go for three years. It takes a lot out of the production value. So I think, I think *Elephant Man* shows what he can do with a budget.

KGG: Yeah. But still, I mean, *Eraserhead* certainly looks much better than a lot of low budget films.

DS: Oh, yeah.

KGG: Considering the amount of care that's gone into it.

DS: Yeah, he wanted everything to look sort of that kind of – the black not only in *Sunset Boulevard*, the film – what? it's *American Tragedy*? I think it's what the Dreiser story is called, the one with Shelley Winters out on the lake with Montgomery Clift, where that lake is so black and so silvery at the same time, that kind of richness, that kind of deep satiny black. That's what we kept on thinking, you know. We all walked around – some of the nights on the set, it would've been fun to see when we had a dolly shot with a – we had – when we had to work the boom, we had a little gas tank. So it would be me riding on the dolly operating the boom, being pushed by David, me – had my stopwatch trying to get all those things going at the same time. There was no one – we never had any extra crew. Every once in a while when we had, when we did like the milk bath scene, we had a couple of extra people around because David – did David tell you how we did that?

KGG: No.

DS: Well, the way he did that was he rebuilt Henry's set outside, where the X's – where he built the X's house, the front of the X's house, right in front of the garage to the stables. He rebuilt Henry's house, Henry's set, and we got this big vat and filled it up with water and milk. And – freezing, it was cold, it was cold for southern California. And just so that these people would not die, David consented to hire a couple of extra people. Not that he didn't – he never cared about paying people, but he didn't want people around to see what he was doing. He wouldn't let the big boys up at the AFI see the baby when they were dying to see the baby. And –

KGG: I heard he kept the set locked.

DS: Not locked. I mean, they couldn't really keep it locked. It was their stables. They actually threw me – I was living there. Because I was living in a place called Topanga Canyon which is a little difficult to get to from Beverly Hills. And I couldn't drive all those hours and, having no sleep, so I was living in Henry's room. And they said I was a fire hazard. It was like a raid, I was sleeping. They kept coming after me, Well, I don't know – I'll – if you ask I'll tell you. I just don't want to, you know, ramble on about things that you're not interested in or –

KGG: Yeah. It's a little hard to – I mean, I wasn't quite sure exactly what your duties had been on the film as production manager, you know, what it had entailed.

DS: Well, it was always sort of *deus ex machina* in a way. But I was the producer; that was my job. The executive producers were the American Film Institute. I was the producer. I was responsible for everything. All of the money. All of the SAG reports. All of the food. All of the equipment. Everything that a regular, you know, that a producer does I did. The American Film Institute gave David the original grant. After the original grant ran out, I had to hustle up more money. David had to hustle up more money. We all had to hustle up more money to keep it going. The film was on, was on deferment. The equipment was the AFI's, so that was deferred. The SAG actors had to get a certain amount of money, then the other payments were deferred. But the reason Catherine – well, I don't – no, that's too personal. I don't want to talk about personalities, but – anyways – David talk about his new project? He's doing *Red Dragon* or something like that.

KGG: Well, he's doing *Dune* right now, and then *Red Dragon* is due after that.

DS: Who's writing the script for *Dune*?

KGG: David plus Eric Bergren and Chris DeVore, you know, the same guys who wrote *Elephant Man*.

DS: And who's the executive – is Brooksfilm doing this one too?

KGG: No. Dino De Laurentiis.

DS: Oh fuck.

KGG: That's what I thought too.

DS: That's too bad, isn't it? Like poor *Ragtime*.

KGG: Well, I sort of hope that David is strong enough to overcome any problems there.

DS: David's strong enough to overcome anybody. David is strong enough to overcome anybody. Really, David is – he is so sure that – well, he doubted himself for a while when *Eraserhead* was not – when he couldn't market it for a while, things were getting a little bleak. And David was going to give it up and teach meditation. But all of his – the close circle, we weren't going to let him, you know, he was our prize; we weren't going to let him go. We had – this is it – he also, if he didn't do it, it would have almost invalidated a whole bunch of our lives. But he – he's very tough. He knows exactly what he has. He knows exactly how talented he is. And he knows exactly how smart and how shrewd he is. Dino De Laurentiis, however, has – I don't know, he just seems to have the power to make, to turn good things into bad things.

KGG: Particularly when it comes to fantasy and science fiction.

DS: Yeah, he's going to want it – he's going to want it to appeal to the, I guess, to the most mass market level. I don't know what David's leverage is going to be. I don't know. But I guess Dino De Laurentiis has broken a better man than David. Or two. Or three.

KGG: I hope he can withstand it anyway.

DS: He's tough. I mean, David seems like, David seems like an innocent creature from Missoula, Montana, but he's nobody's pushover. And he's – and when he – he shouldn't fool you into thinking that he's not verbal at all. If he's done that. Because he is.

KGG: No. As I say, I have six or seven hours of interview on tape with him and I found him extremely articulate.

DS: Oh, did he – we all had to have our charts done before –

KGG: Why was that?

DS: Yes, we all had to go see this guy James up in one of the Hollywood hills someplace. And we all had to have our astrology – David was born, I think, on the same day Federico Fellini was born, on January twentieth. David's on the cusp of two odious creatures. I don't know. I – mine was – I had to tape mine, that's what reminded me. We had to put it on tape so he could hear what the astrologer said about us and see if we were compatible or not. But anyway we were – David and I were very very compatible. I think we – you see, we got along just about as well as two people can. We spent – we worked together, we – just our whole lives were completely intertwined for those three years. With no regrets. No regrets.

KGG: Do you ever think you'll work with him again?

DS: I think that's completely up to David. And I think that David is going to do what's good for David. I don't know what his – I don't know what David wants.

You know, he used to have this wonderful dream that he would own a studio – I guess like Lucasfilm, you know. And he'd build a studio, I guess, like he's building up in Marin, and it would be where he'd have a shop for building props and sets and we'd all work together and – but I don't know. I haven't known David since he's done *Elephant Man*, I really haven't. So I don't know what he wants. It would – the ball is not in my court. And I think that there is – let him be happy, let him do what he wants to do. I've got my own life, you know. And I think it never gets any better than *Eraserhead* got. You know, we'll all make more money than we made on *Eraserhead*, lord knows, but it'll never feel as good, I think, or better. Maybe it'll feel as good, but I don't think it can feel better than that. So committed to something, so proud of something. Yeah, if he wants it, fine. If he doesn't, fine.

KGG: Well, thanks very much for talking to me.

DS: You're very welcome. It was fun to talk about.

Jack Fisk

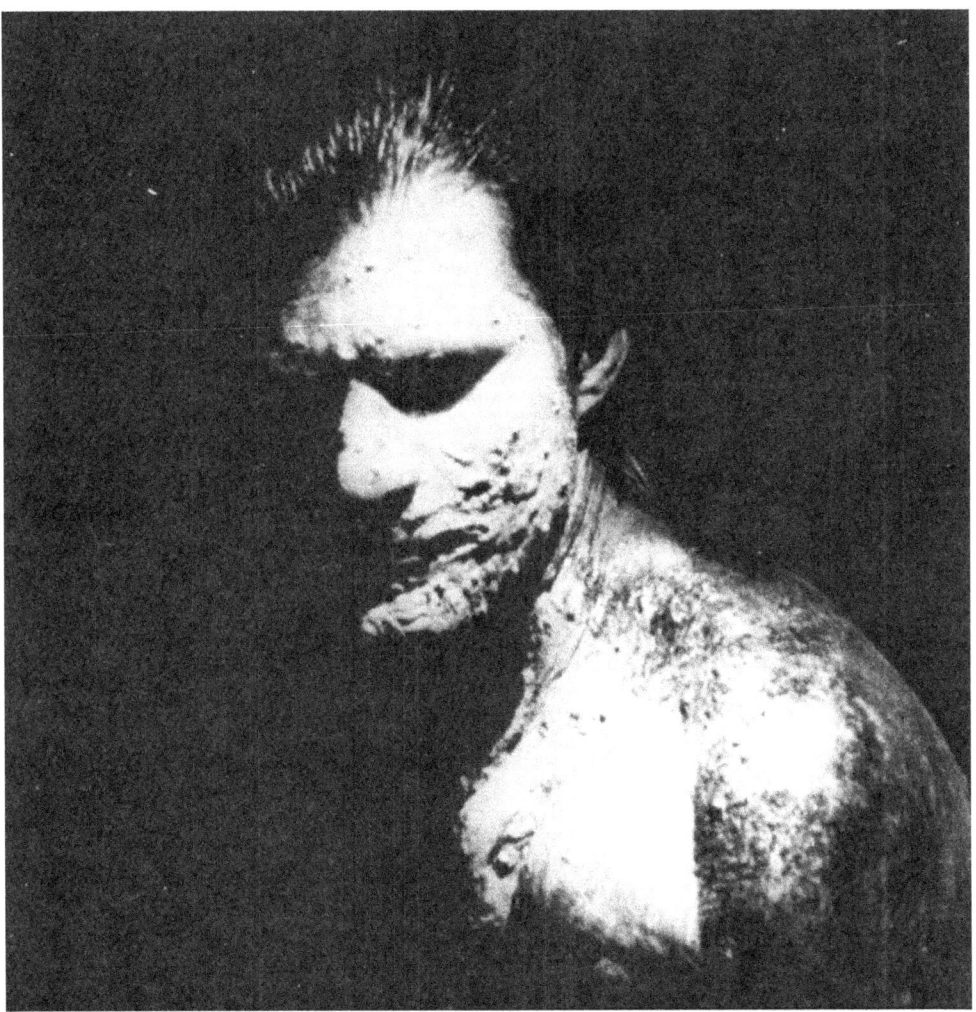

Jack Fisk as the Man in the Planet.

December 12, 1981 (by phone)

Jack Fisk, who has had a major career as an art director and production designer, played the Man in the Planet in *Eraserhead* as a favour to his old friend David Lynch.

Jack Fisk: I apologize for not getting through to you last night. I guess it was – I don't know what happened. I completely went blank.

Kenneth George Godwin: How did you meet David Lynch?

JF: I met David in high school, in 1960. And – we went to the same high school together. And we were both interested in drawing.

KGG: How did you get involved with his filmmaking?

JF: Well, David and I, we – after high school, we went to art school together – in Pennsylvania Academy. And then we moved out to L.A. at the same time. In fact, in the same truck. We put all our stuff in a big U-Haul van and moved to California, you know, with his wife Peggy and Jennifer. And that's, I mean, David and I have been real good friends for over twenty years, and when he started working on that film, I was working another film – I'd started working as an art director, but later he'd gotten so far in the film and was having trouble getting it finished, that Sissy and myself helped him financially. And I also did that small part in there – the Man in the Planet. And Sissy worked one day as a script clerk – I don't know, it's just everybody wanted to do whatever it took to help David get it done.

KGG: You hadn't worked on his earlier films?

JF: No. No, 'cause see David and I, we've always been real competitive. You know, we went to art school together. But we shared studios, like when we were in high school we had a studio – it was an old house – we shared it. We've always worked together, I mean, like side by side, but we haven't worked on very many projects together. You know, just because we – I don't know, it's sort of a professional jealousy. You know, it keeps us working, but we work better side-by-side than on the same projects.

KGG: What exactly was your work on *Eraserhead*? did you do much behind-the-scenes work?

JF: No. I – the only thing that I did was that Man in the Planet. And then we put up some money to help – Sissy and I put up some money to help him.

KGG: What kind of a makeup thing did you use for the Man in the Planet?

JF: I don't know. Because I'd just started growing a beard and I'd had it about two weeks. He got this stuff and it was like a latex and he brushed that on my face so it didn't look like I had a beard, but my skin was kind of deformed. I remember that then he built out my chest – he built some kind of cavity effect, like something was bulging out of my chest. And when I went home after doing this – that Man in the Planet; it just took one day – I went home and I was trying to get that stuff out of my beard, and it was impossible to come out. Sissy didn't want me to shave my beard off, and I always remember I was in a tub of hot water just like in this tub and pulling it out a little piece at a time. I've never really forgiven David for that. We still joke about it.

KGG: How did he explain it to you? what you were doing on the film. I mean, it's kind of a strange character to play.

JF: He never really did explain it to me. He just told me what he wanted me to do. I never - I've never completely understood the film. You know, there's so much personal stuff in it too. I mean, a lot of stuff in the film I recognize, you know, having lived with him so long. I mean, the address on the house, that was the address on the house we lived in in Philadelphia. And some of the visuals reminded me of things we'd seen together, you know, we'd been involved with. And there seemed to be a lot of personal stuff in the story, which when I saw the film, you know, I recognized. And I'd probably have made a different film out of it than what he'd originally thought of.

KGG: Would you like to work with him again?

JF: Well, I like - like I said, I don't think we could work very well together because we - I don't know - you know how it is when two people are both sort of artists or whatever. I want to do my own things and I want David to do his own things. I just have so much respect for him. I'd do anything that, you know, that he needed. But I'd never start out to do a project with him. But I'd love to - you know, I'd be real supportive of it. And I'd love to see it when it was done. He has a real neat vision. It's all in his head and - I don't know, especially filmmaking, it's so collaborative that everybody would have to bend around and follow the director, and it's hard for me to do. One thing he did - I lost my finger a couple of years ago, in an accident with a spray gun - so we made a fake finger - I use that every once in a while for a joke. I'm really glad you're doing this article on David - I'd like to know more about him. David's really my best friend, I guess. Because we've been through so much together. We lived in a lot of houses together. We've been together in Virginia, Pennsylvania, and California. It's just real neat, but I think we found out at an early age it was better to be together and working separate. I'm really excited what happened. He got - you know, he did that *Elephant Man* in, I'm not kidding you, two months - December, it was in December that he decided he was going to start looking for a job. Before that he was delivering newspapers, you know, living in a garage. And the weird thing is, you know, he married my sister after all those years we were friends. I don't know - I can't wait to read your article.

Laurel Near

Singer Laurel Near as the Lady in the Radiator.

December 15, 1981 (by phone)

Laurel Near was a singer when she became involved with *Eraserhead* through her friend Catherine Coulson. She portrayed the Lady in the Radiator.

Kenneth George Godwin: I'm doing an article on David Lynch and *Eraserhead* and, you know, I'm trying to talk to everybody I can. And so if you don't mind talking for a little while, maybe I could -

Laurel Near: Okay.

KGG: Could you tell me first of all how you met David?

LN: I was down in Los Angeles with my two sisters, Timothy and Holly, and we were singing in a trio called the Near Sisters, and I think it was Holly or Timmy that knew him through acting and theatre friends. But he came to a concert we were doing - I think I'd met him before that, but that's sort of where I officially met him.

KGG: What did he tell you he wanted?

LN: What did he tell me he wanted? Well, basically he said he liked my smile. And I was much younger then. So I didn't - I'd never done any films or anything like that, and it was like supposed to be a real small movie, you know, just practising. And so that's, yeah, basically it. And I said I'd do it. I didn't know what I was getting into really. In fact, I really didn't know what I was getting into until after I saw the film, because I only pretty much knew my own part in it. I didn't know anything about the film.

KGG: Had you done any film work before?

LN: No. No. I'd done lots of theatre and dance before, but not anything like this.

KGG: How complicated was the makeup that you had to wear?

LN: Oh, it was real complicated. That's one thing I didn't realize that I was getting into, you know. I thought I was just going to go and sort of dance across the stage. But the makeup was - I can't even remember the name of it, but they put - it was like warm - hot, and it was - they had to - I think I did it about five or six times and it was real thick stuff that when you took it off it just sort of peeled your whole face off with it. My face hurt a lot after the sessions. But they took a lot of time and they were real sweet to me, you know, they took care of me. But -

KGG: David did all that himself, did he, the makeup?

LN: David and someone else, yeah. Mostly David though, I recall. This is a long time ago and I can't really even remember that much about it.

KGG: How long were you working on the film?

LN: God, I think it was only maybe ten days. It wasn't very long, even if that. We worked real late at night, I remember, so that we could get all the lighting and stuff just right.

KGG: Can you remember any sort of particular incidents that stick out from your time on the film?

LN: Just working with David was a real treat. I love his sense of humour and just he's real - he's real sincere, he's a real sincere person. You know, basic. I just remember liking him as a person, you know, and he was - I remember he was - to make the film, he was throwing a paper route. He was really working hard throwing this paper route out of this little tiny Volkswagen that - I don't think the doors closed. And he was just - he was like a beautiful character, you know. I'm sort of glad I met him.

KGG: Have you worked with any of the people on the film since?

LN: No. I know Catherine Coulson, who did the lighting.

KGG: Yeah. She's the one who gave me your number.

LN: Yeah. She's real good friends with my family. We haven't worked together.

KGG: What are you doing now?

LN: After I did that, I joined a dance group in Oregon and we toured around a lot. It was a collective group of people and we created our own stuff, and I did that for seven years. And now I'm in a transition. I'm not sure what I'm up to. I came down to - I was living in Oregon and it's a real culture shock, coming down here, because it's very different, the cultural climate. I feel pretty square. And I came down here with my boyfriend. I thought maybe I could get more dance input and work down here, but it's not really happening. I don't - I think I'm more of a northern California person, and Oregon. So right now I'm just working at a health food store, trying to make enough money to probably leave.

KGG: Are you interested in doing any more film work?

LN: Yeah. Yeah, I am. I don't have a - I don't have a whole get up and go to go and dress up and go out and stuff to go get parts. So that's my problem.

KGG: I guess your role in *Eraserhead* hasn't produced many offers.

LN: Certainly right. I guess they can't see the real me in there. Or maybe they can. But I was real surprised when the film came out because I had no idea -

KGG: That it was a real film?

LN: What it was going to be like, this whole plot line. And it was real wonderful watching Jack Nance work, because - I don't know. Have you interviewed him?

KGG: Oh yes. I spent two afternoons with him,

LN: Yeah, he's really wonderful. So I felt like I was working with real unique, wonderful people.

Jeanne Bates

Jeanne Bates as Mrs. X (right).

December 9, 1981 (by phone)

Jeanne Bates played Mrs. X, Mary's mother, in *Eraserhead*.

Kenneth George Godwin: First of all, how did you meet David Lynch?

Jeanne Bates: Well, now, let me see. This was quite a while ago. Okay, well, I guess how it happened – and I can't remember her name now – it's been so long ago – but I was a member of Theatre West, which is a theatre workshop and one of the young women that was in the group at the time knew David and recommended me, and I interviewed David up at AFI and that's how it happened.

KGG: How was the project first presented to you?

JB: Well, only that it was the AFI and he was a young man and he seemed very enthusiastic and then I said yes, sure, because it seemed like an interesting thing to do. And then he showed me a film that he had done back in his home – now, I don't remember where that is either –

KGG: Philadelphia –

JB: Yeah. And he had done it with some friends of his and it was called **The Grandmother** and it was just wonderful. I was so impressed, not only with the picture itself, but with the sound and all that they did. And I was very impressed with David too because he seemed to be a very individual young man. That's kind of how it came about. And so they worked up at AFI which was the mansion of Mr Doheny and they shot it in the stables, up in a loft and it went on and on. It was kind of an interesting experience.

KGG: Had you done film before?

JB: Oh, yes. I mean, I'm a professional actress. I was under contract to Columbia for – I did twenty-two films for them. I starred in radio in San Francisco and – yeah, you know. But it was just I like to work and, you know, when something like that comes up, it's new and different and out of the ordinary, and if you're not working, making a buck – but David was kind of wonderful. I think he had some kind of a stipend and he insisted on paying the actors whatever – I can't remember now what the amount was, but he was very conscientious about wanting to pay the actors a stipend, for gas and whatever. And that was one of the things that was kind of dear about him. Because I don't know, you know, what his budget was, what they gave him, but he wanted to pay the actors.

KGG: Was there any problem, considering the sort of strange nature of the subject, in getting into the role?

JB: Oh, no. I thought it was divine 'cause I usually played, you know, the dear young thing, and nice young – well, at that time young – mothers and so forth. And I thought it was a ball because we put on moles and we put hair coming out of – and actually when I saw it it didn't look as dreadful to me as I kind of anticipated it would. It was pretty dreadful but, you know, I thought it was even worse than what I finally saw. But, oh no, that was the great part of it, the macabre-ness of it all.

KGG: Did he sort of define your character for you or was it pretty much left up to you?

JB: Yeah, he kind of suggested what – well, the script itself suggested that this lady was not fair and lovely. The whole situation was kind of – so it was, you know, half and half I guess. In other words, anything gross that I could think of or anything gross that he could think of was fine. I thought it was great. I have a still of my closeup with one eye drooping and the mole with the hair coming out of it and I loved it and I showed it to my husband and he said, "Tear it up. Throw it away." I still have it somewhere because I thought it was wonderful. I wanted to get out of doing nice ladies because I think in all of us is the feeling that you'd like to do something that's, well, like a heavy, or like an off-beat character.

KGG: What did you think the film was about while you were making it?

JB: Well, actually, I don't know if I can answer that because after seeing the whole thing put together – I think I came away with – it was just that this poor young man who didn't have all his marbles got involved with – well, it's kind of the off-beat people, I guess, of the world. You know, the people that really don't have a chance and they don't know – let's see – well, they're living and they're in life but they're kind of, they don't have a chance. They're sort of off-beat people but they're still in there – because they're alive, they're still in there living.

KGG: Did you like the film when you saw it completed?

JB: Well, yeah, I thought it was kind of fun. The baby with all of that – whatever – and I was intrigued as to how he got that effect. Yeah, you know. I mean, yeah, I liked it because I kind of admired what he was doing and the off-beatness of it. Yeah, I liked it because of his effort and the effort that was put into it. I don't know if that makes any sense.

KGG: Did you know any of the other people involved before –

JB: No, I didn't at the – oh, yes, one person; the man that played my husband Bill, Alan Joseph. I knew him from Theatre West. Oh yes, and I also knew the young woman that played – and I can't think of her name now, it's been so long and I haven't seen her since then –

KGG: Who played the daughter?

JB: No, no. I didn't know her, nor did I know the young man who played her husband. But the young woman that he kind of got involved with in the boarding house there where he was staying [Judith Roberts]. Anyway, I knew her. And she was the one that actually told David about me and at first David said, "Oh no, you're too pretty," or whatever it was. I mean, I said that's just your illusion.

KGG: Can you remember any particular incidents during the filming?

JB: Only that it was in this stable and it was in, not like downstairs where the horses were, but upstairs where they kept the hay and everything. And it was very close. That's all I remember about that really.

KGG: How long were you involved in the production? I mean, the whole thing went about five years –

JB: I know it went on because I saw David like two years later and he said that they had to stop because, you know, he didn't have the funds to go on, but I think – I can't really remember – two or three weeks I guess. Maybe four weeks. I can't really remember. Because I was only – well, yeah, the first set – our home, if you can call it that – anyway, where the chickens were all done and where the young man came to call on my daughter, was in the hayloft of the stable. Then there was another scene that they did at somebody's home way out in Los Angeles someplace – I don't remember now where it was – so, I guess it was over a period of two or three, four weeks.

KGG: Has being connected with a cult film had any effect on your career?

JB: No. I wouldn't say so. No, that was just, you know, one of those things that you did. However, a friend of mine sent me all of this – that's how I knew in a way it was a cult film, because I didn't know. David invited us to the showing, and then he cut the thing and then I think we saw it again. And then this friend of mine – there was a lot of publicity on it and my husband and I went to see it out in the valley when it was suddenly a cult film. That's all I really know about that.

KGG: What are you doing now?

JB: Well, at the moment I have a recurring role on *The Young and the Restless*. I had been on a series before that, *Ben Casey*. Well, I've been acting all my life. I was under contract to Columbia Pictures. I'm now in rehearsal to go out on the road in *Seven Brides for Seven Brothers*. We leave on the twentieth [December] to go down to San Diego for previews and then it's going to be six months on the road. My agent is about to kill me.

KGG: So, *Eraserhead* is probably the strangest thing you've done.

JB: Oh yes. Well, when I was under contract to Columbia, I did some mysteries and strange things. My husband was a radio writer and director – that's how I met him in San Francisco, he was doing a murder mystery called *Who Done It?* – and the show was so popular there, they brought it down to Hollywood, and the agency said, you know, if you want to come down and get a – we'll give you a few jobs, so come on down. So I did. But at Columbia I did some strange films. And then I did a film with Eric von Stroheim called *The Mask of Dijon* and that was kind of strange too. He was a hypnotist and I was married to him. And this was just after the war, before he went back to Paris. And I played his wife and he was a hypnotist – and it was very strange. Yeah, no, I'm into strange and eerie things.

Peter Ivers

December 10, 1981 (the Beverly Garland Howard Johnson's, North Hollywood)

Although Peter Ivers was a well known *avant garde* and New Wave musician, when I met him in December 1981, all I knew about him was that he had written the music for and sung "In Heaven", the song performed by the Lady in the Radiator in *Eraserhead*. Knowing next to nothing about someone you're interviewing isn't a very good idea; doing the interview in a busy, and loud, restaurant in a Howard Johnson's hotel just compounds the problem. Needless to say, my interview with Ivers was not my finest hour during the week I spent in Los Angeles researching the production of David Lynch's debut feature, although Ivers was an engaging lunch companion. After that meeting, I managed to track down several of his records, which I liked a lot and played frequently for years.

It was shocking to learn, a year-and-a-half after our meeting, that Peter Ivers was brutally murdered in his apartment less than three weeks before I arrived back in Los Angeles to start working on *Dune*. His killer has never been identified.

Kenneth George Godwin: The first thing I should ask is how you met David?

Peter Ivers: The AFI. Tim Hunter was the first person to make a film at Harvard, and he came out here the first year of the AFI, which included many, you know, luminaries that first year – Jeremy Kagan and Tim Hunter and Stanton Kaye and Howard Smith, who I still work with. Tim brought me out and I did a score for him and other people admired the score and I did maybe five or eight that first year for various people. I wasn't really connected with the AFI, and Alan Splet was the AFI sound guy. He had recorded me many times and he was an admirer of mine and he kind of told David about me and really that was the setting in which we met, the old Greystone Mansion.

KGG: How was *Eraserhead* first presented to you?

PI: Well, we all knew David was working on some weird project. A lot of people really were more familiar with the script, or had seen ***The Grandmother***, but when I did this I hadn't seen ***The Grandmother***. And I'm a total creative soul … you know, I'm interested in all collaborations and he just came to me with the lyric, and explained the kind of sound concept having to do with the organs and those sustaining hums that he builds. And he wanted … he knew it was the girl in the [radiator] and he wanted me to sing it. It is me singing, and …

KGG: I didn't know that until just the other day.

PI: Yeah, yeah. I sing in a high ... I made albums that are much more rock and that, and I wrote it and I came to him like the next day, I think. And he said "fine, that's great, that's it." And, you know, I know how to accept that, and that's it. And then I was making an album and we ... you know, David at that time was, he would go through ... I'd bump into him on the Warners lot and he would be stealing, he would be taking film stock out of the trash cans to use as leader on the sound reels and stuff like that, and I was making an album at a studio in Hollywood and just after our session we used the organ and stuff in that studio. A pal of mine from Harvard, [Brad Berg?], came and played the organ, and the engineer for that Warner Brothers album recorded us and I laid it down a half-hour or an hour after a session.

KGG: Was it a lot different from the usual music you write?

PI: I have done a lot of theatre and I've done a lot of films and my natural stuff is more rock, but I've always been *avant garde* and I have tons of weird material that maybe doesn't equal that because of the orchestration perhaps, but, you know, I've made an *avant garde* album in '69 that had oboe, bassoon and harmonica as the harmony section, no guitar.

KGG: What exactly did he say he was looking for in the music?

PI: That was a long time ago.

KGG: When did you first get onto the film?

PI: This was in '71 or '72.

KGG: So it was right around the beginning?

PI: Yeah, 'cause they shot to the sound. You know, it was in ... we talked about it and maybe even had written it, then we got to the point where he was going to shoot it and we needed to record it, and that was in '74, when it was recorded. In the Spring. I can't remember his exact words. You know, you read the script and you talk to David, he gives you a good idea. You don't really know where his ... he has his own logic. But I'm somebody who is intuitive ... I'd like to do more with him, I was hoping that *Ronnie Rocket* would be his next picture and then ... there may have been many composers, but I was hoping to do something in that. I play harmonica so ... and he really loves the blues, you know, we used to listen ... well, I think at the time Sonny Boy Williamson helped me. You know that record? It's a blues that has an organ in it, was a reference point. And I was influential in the Fats Waller, as I recall now. I was living with a guy who owned that Fats Waller record and I, either he mentioned it to me and I knew he had it or I turned him onto it, I don't really remember how Fats came into it, but I did loan him the record.

KGG: I find it interesting the way he uses sound in the film, very different from the way most filmmakers use it.

PI: Most filmmakers use underscore where he has the music, that hum be part of the fabric of it. In the sense that industrial hum exists and in the sense that he likes to keep his thumb on the dramatic ... you know, I host this New Wave TV show called *New Wave Theater* – it's on in all fifty states, it was named one of America's top twenty-five cable stars – and David has, we have what we call ghost hosts, we have this wild Andy Warhol-style shooting thing that we do and who's ever around, there's no set, who's ever around stands with me when I'm introducing the bands and he was there for, I forget what, he was my [...] for the band, but I said "David", he told me to ask him what New Wave was, so I said "David, what's New Wave?" and he said, if I look at the video I tell you the exact quote, he said "picture a truck packed with cows, maybe fifty or sixty cows going down the highway, fifty or sixty miles an hour, and one of the cows gets his head down in between the floorboards and his face is rubbing on the asphalt, and the sound and the stench, that's New Wave."

KGG: Was that complimentary or ...?

PI: And the other thing he did on the show was [*makes a gesture with his hand*] ... this was the configuration it was in; "remember, you saw it here first" and he had his hand in some weird, as if it had been sawed ... David's a poet too, you know.

KGG: I know he paints.

PI: He writes ... his paintings are great, but he writes lyrics too. He did the paintings in *Heartbeat*.

KGG: I haven't seen that.

PI: It's a scene where Kerouac and, you know, the other characters are at an art opening and the art on the wall is David's. They're big canvasses. Jack Fisk, I think, was the art director. You talking to Fisk?

KGG: I haven't been able to get hold of him yet. I'm not even sure if he's in town right now. I'd like to of course. In *Eraserhead*, as I said, the sound is very different from the usual thing because the effects aren't used the way effects are usually used just to ...

PI: The effects become music.

KGG: Yeah, the effects become music and so the music is sort of relegated to another effect in the whole pattern.

PI: Well, no, he uses them, he uses the music for psychological mood. I mean, even though he puts on that scratchy record in the room and a couple of places where you hear this very distant, very echoey mysterious organ, but not so much music as opposed to what David and Alan created. I mean there's some, the Fats Waller stuff and there's the song by me and him, he wrote the lyric. You know Devo performed that song in their act for a whole year on the road.

KGG: I didn't know that.

PI: And a band called Tuxedo Moon, which is an *avant garde* San Francisco band, also recorded it.

KGG: What other films have you done?

PI: *Grand Theft Auto*. A lot of student films, some episodic TV. I produced the songs in *Airplane*, you know the singing nun. There's tons of credits; the next to last credit is mine, just in a thank-you list of about ten people. And then I wrote two songs in Paramount's *Jekyll and Hyde Together Again*, which is a comedy, and it was choreographed for twenty punk rock dancers, with a girl whose costume lit up different parts of her body. That's coming out next Spring. I'm really known in the underground. My own albums have been very advanced. *Eraserhead* is definitely a cult credit. And I'm trying to do more mainstream work now, like David, as well as doing the underground stuff because it doesn't ... I need more money.

KGG: Do you like working in films?

PI: Yeah, I like to collaborate. I like to ... if I understand what they want, I can deliver. A composer always works with intuition, get the vibes. Because people know music but they don't really know music, it's not like ... in almost any musical work anywhere.

KGG: Yeah, when you hear it, you know it's what you want, but it's hard to describe it beforehand.

PI: Yeah. Most people who come to me want my, want me. Now I'm hustling in another ... I was supported for a few years by various art patrons and products, and now it's kind of run out and I have to get that money somehow. I wasn't generally for hire at that point. I was more, you know, an artist, somehow I'd do it myself. You know, that's one of my most famous things, that movie.

KGG: How do you like the film?

PI: I've seen it about forty, fifty, you know, yeah, when it first came out, I took everybody to it. Now, I'm OD'd basically. I saw it about a month before it closed at the cinema. You know, I [...] some musicals myself. I'm kind of the Mike Todd of the underground. I do video, art videos, stuff like that.

KGG: I can't really think of any questions about the music in the film. It hasn't really got that much music.

PI: Right. No, sounds become music... German art music or Eno related to David's musical ideas, he has an instinct for ... And the sound on *Elephant Man*. Of course Alan Splet won the Academy Award and when he didn't show up Johnny Carson made jokes about it, he was hosting the Academy Awards. Tremendous three-dimensional sense of space, which you see ... all that churning underneath is like the inner mind. You know how everybody's inner life is always going wild and that's constantly part of this watery mystery going on, a little disturbing, and sometimes a little relaxed and then you get disturbed again, is like the mind itself. It adds a dimension.

KGG: That's what in *Eraserhead* draws you right into it. It's like having someone's dream running in your own head.

PI: And some of the ambiguity of that is what's so modern and interesting about it, and what gives it its shades and colours beyond the flat and the two-dimensional. It's not like ... it's true art when you see that movie, every frame is an architectural, geographic design, but it doesn't have any of the unrealism ... it has surrealism, it doesn't have what, say, a Roger Corman film has or one of those dumb horror movies where, where ... not camp ... it has total seriousness and conviction, even though it has a lot of humour in it.

KGG: Yeah.

PI: I forget what I was going to say about David. He's ... you met Mary and everybody? Mary, his wife.

KGG: So far it's just been people who worked on the film.

PI: He has a very clear idea of what he wants. I noticed in a John Hurt interview somewhere, he said that David mostly takes first takes, first or second takes, which is great.

KGG: He's extremely good at getting across his ideas in an interview, even when he's talking about things that aren't specific that you can pin down. His whole thing with feeling rather than sort of an intellectual knowing of what he's after, he feels what he wants.

PI: The artist.

KGG: He's still very clear even though that's not something you can pin down and label, what he's trying to get across. Which is why his films are, they're sort of abstract in a way but they're extremely clear. There's nothing sort of confusing in *Eraserhead*, even though it's so strange.

PI: No, it's not ... it's a simple story. Guy gets his girl pregnant and they have a premature baby, and told through this nightmarish inner life of David, which kind of expands and engulfs the story and, you know, blossoms into this industrial ...

KGG: You've seen *The Grandmother*, I take it? That's even stranger, but it's still very clear.

PI: The dirt in her room. ... I didn't spend that much time, I mean, he and I connected but we don't spend a lot of time together really. In those days, you know, I'm kind of fast and direct and so's he, there's no bullshit, which I like. What magazine is this for?

KGG: *Cinefantastique*, out of Chicago.

PI: They fly you into Hollywood to actually do it.

KGG: They flew me in because David insisted on it. I was supposed to do it through a third party.

PI: What was the third party?

KGG: Well, I wrote this essay about *Eraserhead* last winter, which I sent to the magazine and the editor sort of liked it and wanted to expand it, do something on the film. So he sent it to David to see if he was interested, and David considers it the best thing he's seen on *Eraserhead* so far, so he wanted to do it with me and the magazine, they just wanted me to send down my questions and their guy here would do the interviews and I'd just take the ...

PI: And David actually ...

KGG: David called them up and said, you know, "give him a ticket", so they did. It's a great thing for me.

PI: So what was the essence of your article?

KGG: Well, it's split up into parts. The first one ... it's very difficult to put into, to put what I was trying to do into words, even in the essay ... how it works in its dream-like way, you know, how he creates that feeling. And then I tried to get at some kind of analysis of the symbols in it, which ...

PI: What do you think of the girl in the radiator? The lady in the radiator ...

KGG: Well, this is tough ... see, in my analysis there's a strong sort of sexual thing running through the whole thing, and sex is something fearsome in this film. And his dream of this woman in the radiator is, I mean, it is his heaven, but it's a sexless heaven.

PI: I can't show you any, but he has a bunch of, I don't know, he'd be angry if I revealed this ... he writes poems that are like "pus", "moon", "suck", "flame", "asshole", "groin" ... you know, very, total anger, which he wouldn't really express ... you know about his family or anything?

KGG: Well, he's told me that he had a very clean, clear background, a happy childhood and all this sort of thing.

PI: His dad worked for the forest service, you know, runs one of those forests in Virginia or someplace.

KGG: That's what I was saying, he seems so normal.

PI: Did you talk to Sanger and Stuart Cornfeld?

KGG: I talked to Stuart Cornfeld, yeah.

PI: Did Stuart get his true ... I mean, Stuart ... I don't know what and why it happened that he didn't end up producing the movie. He got Mel ... he brought me in ... he saw the movie and he had me and David ... I had known him from somewhere way in the past, he was at CalArts, he was a friend of a friend. We went and talked to him and a few months later he got Mel to, actually got Mel to see it and really did a job to put that together, but I think Sanger might be more able to execute David's will. I'm not sure how they work together. I wasn't involved in all of that.

KGG: Cornfeld said that once he sort of put it together, that was pretty well it for him. And Sanger was there on the set working all the time.

PI: What does David say about the music?

KGG: For *Eraserhead*?

PI: Yeah. Did he elaborate about his and Alan's concepts at all?

KGG: Well, basically just that thing of getting sound that is halfway between sound effect and music, that's very sort of plastic and ...

PI: Mold it.

KGG: Yeah, the way it's used to guide your mood through the visuals. It's sort of hard to remember the specifics now. The last few days I've talked to lots of people.

PI: [David's assistant] Steve Martin?

KGG: He wasn't quite what I expected either. I talked to him on the phone a bit before coming down here.

PI: He hosts ... I started my TV show on public access and we had to go off public access when it went national. And now there's a show in that time slot called *Brown Box Theater*, which Steve Martin hosts as Eddie, and it's a real conceptual ... they trip out for thirty minutes. Public access, you can do anything, you know, it could be Steve in a dress dancing with a cowboy, stopping traffic ... you know, they go and they do ... and then he can just get totally, he can talk about ... I saw this one *Brown Box Theater* where he talked about kids and violence and the violence folding back on the kids and it was extremely articulate. He's a good writer too. He makes things happen, he's an excellent producer. Good at following up and putting people together, putting stuff together. His brother designs the ... you ever see the posters for the Fox Venice or the NuArt, like, they have a different movie every day and they're usually classics?

(After ordering dessert:)

PI: I lived in Boston. You could drive from New York to Boston, there's a Howard Johnson's on the road.

KGG: You originally came from the East?

PI: I was born in Chicago. My father died when I was about three-and-a-half and my mother remarried a Bostonian. So I grew up in Brookline, Mass, went to Harvard. I studied Latin and Greek and learned to play rock-and-roll. I made a couple of albums in New York and then in '71 Tim Hunter invited me out to the AFI and it was ... drove out again to do some more scores over the next year and then ended up staying.

KGG: Been here ever since ...

PI: About '72. My ex-girlfriend is Lucy Fisher, we'd been together about eleven years, she's now vice president of Warner Brothers, but she was the head of Zoetrope when David was there, only one adventurous enough to believe in *Ronnie Rocket*.

KGG: It'd be nice if that could get off the ground sometime, it sounds really interesting.

PI: It will, but *Dune* could be another five years. They haven't cast it yet, have they?

KGG: No, he's only just got the first draft script in to Dino De Laurentiis, so ... he wanted to try and start shooting next summer, but that looks as if it's not going to come off. Wanted to get into pre-production next Spring sometime.

PI: Well, corporate time moves much slower than the artist's time. And you either rail against it or you can figure out a way to hang in there.

KGG: It must be pretty frustrating.

PI: When you're spending millions of bucks, you have a lot of points of view to consider. It's not like ... I don't know ... he had no problem handling *Elephant Man*. On budget, on time. Yeah, he had problems, but ...

KGG: He seems to be extremely good at handling ... I mean, each film he's done has been vastly bigger than the previous one ...

PI: Yeah, and now he's going for vastly bigger. Probably go smaller after *Dune*.

KGG: He mentioned he already has a project lined up to follow *Dune*.

PI: Not *Ronnie Rocket* then?

KGG: No, it's about a mass murderer ...

PI: He's attracted to those themes. ... I mean, it's great to see that something with true artistic merit was discovered by the public and maintained really all its artistic ... I mean, yeah, it has shock value like *Rocky Horror Show*, but it's a much more serious piece ...

KGG: The only relation between those two really is that they're both cult movies.

PI: One plays Friday, one plays Saturday.

KGG: One's a lot of fun and one is something that you go to really get into.

PI: I believe they're actual umbilical cords dropping from the ceiling, they got from the hospital, that are stepped on by the lady in the radiator. I asked him about that. I'm pretty sure that's ...

KGG: I know he got a real dead cat for one scene.

PI: You mean "real dead" as opposed to, you mean a very dead cat ...

KGG: Yeah, he got it from a vet. It's not a stuffed cat from an antique store or something.

PI: His wife Mary, I believe, is a great aid to him. I really like her too.

KGG: Is she in the business as well?

PI: Not really. She does stuff ... she seems to handle some of his business. I've got phone calls from her about them publishing this *Eraserhead* album.

KGG: There's an album?

PI: Hasn't Steve Martin told you that?

KGG: No.

PI: Maybe it's a secret. They've either made a record deal or there've been discussions about putting out an album. I guess that isn't official, so ... I mean, I wasn't really involved. I wonder if there were ever royalties from, whether Libra has actually made, is in profit from Libra or not.

KGG: I haven't talked too much about money to him.

PI: I think ... I'd be personally interested just to know ... you make one of the farthest out underground hits, is there any, I mean, is it totally art or is there ...? I'm sure there's value over time if he owns the rights or something like that. I know people don't really talk about money versus art, but they have to be reconciled, and it's a very ... you know, there are diminishing resources. What the relationship is, it's just a major factor that has to be considered in any project. Expenses of doing anything are really high. Post-production, production, stock, actors ...

KGG: The bigger you get, the harder it is to maintain the art. Whereas with *Eraserhead*, where he was working so slowly and privately, I mean, that's probably going to remain his purest film, his purest feature no matter how much he does.

Additional Interviews

The final group of short interviews I did for my article were with people who connected with David Lynch after *Eraserhead* had been finished: Ben Barenholz, who distributed the film; and Mel Brooks, Stuart Cornfeld and Jonathan Sanger, who put their trust in Lynch because of *Eraserhead* and gave him his first chance at directing a commercial feature, *The Elephant Man*.

Ben Barenholz

December 16, 1981 (by phone)

Ben Barenholz, through his distribution company Libra Films, practically invented the concept of the "midnight movie" with his release of such films as *El Topo*, *Pink Flamingos* and *The Harder They Come* in the 1970s.

Kenneth George Godwin: My name is George Godwin. I'm doing an article on David Lynch and *Eraserhead* and I wonder if I could just talk to you for a few minutes?

Ben Barenholz: Sure. What – where are you doing this article for?

KGG: It's for a magazine called *Cinefantastique* out of Chicago. Yeah, I was down in L.A. last week talking to David Lynch and other people about it – I wondered if you could first of all tell me when you first saw *Eraserhead*? when you first encountered it?

BB: You mean, in a date aspect?

KGG: Well, no – where and how you came across the film?

BB: I think somebody mentioned it to me and we called David and he shipped in a print. I think it was after – the only previous showing of that was at Filmex.

KGG: Yeah.

BB: And somebody had seen it at Filmex and told me about it and we called David and a print was shipped in.

KGG: What was your reaction when you first saw the film?

BB: Honestly? I was in my screening room with somebody who was working for me at the time and about halfway through the film I told him to get on the phone and make a deal for the film. I liked it.

KGG: What was it about the film that appealed to you?

BB: Oh, I think basically it was its originality. I know a bit about those kinds of films and I just thought it was so original and so – there was so much in it and I just thought I could do something with it.

KGG: Did you have any reservations about being able to sell it to anybody?

BB: No. I didn't have any reservations about being able to sell it. My reservation was that the film was so far out that it wasn't going to be an easy sale, that it had to be worked. And that the process was going to take a long time, that it was going to be very slow.

KGG: How did you go about that?

BB: Well, basically it was in the way I've handled quite a few other things, like *El Topo*, *Pink Flamingos*, *The Harder They Come*. Essentially it's through the midnight circuit that you create a discovery aspect of it. The film had to be discovered, not only by the distribution end but by an audience. And the only way to do that economically is to put it on at midnight. And get it out to an audience economically. The film has – even to date, it's a limited audience film. Just not that many people see it. If you go through the normal process many films are killed that way, that are limited audience. The problem is how to reach that limited audience economically.

KGG: Has it continued to build steadily?

BB: I have a feeling it's been playing very steadily now for the past four years. It's still as strong now as it was four years ago.

KGG: And it's now being seen overseas, I understand.

BB: Oh yes, we have it in about twelve countries.

KGG: What kind of response is it getting in other countries?

BB: Okay. But it's still a – I think wherever it's been handled properly in relation to the limited audience aspect, it's done well. It's doing very well in England, for instance. Because the people who are handling it understand how to handle it. But you can't go out there in a fifty theatre break with it. I mean, it's funny – the French tried it.

KGG: It didn't work?

BB: It actually – we don't know. The results aren't in yet. But I don't think it'll work. I don't think it lends itself to that.

Mel Brooks

December 8, 1981 (by phone)

Mel Brooks used the resources of his own production company, Brooksfilms, to give David Lynch his first chance at a mainstream directing job, *The Elephant Man*.

Mel Brooks: All right, I have a couple of minutes if I can be of any help. What're you doing? interviewing David Lynch?

KGG: Yeah. I'm doing an article on him. The main reason I wanted to talk to you was I just wanted to find out why you would have chosen him to direct your sort of first serious production – *Elephant Man*.

MB: A man called Stuart Cornfeld. Stuart Cornfeld was my associate producer on *History of the World*. While we were doing that and I was putting together *The Elephant Man* with Jonathan Sanger, the producer, Stuart also was the executive producer of *The Elephant Man*. Stuart was a big fan of this fellow David Lynch who I'd never heard of and I said, "Why have I never heard of him?" and he said, "Because he's an underground filmmaker." He's made two films that Stuart knew of called *Eraserhead* and *The Grandmother*. So I said, "Well, why do you think he'd be good for *The Elephant Man*, Stuart?" And Stuart said, "Because he has an understanding, a clear understanding of the unconscious mind." So, a lot of that is happening in *The Elephant Man*. So I said, "I think you're crazy and I'm not going to take a chance on a new director and you're an asshole and a fool but I'll take a look at this *Eraserhead*. So I went to see *Eraserhead* and I was flabbergasted. I said, "This is clear, it's very clear. It's beautiful and it's clear. It's like Beckett, it's like Ionesco. And it's very moving. And very, very well done." I mean, I said this is really kind of Max Reinhardt, expressionistic filmmaking. So I said, "What else has he got?" Then I saw *The Grandmother*, and I thought that was lovely, touching, and weird and beautiful. Then I met with David and I expected to meet a grotesque – you know, I expected to meet a, I don't know, a fat little German with fat stains running down his chin and just eating pork. And I meet this clean American Charles Lindbergh with a leather jacket who walks into my office – I can't believe that this WASP kid could ever – I mean, it's like Jimmy Stewart thirty-five years ago, you know. And he sits down and he has an "r" in his speech – New Yorkers, we don't have an "r" in our speech – and he had this "r", and little by little I began to see that it was the same person, that it was indeed David Lynch. Because when he spoke about our unconscious feelings, our ever-present underneath feelings, I mean, he was very clear, very simple and eloquent. And when he talked about *The Elephant Man*, he convinced me that it was something that he should do. So, when I told the people, the backers, you know, that I'm just going with a new underground filmmaker, I mean, I had to fight, literally fight them – fist fights, sword fights, all kinds of fights. And I said, "No. I believe that this is the young man to do it."

KGG: So you didn't have any reservations about using him?

MB: Never! I never did – everybody else did. And he was also valuable in the writing. He sat down with Chris and Eric – Christopher DeVore and Eric Bergren – and they put their cards up on the wall like I taught them to. And little by little they made – I must say with a little help from me in the writing – they made a wonderful script and, I mean, the rest is history.

KGG: And you're satisfied with what he produced?

MB: Oh, are you kidding? Satisfied – I'm head over heels in love with it. Satisfied is a very meagre description of my feelings for his contribution to that picture. I wish we could work again together. We haven't found a subject that both of us want to work on, but the minute we do we'll be working again. I mean, he's the wildest combination of a child and an old Einsteinian genius that I've ever met, you know. He's fucking weird. But he's the most decent, honest, hardworking crazy man you'll ever work with.

Stuart Cornfeld

December 9, 1981 (by phone)

Stuart Cornfeld was the executive producer of *The Elephant Man*.

Stuart Cornfeld: I heard about the film from a friend of mine at the American Film Institute, who had seen a rough cut of it, and said that I would probably like it. And then I – I knew that it was going to open up at the NuArt Theatre in Los Angeles, at this midnight screening. So I went to see it and I think there were about twenty-five people in this audience. This was the first time that it had been shown and I – I looked at this friend of mine who I went with and I said, "Jesus, I've never seen anything like this before." And I thought it was the best film I'd ever seen, and certainly the most unique. You know, the guy did so many things that had never even been tried before, let alone executed. So the following Monday – I knew that David had attended the AFI, so I called them up and asked for his phone number, and called him up. And he was out in Riverside, repairing roofs with his father, and I said, "Listen, I just wanted to tell you I thought your film was incredible." And he thanked me, and I asked him what he was doing, and he said well, you know, he was repairing roofs and that the initial reception that the film had had, like a year before that when he had finished it and screened it for people was, you know, somewhat disappointing and that he hadn't received any offers to do anything. So, we got together and we had lunch, and we, you know, we basically became very good friends. And he decided that – I mean, I thought he was great and, you know, I asked him what he wanted to do next and he said, well, he had this idea for a film called *Ronnie Rocket*. So, he then decided that he would write the film and he wrote the screenplay, which is, I would say, the most unique screenplay I've ever read.

KGG: Stranger than *Eraserhead*?

SC: Much stranger – I don't like to use the word strange, but – let's just say more things happen in *Ronnie Rocket* than happened in *Eraserhead*. And, you know, we tried to set that up, but nobody was very interested in it. And then we – then after this kind of disappointing period of trying to get people to put money into *Ronnie Rocket*, we had a conversation where David said, "Gee, you know, maybe I should consider directing something somebody else has written." And I thought that that was a good idea.

KGG: Did you have any projects then that would have –

SC: At that point no, but two weeks later Jonathan Sanger gave me the script to *The Elephant Man*, and I read it and said, "Look, I know the guy to direct this. I mean, there's no question in my mind that I know the absolute perfect director for that film."

KGG: Well, what was it in the script that made you think of David?

SC: Well, I think basically his ability to deliver a character as being sympathetic even if they're – you know, even if they're just sort of – I don't know, cut from a different swath. I mean, it was basically that and it was also the tone of the piece. You know, David is so good with sound and that was just the right time for – you know, I mean, that – the end of the Victorian Age. You know, you get all these great sounds. And the fact that it was a seemingly bleak yet ultimately transcendent piece, which is where I feel that David has his greatest strength.

KGG: Did you have any trouble convincing other people of that?

SC: No – well, I – yes and no. I didn't have any trouble convincing David that it should be – that he should proceed with that script. I didn't have any trouble convincing Jonathan that he should be the person to do the film.

KGG: He'd already seen *Eraserhead*?

SC: No, he hadn't. But he met with David and David's discussion of what he wanted to do with the film was, you know, real specific and he was very clear on what he wanted out of the film and I think he impressed everybody about it. It was impossible to convince anybody at any studio. I mean, it wasn't a problem because it was an impossibility. But that had to do as much with the subject matter of the film itself as with David. I mean, I – it was the kind of film, the kind of screenplay where the initial reception was basically, people weren't really interested in it, didn't think it was a commercial work. I'm sure the only reason they would have done that film is if a director of some renown had said, "This is my next film. Do you want to do a film with me?" And, you know, nobody was very interested in working with David Lynch who they would just sort of write him off as some strange, you know, breed of non-director. However, I didn't have any problem at all convincing Mel Brooks.

KGG: You were already connected with him at the time?

SC: Yeah, I had worked with him for two-and-half years at that point. And I told Mel that I knew the guy to direct it and Mel really – Mel said, "Okay. It sounds good to me." And actually we, you know, he met David and he was, again, impressed with David. And at a certain point, just before we signed the contract for *Elephant Man*, I said, "Listen, Mel, you know you should really see *Eraserhead*." And Mel loved it. Mel loved it. I'll tell you, the two people – I mean, other than myself and a couple of friends of mine – the two people who really had the biggest reaction to *Eraserhead* in terms of it being the work of a mature mind were Mel and my mother, who both really loved the film, and who both – it was strange, they both really understood the film in exactly the same way, and it was a way I didn't even see it in terms of, you know, really being specifically a parable of responsibility. You know, I mean I was a little too young to appreciate that kind of stuff.

KGG: Once Mel Brooks was connected with it, did everything go quite smoothly? or did you still have any trouble raising the money for it?

SC: Well, I don't know. You know, we ultimately got the money and we ultimately got the money in a way that was very beneficial to the production, because we were completely autonomous. The film would not have been done had it not been for Mel Brooks. I mean, there is absolutely no question about that. I mean, he was – basically, he made a deal where he ended up having to promise services of his own in the future to raise the money, which I don't know of anybody having ever done, you know, to get an unknown – you know, to get their first break. But, you know, we ended up raising the money.

KGG: Were there any serious problems during the filming? or did it all go quite smoothly?

SC: Yeah, I mean, it went smoothly – well, there was initial – there was an initial problem with the makeup, but that was resolved down the line. But I was not that involved with the actual day by day production. I basically was working on *History of the World* by that time so, you know, Jonathan and David would be the people you should ask about that.

KGG: How do you like the film?

SC: *Elephant Man*? It's a great film.

KGG: You're quite happy with what he did with it?

SC: Absolutely. You know, I always knew that he would deliver something great. You know, it was nice that, even seeing the film – you know, that I had contributed to – I could still look at it as a fan of David Lynch. But I was really pleased with it.

Jonathan Sanger

December 10, 1981 (by phone)

Jonathan Sanger was the producer of *The Elephant Man*.
KGG: How did you first hear of David Lynch?
Jonathan Sanger: Well, I'll tell you – I first heard about David from a fellow by the name of Stuart Cornfeld who was an assistant to Mel Brooks at the time and he had mentioned – I had already optioned the screenplay of *The Elephant Man*, and I was looking for a director and Stuart just suggested I see *Eraserhead*, and told me where it was playing, he said I should see it. So I went to see it and I was fascinated by the movie and asked to meet David. I mean, I tried to find out where he was, and set up a meeting and gave him the script to read just to see – I sent him the script and decided to have a meeting with him. After the meeting – when I did meet him I was astonished; he was not at all what I had expected he would be. And we just started talking about the script and everything I felt about it he felt about it too. We had very, really good discussions. We met at Santa Monica Bob's Big Boy and then spent the whole afternoon together talking about music for the film and all kinds of things about the movie. And I really had a very good feeling about him right from the start. So, after that meeting, we continued to meet and I felt real good about him and decided that I wanted to see if we could – if I could convince whatever company it was that I was going to be working with that I wanted David to direct it.

KGG: What was it about *Eraserhead* that made you want to meet him with regard to *Elephant Man*?
JS: I'll tell you – when I saw *Eraserhead* initially, it was the kind of movie where just his use of film technique to me was astonishing for somebody who'd never really had very much film experience before. And it was confirmed very soon after that when he let me see *The Grandmother*. I mean, I said, "Jesus, he's not a flash in the pan. This is somebody who has a real consistency of vision." I mean, there are images that are repellent and images that you may not like, that you can't – I couldn't come out of *Eraserhead* and say, "Gee, I loved it." It's not that kind of a movie. But it's the kind of movie where, I mean, I was quite impressed with his grasp of a language which he'd developed himself. I mean, it was – having talked to him, knowing a little bit about his background subsequently and finding out that we had a lot in common, because he's – we were both as it turned out in Philadelphia at the same time. I was going to the University of

Pennsylvania, the film school, and he was going to the Philadelphia Academy of Art. And we were both in Philadelphia at the same time and, you know, I had seen one of his very early films at a screening back in the Sixties, not knowing who he was and never making the connection, because it was only shown once and I saw it at a place called the Bandbox in Philadelphia.

KGG: That was his sort of moving art piece, was it?

JS: Yeah. But knowing his background was not a film background, you know, he was to my mind very little influenced by other filmmakers. He was much more influenced by works of art and animation, things that he was toying with, you know. And in the beginning I was real interested in his approach to film, and *Eraserhead*, just technically, I just found astonishing in many ways, things about it that really were quite wonderful. One obvious fact, I mean a simple thing, was the fact that we had a major monumental makeup test that we were trying to figure out how exactly to do when we started the picture and having David of course designing makeup, designing a monster – I mean, a child in *Eraserhead*, was somebody who – I mean, he had a lot of strong feelings about that and a real good sense of what ought to be done, which was something that I didn't find from many directors. They were just content to leave it to somebody else to do, but David really wanted to get into it, really wanted to think about materials and textures, and other things that I don't think a lot of other directors would have gotten into, and it was things that I really felt were important. So, for just those variety of reasons and the fact that for me it was an exciting chance to work with somebody who I could work really closely with rather than hiring a director who would then kind of take over and kind of shunt me off to the side. I mean, you know, it was my first producing thing. It just seemed like a very good thing. What really confirmed it though was that I knew we needed another draft and like two weeks after I met David, and decided that I really wanted him, I introduced him to Chris DeVore and Eric Bergren at Bob's. We had a meeting at Bob's on a Sunday and the three of them hit it off also really well, and they were prepared to write another draft. And I said, well, you know, I'd like David to be working with them. And so they were a little sceptical until they met David and then they just, all three of them really took to each other and I think all of the things that were David's strong suit, all the things that he was really best at came out in the next draft. I mean, he refined the work that they had done – their work was terrific and I was very pleased with their initial work, but David added certain elements and helped refine a lot of the work. And I think he was a real – I mean, he helped shape the final script very very much, and obviously even more so when he got to the filming. But it was just a very good working relationship for all the people who were involved at that stage 'til we went to England. And then, going to England, it was just David and I. You know, we had to put together a film crew and it was another case where, all the casting we did together pretty much – I mean, you know, all the people would come in and meet us both and we'd make notes. You know, we'd have – the casting director would bring people in and invariably after, at the end of the day, we'd go through our choices – the people we liked – and they were invariably the same people. There were no major arguments or fights about how to go about doing it. A large part of the success of it was the fact that we were two Americans in a sea of foreigners in London, and things that might have been difficult to accept by an American – I mean, an American crew might have had trouble accepting certain things in David, for example, because he was young and new and had never worked with a normal sized film crew – were easier to take because they just took it as, "Well, they're Americans, they're eccentric," not realizing that, you know, that eccentricity had nothing to do with the fact that David was American. That's just the way he is, you know. But it gave us a lot of room and they were very very helpful, all the English people on the crew. But it was a good experience too for me because I had – my experience before this had been production managing, assistant directing – I had done a lot of documentary films even before that, I mean, I'd worked on professional film sets for ten years with lots of different people so it was easy for me to help orient David to the tasks of filmmaking as they are, you know, when you're working under a pressured schedule and you've got to get a certain amount of work a day and you've got eighty people asking you where you want the camera. At least getting him through that transition was something that I tried to help do.

KGG: Did he adapt quite quickly?

JS: Oh, he adapted right away. We had some wonderful people on the crew too. I mean really, Freddie Francis was a very strong element in the mix, the cameraman who was somebody that David and I interviewed fairly early, someone had brought him in, mainly because we had both seen *Sons and Lovers* and both really loved it and David had felt that that was the kind of – once we had decided we had wanted to go in black and white – that was a look that he kept mentioning to the other cameraman, saying, you know, he liked the way that picture looked and it should look something like that. Someone finally said to us, "Well, why don't you call Freddie Francis? He shot it." We didn't even know he was still working. I mean, it had been twenty years since he had shot a movie. But we brought him in, and he had been directing pictures but was very much interested in getting back into cinematography on a picture that was really worth doing. And so ultimately we hired him, you know. But he was a very strong element because he was somebody that was highly respected in the British film industry and things that other crew members might have objected to – if Freddie was willing to do something, everybody would do it because they, you know, they really respected him greatly. It was helpful.

KGG: Were there any major problems on the production once you got to England and were rolling?

JS: Well, sure, there always are. I mean, there were problems in that the makeup which was being designed wasn't ready in time. We had a stop date on Tony Hopkins, so we had to lose – get rid of him early for another picture, so we had a lot of things that were – not having the makeup on time might have – I mean, in another situation we might have been able to shut down and wait; in this case we couldn't wait. We had to shoot anyway because we were going to lose Tony Hopkins if we didn't. So, we were really under the gun all the time. I mean, the material was terrific right from the start. I mean, it always looked good, the dailies were great. We were all excited about what we were seeing. And there were no conflicts between David and the set designer or, you know, anybody like that because they all pretty much shared the same vision about what the picture should look like. But just the fact that we shot seven-and-a-half weeks without ever knowing what John Hurt was going to look like as the Elephant Man was a little bit scary. You know, because if it didn't work – I mean, it was the whole centre of the picture and if the makeup didn't work we didn't have a movie. So it was a very precarious kind of a – I mean, the first seven weeks we were very very apprehensive, not really knowing what was going to happen, just hoping that it was going to work out.

KGG: Considering the subject matter, it must have been a fairly hard project to sell. How long were you working on it before you actually made the film?

JS: Actually, not that long, as it turns out. I mean, I originally read the screenplay around the end of the summer, 1978, that Chris DeVore brought to me. And I liked it immediately and optioned it. And I was working at the time and I was trying – I took it around to a couple of places, to two or three major companies. And the response was not negative, but it wasn't positive either. I mean, it was interesting but we didn't have any elements attached to it and I wasn't really getting very far. But no one had turned it down yet. I mean, they all said it would take some time, they needed to think about it. Then in January the play came out – and when the play opened off-Broadway we thought that we didn't stand a chance. I mean, we just – no one would be interested in doing the thing that we had. But just before that I had – I mean, I took it to Mel Brooks who I knew and he had told me he was looking to do other projects other than his own films. And as soon as he read it he said, "Yeah, this is a project I'd love to do. Let's do it." So I said, "Well, what do you mean?" He says, "Well, you know –" he says, "we'll get it financed independently and then we won't have to deal with any studios. We'll be able to do what we want." So, as soon as he said that, it sounded like a – you know, I said, "Geez, that's terrific. I love that." So I then said, "Well, as a director I'd really like to use –" and, you know, I told him about David and he wanted to see *Eraserhead*. And I was apprehensive about that too, but he loved it. He just flipped over it. He said, "Yeah, absolutely. That's the guy. Let's use him." And at that point we didn't go back to any studios for major financing, that's why it didn't take that long. Mel said, "Look, what we're going to do is, we'll go round to all the majors and ask for a distribution deal only, but we don't want anybody financing it because then they'll have all the say about who's in it and how we shoot it and everything else and we don't want that." So, I mean, I was a relative neophyte and I said, "Great." You know, and I went with him to all the majors – we talked to everybody and we got offers from Universal and Paramount immediately to finance or to distribute, either way. We said we just want distribution. And even in that case we didn't want to give them the whole world, we said just the U.S. and we'll get a separate distributor for foreign so that we don't cross-collateralize, and don't, you know – and EMI was interested so we gave EMI the foreign rights and Paramount the domestic rights and EMI put up an advance against distribution. And the big thing was that Mel was able to get a pre-sale from NBC television – and that pre-sale was virtually enough, with the advance from EMI, to make the movie. I mean, Mel put up some of his own money, but basically the big money came from NBC and EMI. And no one had any say in how the picture was to go. Mel was very supportive of David and I and left it to us.

KGG: So you never really had to fight with anybody to get David to direct?

JS: Absolutely not. I mean, Paramount had some concern about it, but they were just distributing the picture. Their concern evaporated pretty fast. They wanted David to meet some people who – Pauline Kael, who was working for them, and other people – it never came about. And once they saw some of our dailies, which they did on one occasion in London, I mean, they came over to visit Warren Beatty who was shooting *Reds*, they were very pleased and that was it. We never heard another thing. But once Mel supported David there was really no problem in terms of his doing the picture. He was really a godfather of the project and he kind of helped it going. And, as I say, once David and I left for London we didn't see Mel again really until we finished shooting. I mean, he wasn't involved in setting it up or anything like that, but was tremendously supportive if we needed anything or, you know, if we had any problems. So, it made it a very pleasant working experience.

www.ingramcontent.com/pod-product-compliance
Lightning Source LLC
Chambersburg PA
CBHW080634230426
43663CB00016B/2865